ASP.NET E-Commerce Programming
Problem – Design – Solution

Kevin Hoffman

Wrox Press Ltd. ®

ASP.NET E-Commerce Programming

Problem – Design – Solution

First Printed January 2003

Published by Wrox Press Ltd.,
Arden House, 1102 Warwick Road, Acocks Green,
Birmingham, B27 6BH
United Kingdom
Printed in the United States of America
ISBN 1-86100-803-1

Trademark Acknowledgments

Credits

Author
Kevin Hoffman

Technical Reviewers
Marco Bellinaso
Cristian Darie
Mark Horner
Andrew Krowczyk
Shefali Kulkarni
Saurabh Nandu
David Schultz

Managing Editor
Louay Fatoohi

Commissioning Editor
Daniel Kent

Technical Editors
Gerard Maguire
Douglas Paterson

Project Manager
Charlotte Smith

Production Coordinator
Sarah Hall

Production Assistant
Paul Grove

Cover
Natalie O' Donnell

Indexer
Andrew Criddle

Proofreader
Chris Smith

About the Author

Kevin Hoffman

Kevin has always loved computers and computer programming. He first got hooked when he received a Commodore VIC-20 from his grandfather, who had repaired it after finding it in the trash. He then started a prolific but unprofitable career writing shareware games and utilities for electronic bulletin board systems.

He started working as a programmer while still in college, writing computer interfaces to solar measurement devices and various other scientific instruments. Moving to Oregon, he did everything from technical support to tuning Unix kernels, and eventually working as an ASP programmer for 800.COM, a popular on-line electronics retailer. From there he moved on to working on large, enterprise ASP applications.

Then he finally found .NET, which he now spends 100% of his programming and learning efforts on. A big C# fan, who would use it to do everything including brush his teeth if only he could figure out how, Kevin has been writing on .NET for Wrox since the middle of Beta 1. He plans to continue until we get tired of him. He's currently in Houston, Texas sweating a lot and working on web services and other large-scale .NET applications.

I'd like to dedicate this book to the rest of my "family", without whom I could not have accomplished many of the things I am proud of today. I would like to thank Gerald for all his support – a best friend in every sense of the word – and his daughter Keely for making me laugh. I would also like to thank Jen, Jocelyn, and Emily for their support and being there for me. And as always I want to dedicate my work to my wife, Connie – without her support I would never have published a single word.

TABLE OF CONTENTS

Table of Contents

Introduction

Introduction

Welcome to ASP.NET E-Commerce Programming. In this book we will create an e-commerce solution using expandable "modules" built upon a robust architectural foundation.

This book follows the approach of the acclaimed ASP.NET Website Programming, by Marco Bellinaso and Kevin Hoffman. Each chapter in this book follows a Problem-Design-Solution pattern, where:

- We identify what we need to achieve
- We sketch out how we will achieve it
- Finally, we build the software in Visual Studio .NET.

By the end of the book you will have developed your ASP.NET skills for producing your own well-engineered, extendable e-commerce website, and have a better understanding of the underlying design of such a website. This book is not just about code, or design, it is also about how to create your site to realize business needs.

What Does This Book Cover?

In **Chapter 1**, we start by giving you some idea of what kinds of things we're going to develop in this book, why we're going to develop them, and finally how we're going to develop them.

Chapter 2 takes you through the process of identifying the various needs for an architecture, designing an architecture that is suitable for the application we're building that might also be reusable enough to use with other applications, and finally, we'll take you on a tour through the source code that makes up the architecture that we will have built throughout the course of this chapter.

For the data access portion of our architecture, we've decided to go with the use of Container-Managed Persistence (CMP). Container Managed Persistence is a design pattern whereby business objects have no direct knowledge of where their data came from and how it will be persisted. As you move on through the book, you'll find that the time we spend on this architecture pays us tremendous dividends.

In **Chapter 3** we get down to dealing with the content of our e-commerce site, beginning with the product catalog. This chapter takes you through some of the challenges of creating a product catalog that is fast, efficient, and flexible enough to support a fully functioning e-commerce website.

One of the most important things to consider when designing your website is the ease with which your customers can find your products. This may sound like a simple task, but there are many different aspects of it that need to be considered when developing a good product searching design and solution. In **Chapter 4** we take you through an analysis of the common problems found in developing product search solutions. Then, we will implement the product search design for our site.

Now that customers can browse for your products and search for them, we need to put them into the shopping cart. **Chapter 5** sees us begin with a discussion of the issues surrounding the building of shopping carts in general, before we look at a design that we came up with for our own shopping cart implementation, and finally, look at the source code that we produced in implementing our design.

In **Chapter 6** we look at one of the main tools that allows websites to provide for, and encourage, the planned purchase: the wish list. We're going to take a look at the problems that wish lists solve, as well as the kinds of problems that wish lists create. Following that, we will design and implement our own wish list solution.

Chapter 7 is about discounts, coupons, and sales. You need to accept and prepare for the fact that any customer can probably compare your prices against all of your competitors without ever having to get up out of their chair! In this chapter, we talk about the problems involved with discounts and coupons, and then we tackle the unexpectedly complex problem of designing a good, reliable, efficient way of managing sales.

Chapter 8 takes us through the complex problem of taking orders, processing them, and providing customers with feedback on the status of individual orders and their order histories with the site.

Chapter 9 is about building a community around your site, to encourage your customers to keep coming back to your site.

Chapter 10 is all about working with affiliates and creating partnerships – these will expand the influence and reach of your website. We'll talk about the problems involved in creating affiliates and partnerships and the issues involved in dealing with them. The design of our affiliate system is going to be fairly simple. Essentially, we're going to have two features: referrals and a Web Service. The referral system will allow affiliates to link into our site. Once they've linked to our website, we'll keep track of which affiliate and affiliate campaign the current user came from. The Web Service is provided as a value-add for affiliates, giving them the ability to query our product catalog to enhance the content of their own site with live product information from our database.

Chapter 11 is all about the administration of our solution. We'll take a look at the problem of creating an administration tool and the issues that are involved. Then we'll take a look at the design alternatives facing us when creating an administration tool and the design that we decided to implement. Finally, we'll walk you through the source code to our administration application.

Chapter 12 is a review of some of the things that we went over throughout the book. If you followed the book over a long period of time, some of the material from the earlier chapters might not be as fresh in your mind as the later chapters. It will hopefully refresh your view of the "big picture" and give us a chance to step back and look at the website as a whole.

> *Note that there is one thing that we will not be covering in this book – actually charging a customer. Our shopping cart example should be able to accept actual billing and charging code very easily, but we haven't coded it into the site. The number and varying complexity of all of the different ways in which you can charge customers for your products is too great to do it justice here.*

Who Is This Book For?

This book is for developers who have a reasonable knowledge of ASP.NET, and want to apply that knowledge to building an e-commerce solution. You will get the most from this book if you have read a decent amount of Wrox's *Beginning ASP.NET 1.0 with C#*, or *Professional ASP.NET 1.0 Special Edition.*

> **You should be comfortable using Visual Studio .NET to create ASP.NET projects, and have a working knowledge of C#.**

What You Need to Use This Book

To run the code samples in this book you need to have the following:

- Windows 2000 or Windows XP Professional (or better), with IIS installed
- Visual Studio .NET Professional Edition (or higher)
- SQL Server 2000 – although most of the techniques we use could apply to other database systems

Conventions

We've used a number of different styles of text and layout in this book to help differentiate between different kinds of information. Here are examples of the styles we used and an explanation of what they mean.

Code has several styles. If it's a word that we're talking about in the text – for example, when discussing a `for (...)` loop, it's in this font. If it's a block of code that can be typed as a program and run, then it's also in a gray box:

```
if (categoryTable  == null )
```

Sometimes we'll see code in a mixture of styles, like this:

```
if (categoryTable  == null )
{
```

```
        categoryTable = GetChildCategories(-1);
        System.Web.HttpContext.Current.Cache["categories"] = categoryTable;
    }
```

In cases like this, the code with a white background is code we are already familiar with; the line highlighted in gray is a new addition to the code since we last looked at it.

Advice, hints, and background information come in this type of font.

> **Important pieces of information come in boxes like this.**

Bullets appear indented, with each new bullet marked as follows:

- **Important Words** are in a bold type font.
- Words that appear on the screen, or in menus like the Open or Close, are in a similar font to the one you would see on a Windows desktop.
- Keys that you press on the keyboard, like *Ctrl* and *Enter*, are in italics.

Customer Support

We always value hearing from our readers, and we want to know what you think about this book: what you liked, what you didn't like, and what you think we can do better next time. You can send us your comments, either by returning the reply card in the back of the book, or by e-mail to feedback@wrox.com. Please be sure to mention the book title in your message.

How to Download the Sample Code for the Book

When you visit the Wrox website, www.wrox.com, locate the title through our Search facility or by using one of the title lists. Click Download Code on the book's detail page, or on the Download item in the Code column for title lists.

The files that are available for download from our site have been archived using WinZip. When you've saved the archives to a folder on your hard drive, you need to extract the files using a decompression program such as WinZip or PKUnzip. When you extract the files, the code will be extracted into separate folders for each chapter of this book, so ensure your extraction utility is set to use folder names.

Errata

We've made every effort to make sure that there are no errors in the text or in the code. However, no one is perfect and mistakes do occur. If you find an error in one of our books, such as a spelling mistake or a faulty piece of code, we would be very grateful to hear about it. By sending in errata you may save another reader hours of frustration, and, of course, you will be helping us to provide even higher quality information. Simply e-mail the information to support@wrox.com – your information will be checked and, if correct, posted to the errata page for that title, and used in reprints of the book.

To find errata on the web site, go to www.wrox.com, and simply locate the title through our Advanced Search or title list. Click the Book Errata link below the cover graphic on the book's detail page.

E-Mail Support

If you wish to query a problem in the book with an expert who knows the book in detail, then e-mail support@wrox.com with the title of the book and the last four numbers of the ISBN in the subject field of the e-mail. A typical e-mail should include the following things:

- The **title of the book**, the **last four digits of the ISBN** (8031), and the **page number** of the problem.
- Your **name, contact information**, and the **problem** in the body of the message.

We need the above details to save your time and ours – we *never* send unsolicited junk mail. When you send an e-mail message, it will go through the following chain of support:

- Customer Support – Your message is delivered to our customer support staff, who are the first people to read it. They have files on most frequently asked questions and will answer anything general about the book or the website immediately.
- Editorial – Deeper queries are forwarded to the technical editor responsible for that book. They have experience with the programming language or particular product, and are able to answer detailed technical questions on the subject.
- The Authors – Finally, in the unlikely event that the editor cannot answer your problem, they will forward the request to the author. Wrox authors are glad to help support their books. They will e-mail the customer and the editor with their response, and again all readers should benefit.

The Wrox support process can only offer support for issues that are directly pertinent to the content of our published title. Support for questions that fall outside the scope of normal book support is provided via the community lists of our http://p2p.wrox.com/ forum.

p2p.wrox.com

For author and peer discussion, join the P2P mailing lists. Our unique system provides **programmer to programmer™** contact on mailing lists, forums, and newsgroups, all in addition to our one-to-one e-mail support system. If you post a query to P2P, you can be confident that the many Wrox authors and other industry experts who are present on our mailing lists are examining it. At p2p.wrox.com, you will find a number of different lists that will help you not only while you read this book, but also as you develop your own applications. Particularly appropriate to this book are the aspx and the aspx_professional lists.

To subscribe to a mailing list, just follow these steps:

1. Go to http://p2p.wrox.com/.
2. Choose the appropriate category from the left menu bar.
3. Click on the mailing list you wish to join.
4. Follow the instructions to subscribe, and fill in your e-mail address and password.
5. Reply to the confirmation e-mail you receive.

6. Use the subscription manager to join more lists and set your e-mail preferences.

Why This System Offers the Best Support

You can choose to join the mailing lists, or you can receive them as a weekly digest. If you don't have the time (or the facility) to receive the mailing lists, then you can search our online archives. Junk and spam mails are deleted, and your own e-mail address is protected by the Lyris system. Queries about joining or leaving lists, and any other general queries about lists, should be sent to listsupport@p2p.wrox.com.

CHAPTER 1

1

Building an E-Commerce Site

This book will take you through the process of building an e-commerce website. This chapter will give you some idea of what kinds of things we're going to develop, why we're going to develop them, and finally how we're going to develop them. This book assumes that the reader has some familiarity or previous experience with ASP.NET and C#. All of the code is written in C# and all of our examples are compiled and tested using Visual Studio .NET. The entire backend of the sample site we're developing in this book is developed in SQL Server 2000, so it will be helpful (but not necessary) for you to have some prior experience with that database tool and developing stored procedures in Transact-SQL.

Priorities

Before we begin our new e-commerce site, we need to figure out what our priorities are. Thankfully, the priorities of most e-commerce sites are pretty much the same. No matter what you're selling or why you're selling it, there are four main things you need to do in order to be successful:

- Bring in the customers
- Keep the customers
- Charge the customers
- Bring them back again

Bring in the Customers

No one is going to buy your product if they don't know you have anything to sell. Advertising, marketing, and word of mouth are key here. The one thing that you need to do here is to identify your target audience and advertise in the places where they would go. If you're selling movies, advertise in a movie theater, or if you're selling sports equipment, advertise on sports websites. The idea is that you need to build a new customer base and you need to pull out every trick and tool you have at your disposal to get customers to come to your site for the first time.

Keep the Customers

After you have probably spent a good deal of money, compromised often, and spent a lot of time and effort trying to reel all your potential new customers into your site, you need to keep them there. If you create a wonderful buzz around the opening of your website, and when everyone gets there they find a horrible, hard-to-use, incomplete website – they're not going to come back. It may be the job of the advertisers, marketers, managers, and other business types to get customers to come to your site, but once they're there, how much the customers want to stay depends directly on the quality of the efforts from the site designers and the programmers. The quality and ease of use of the user interface and the feature set of the website are what will bring customers back for more once they've been lured to the site initially.

Charge the Customers

I can't stress enough that your site needs to accomplish all of its main goals. If it excels in one thing, but lacks the others, customers will go to other sites, and they will probably go quickly. It is far better that your site do everything well than does one thing better than everyone else and lacks in other areas. This is especially true with the actual commerce portion of your website. If you do not have an easy-to-use shopping cart, order fulfillment, order history, and order tracking system, customers will probably not come back for a repeat purchase. Think about it this way: You go into a movie theater, and the exterior is beautiful. The movie you want to see is great. The seats are incredibly comfortable, the food is cheap and delicious. Then, the projector breaks halfway through the movie and the picture quality is horrible. Customers will be upset because they didn't get what they paid for. The same goes for your site. If you don't consistently and reliably give your customers the products they purchase, and give them an outlet to resolve problems in shipping, handling, and order mix-ups, they will leave your site for greener pastures.

Bring them Back Again

After you've managed to convince the customers to come to your site, and they feel comfortable enough with your site to purchase products from you, you need them to come back again. There is not an indefinite supply of new customers from which to make all of your money. In order to keep your site afloat, you need regular customers. In order to accomplish that, your prices need to be competitive, and the community feeling on your site needs to be strong enough to pull the customer back in. We'll talk more about community when we cover the four C's.

The Four C's

No discussion of websites can be complete without talking about the Four C's. Whenever anyone talks about the prerequisites for a good, strong, successful website, people are bound to start talking about a set of requirements that all such sites must meet. They are:

- Content
- Community
- Communication
- Commerce

Content

The phrase "Content is King" should be fairly familiar to most of the modern denizens of the Internet and creators of websites. The first of the four C's is definitely *Content.* In creating a site that has "stickiness" and will keep customers coming back for more, we need to make sure that we have good quality content. In addition to having good content, we need a lot of it and we need it to be dynamic and varying. Nobody comes back to the same site two months later if the content never changes. These days, people (myself included) are so used to getting dynamic content that they get upset when their favorite sites haven't updated by the time they get into work in the morning.

Community

Above all other things, websites need to keep their customers coming back. A customer who comes back to the site on a regular basis but buys nothing is still more important to the site than the customer who bought something and never came back. Building a sense of community gives customers more reason to come back, because they associate with the other customers on the site.

Communication

From my own personal experience, I know that a *lot* of customers will simply leave your site and never come back if the communication between you, your site, and the customer is poor. For example, you can count the remaining seconds of a customer's interest on one hand once they realize that they can't contact you by phone. If the customer doesn't trust their ability to reach you if something goes wrong, or contact you if they have questions, they won't buy from you. There are hundreds of other sites on the web with good communication, and you'll lose most, if not all, of your customers without good communication.

Do the customers know what to do in order to get a refund from you? What if something you ship arrives at the customer's doorstep broken or never arrives at all? What if they want to change their order before it ships but they've already submitted their shopping cart? Do you have your security and privacy policy published in an easily accessible place? Even though everyone hates complaints, do you have some way for customers to send you feedback on things your site is doing wrong? Or even things your site is doing right? If you don't have answers to these questions, you might want to reconsider going live with your site until you do get some answers. Customers have always been discerning, but when your competitor is a click away and the customer never has to leave their recliner to go shopping somewhere else – you need to make sure that you have every base covered.

Commerce

If you've got great, wonderful, and dynamic content, and you've got a thriving community and your customers are communicating wonderfully – your site will still lose money if you come up short on the commerce side. The site needs to make it easy for customers to buy what they want, how they want, and when they want. They need to be able to get order status, modify their order if they like, contact you or your support staff regarding their order, and trust your site.

What we'll Create

The website that we're going to be building is a fully-functional e-commerce website. What we're going to walk you through is the development of a product catalog, product searching facilities, discounting, and coupons. In addition to this we're going to walk through some lengthy coverage of shopping carts and order fulfillment, as well as things like product reviews, ratings, and discussion forums.

To demonstrate all of the various technologies and code we're going to implement, we're going to be building a sample e-commerce website. Our efforts in this book will result in a website devoted to selling gadgets of all kinds, GadgetsWarehouse.COM. This site is designed to sell items that cater to the gadget fan, whether the gadgets are electronic, mechanical, or just plain weird. The site will have a product catalog full of gadgetry, including a sample hierarchy of categories to organize the gadgets into groups like DVDs, Radio Controlled toys, and so on. When we have defined all of our problems, illustrated all of our designs, and implemented all of our solutions, GadgetsWarehouse.COM should provide you with an example of a fully-functional, robust and feature-rich e-commerce site.

What we'll Skip

There are a few things that we just don't have the resources to cover in a book this size with the time and number of pages we have to work with. One of these things is actually charging a customer. Our shopping cart example should be able to accept actual billing and charging code very easily, but we haven't coded it into the site. The number and varying complexity of all of the different ways in which you can charge customers for your products is too numerous to do it justice. There are providers who provide re-direction so that your customers temporarily leave the site to complete the purchase and then return. Models like this are implemented by companies like PayPal. Other companies provide libraries, APIs, and/or services that allow you to charge customers for products without leaving the context of your own site. These services are typically expensive.

The other thing we're not going to cover is Commerce Server. A lot of what we're going to code you can do automatically within the context of Commerce Server. However, there is a cost that comes with Commerce Server. The goal of this book is to teach you ASP.NET and C# as it applies to website programming and e-commerce. We couldn't very well accomplish that if we told you to leave all of the hard work to Commerce Server. Another feature that Commerce Server provides that we are intentionally leaving out is interfacing with the credit card companies for live purchases and card verification.

Summary

This book is not a user manual for a previously existing website. We're not trying to sell a cookie-cutter web platform that we claim you can take to your corporation and put your mission-critical commerce platform on. Rather, this book is an exploration of the process involved in creating your own website. We talk about the issues that you will face when building your own site. We illustrate designs that you might come up with on your own when solving your own company's website requirements. Finally, we take a look at the source code that solves the solutions and completes the designs. By the time you're done with this book, we hope that you will have seen enough problems, designs, and solutions to give you some good ideas about how you'd like to implement your own e-commerce site and hopefully you'll have seen enough code examples solving common problems in C# and ASP.NET to start coding.

CHAPTER 2

2

Core Services

You may often hear that code is only as good as the architecture on which it was built. For the most part, this is true. When we're designing any application, we generally start at the business logic and work downward from there. For example, when designing an e-commerce website, we might be tempted to start thinking about products, shopping carts, wish lists, and all that sort of thing first. However, there is something more important that needs to be addressed before we can get into any of that; the architecture.

This chapter will take you through the process of identifying the various needs for an architecture, designing an architecture that is suitable for the application we're building that might also be reusable enough to use with other applications, and finally, we'll take you on a tour through the source code that makes up the architecture that we will have built throughout the course of this chapter.

The Problem

The problem is very simple: we need a solid foundation on which to rest all of our future code for the website. If you've read *ASP.NET Website Programming: Problem-Design-Solution (Wrox Press: ISBN 1-86100-693-4)*, you'll remember we had this same problem when we built a content/news community website. What exactly is a foundation? What kind of code do you find in a foundation?

In general, you want to think of your foundation as a collection of services provided to calling code. These services are there to provide useful features and functionality that accomplish several goals. A few goals to keep in mind when building any architecture are described next.

Maximize Code Reuse

One of the most important tasks in figuring out what services your foundation code is going to provide is in identifying common, repeatable tasks that will be performed by the many different modules in the application. In our example, we are going to want to take a look at features like Shopping Carts, Product Catalog, etc., and find out what tasks performed by those features will be shared and see if they make for a good fit in the foundation code.

The framework on which you build your website must also be extensible. One thing you never want to have to say to a manager is "our framework won't support that" when you're asked to implement a new feature, that wasn't part of the original design, on the site. If the framework doesn't support it outright, it needs to be designed and coded in such a way that you should be able to add support for the feature without breaking the rest of the code for the framework and the code for the website that builds on it.

Enforce Design Patterns and Best Practices

When you are designing your base architecture for your application, you have a tremendous advantage in that (in the case of creating a new application) you get to design everything from the ground up. This gives you an added bonus of being able to dictate some low-level design patterns and best practices. If you want all of the developers to use a certain design pattern for calling stored procedures, then build it into the architecture. If you want to make sure that tracing calls are made each and every time someone reads a key out of the `web.config` file, then build that into your architecture. You have a wide variety of options at your disposal, so make sure you use the ones that are both available and practical.

Provide Common Functionality

Another benefit of providing a strong architectural framework is that you can expose useful functionality that can be shared by other code. For example, you might want to create your own custom `Exception` class, or a standard `Page` class from which all of your base pages inherit.

Provide Development Sandbox

This added benefit of being able to build an architecture from the ground up goes hand-in-hand with the other benefit of enforcing design patterns and providing common functionality. One problem that many teams of developers have is that they tend to come up with their own ways of accomplishing things. This problem is magnified by the fact that the .NET Framework is so large and provides so many solutions to the same problem.

With a strong architecture in place, you can dictate to your developers exactly how it is they should be accomplishing various tasks. You can provide standardized code that developers must use in order to do things such as utilize the cache, the `CallContext`, or data access – each of these is a great feature that can be easily abused. It will also be fairly easy for you to tell when other developers are circumventing the architecture to perform various tasks. By putting your own architectural control over costly resources and critical-path operations, you can set yourself up for success and a structured, disciplined development effort.

The Design

We've had a quick look at what some of the goals are when designing a foundation, but we haven't yet taken a look at the services that we think an architecture should provide. All base architectures for a web application are going to have to solve certain problems, regardless of what the application itself does. Before we talk about what we think should be in our design, we need to talk about some of the things that motivate our design.

If you're familiar with the IBuySpy portal or website, you might be familiar with the architecture and framework provided for those sites. In essence, the architecture for those sites is much simpler than the one we're coming up with. In general, the more flexibility and scalability your site requires, the more complex the underlying infrastructure code must be in order to support it. In addition, the more complex and powerful the foundation code is, the longer it takes to implement.

This isn't meant to scare you off by saying we're about to implement some monolithic code. On the contrary, it should whet your appetite for a robust, efficient, scalable, extensible framework on which you can build virtually any kind of website. For our purposes, we are going to be building a large framework on which we can place a business application that accommodates e-commerce functionality.

We've taken the list of problems that need to be solved by any such rich infrastructure and turned them into a list of required services. That list is as follows:

Data Services

At the most basic level, the one thing that almost all of your application will be doing is accessing data. There is no way of avoiding this – if you are writing a data-driven web application, then obviously you need to have some way of allowing that data to drive your application. This next section will take you through the design process of the data layer that we created, why we created it, and what the design of it looks like.

If you choose to create some other kind of data tier (for example, a more traditional "stored procedure caller/wrapper" layer, such as the layer you will find in most of Microsoft's architectural samples) you can still use many of the other pieces of the core services, but you may just have to adapt them slightly to your particular data-access methods.

I'm frequently asked, "What is the best architecture?" There is no right answer to that question. There is a perfect architecture *for each situation.* For the purpose of demonstrating the quickest way of creating a data access tier, the samples from IBuySpy, Nile, Pet Shop, etc. are all very good and appropriate. However, for our needs, we want something that is easy to maintain, upgrade, and enhance, and we want to be able to make quick and easy changes to our code if the data structure changes. One thing about commerce sites is that people are always finding more information to store and different ways to store it. Our data-services tier *must* be able to easily handle that kind of situation, and we want our business objects to be readable by people with varying .NET backgrounds. For this reason, we felt a more complex data-services tier was in order.

Container Managed Persistence

For the data access portion of our architecture, we've decided to go with the use of **Container-Managed Persistence (CMP)**. Container-Managed Persistence is a design pattern whereby business objects have no direct knowledge of where their data came from and how it will be persisted.

In traditional data services components, you might find some routines that help developers in creating and executing stored procedures, and in more advanced implementations you might find routines for stored procedure caching, SQL statement repositories, or even things like connection and procedure factories that further abstract the creation and execution of stored procedures.

All of these traditional methods refer to **Component-Managed Persistence**. Component-Managed Persistence is where the component itself initiates the call to some form of persistence provider, such as a relational database or a flat file, or whatever. The important thing to remember is that the component must make use of the persistence provider, and the component needs to know how to supply parameters to that data store such as stored procedure arguments, data types, and sizes. This tightly couples a particular business class to the underlying data store.

Thus, if you have a `Customer` object that builds SQL stored procedures and executes them in order to perform persistence operations, (`INSERT`, `UPDATE`, `DELETE`, `SELECT`) then you might as well call that class `SqlCustomer`, because you'd have to re-write the class to use it with anything other than SQL Server.

Now that we know what *Container-Managed Persistence* is *not*, we can talk about what it really *is*. In a nutshell, CMP is a pattern in which all data objects in a system are completely unaware of their own persistence methods. The business objects are pure business objects; they maintain business data and indicate whether that data is valid according to business rules. At no point is a business object *ever* tightly coupled with a particular persistence layer.

Enter the container. In this pattern, the container is a class that is responsible for taking a data-source-agnostic business object instance and persisting it. By "persisting" we mean taking part in any of the four types of data operations in CRUD (Create, Retrieve, Update, and Delete) functionality.

The basic flow is this:

1. The business object is invoked by some other control – typically the code behind of a web page.

2. This business object then creates a container and a persistable object, namely an object that is allowed to take place in Container-Managed Persistence.

3. Then, the business object invokes the relevant `SELECT`, `INSERT`, `UPDATE`, or `DELETE` method on the container to perform the actual persistence. These four methods are often referred to as CRUD (Create, Retrieve, Update, Delete).

The following diagram illustrates how CMP fits into the overall architecture of our web site:

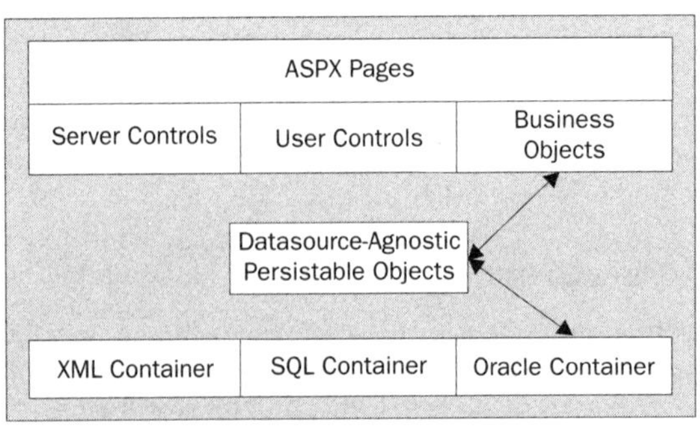

As you can see from the diagram, one of the huge benefits of using a CMP-based architecture is that our entire middle tier of business objects does not rely on any kind of data source whatsoever. All it does is maintain data and validate data. That data could come from a SQL Server database, an Oracle server, an XML file, an XML document out on the Internet, or, even more interestingly from a Web Service. This allows us to easily and rapidly debug, maintain, and enhance our data layer without much effort, and prevents changes to the underlying persistence methods from having a large, negative impact on the rest of the application.

Admittedly, there is also some small satisfaction in knowing that this is a CMP solution implemented in .NET. I once encountered someone who was convinced that Java was better than .NET. This person told me, "Let's see .NET do CMP" as an excuse for clinging to Java. Well, here it is – CMP on .NET with a fraction of the complexity and time to market of the Sun implementation. However, in the interest of all fairness, here is a link to Sun's EJB 2.0 CMP implementation documentation:

http://developer.java.sun.com/developer/technicalArticles/ebeans/EJB20CMP/

So, how does all this work? Well, it relies on the fact that the containers are the only classes that know any intimate details about the persistence methods and the underlying data source. This is accomplished by creating a store of metadata that provides information on how to perform **Object-Relational Mapping**. ORM is a technique that is used to map fields and public properties of class instances to various data constructs such as tables or stored procedures within a database. We'll go into how the rest of CMP is implemented in the *Solution* section of this chapter, where we'll look at the C# code for a SQL persistence container and we'll see the XML metadata that makes it all happen.

We'll break the class diagram for our CMP services up into three diagrams. Don't worry if it all looks a little complex, there is a lot in these classes. Rest assured that we will cover it all in detail throughout the chapter.

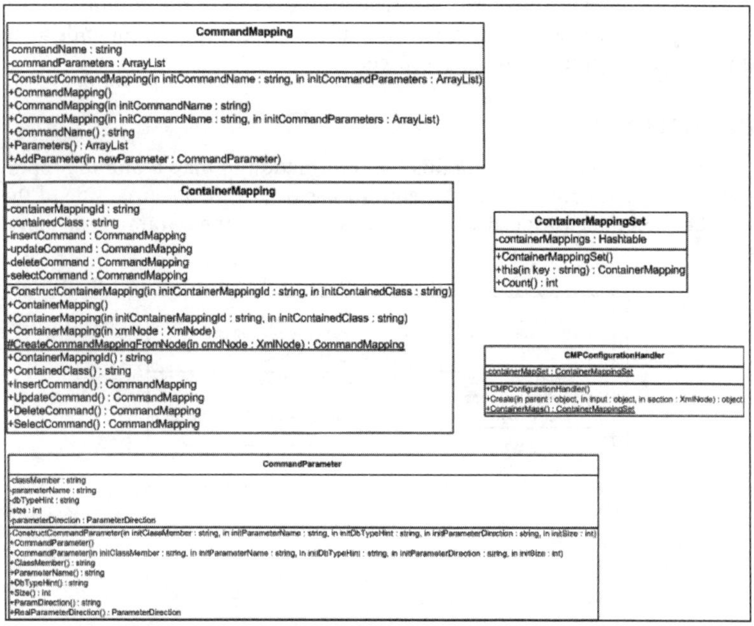

CMPConfigurationHandler

As we'll see when we look at the source code, the `CMPConfigurationHandler` is a class that is responsible for loading the metadata configuration information from a custom configuration section in the `web.config` file. The reason for using the `web.config` file is that we can make use of the functionality already provided through that file. In particular, the feature whereby any change to the file causes the web application to restart, which gives us the opportunity to reload the metadata. This allows us to change the metadata for our persistence code without having to recompile, or even turn off IIS.

ContainerMappingSet

At the topmost level of the metadata configuration is a root XML node that contains a list of container mappings. This collection of container mappings is stored in an instance of the `ContainerMappingSet` class. It exposes functionality that allows for instantiating itself based on an XML node, and functionality that allows for manual loading that can be used for rigging up test harnesses.

ContainerMapping

A container mapping is an abstraction of a single Object-Relational Mapping. It is called a container mapping because it allows a container (like a SQL persistence container or an XML container, etc.) to obtain enough information about the object instances it will be handling to perform the object-relational mapping that allows the object instance to be persisted to the underlying data store. A container mapping contains a list of up to four command mappings (for the four commands in the CRUD standard).

CommandMapping

A command mapping is a representation of a CRUD action that can be performed by the underlying data store. So, for a SQL container, there will be up to four `CommandMappings` defined, providing the support needed for the `INSERT`, `UPDATE`, `SELECT`, and `DELETE` methods. A `CommandMapping` contains a list of parameters and maintains properties indicating the name of the command (which can be mapped to a stored procedure) and a provider hint, allowing different commands to come from different databases within the same container or data source.

CommandParameter

A `CommandParameter` is a class that contains the information to map a public property or field of a class instance to a particular command parameter for use on the data source side of the mapping. A `CommandParameter` contains properties for the class property, the parameter name, data type, size, and parameter direction.

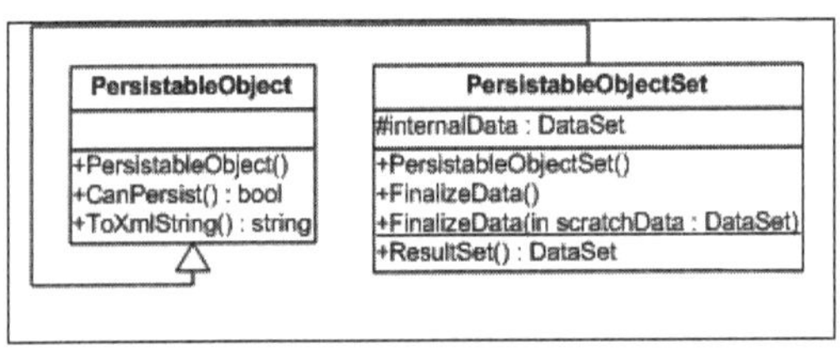

PersistableObject

This is a base class that provides the basic set of functionality that allows an object to take part in Container-Managed Persistence – any class wishing its instances to take part in Container-Managed Persistence needs to inherit from `PersistableObject`. A `PersistableObject` represents a single piece of data to be persisted. For querying multiple results from the database or other data source, a `PersistableObjectSet` is used.

PersistableObjectSet

In a completely pure implementation of Container-Managed Persistence, `Select` operations that returned multiple rows of data would actually return arrays or collections of fully instantiated business objects. While this may be the best option from a pure object-oriented design perspective, we found that there were performance problems there. We didn't want to end up in a situation where we would be instantiating an indefinite number of class instances.

Because it can be expensive to retrieve arrays of `PersistableObject` instances when we don't know ahead of time the size of the result set, we needed an alternative. That alternative was to create a derivative of `PersistableObject` that maintains an internal `DataSet`. This internal `DataSet` serves as a receptacle for data retrieved from a command executed by a container. The containers are smart enough to know ahead of time whether they are dealing with a `PersistableObject` or a `PersistableObjectSet` and can dynamically determine where the results of the executed command should be stored.

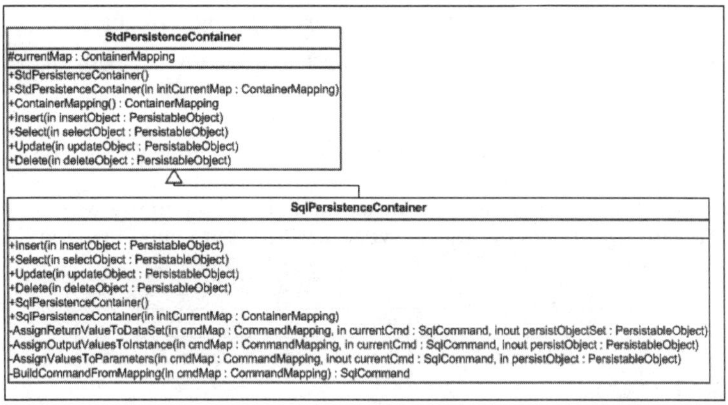

StdPersistenceContainer

The `StdPersistenceContainer` class is a base class that defines the core functionality that all containers must provide. We used a class rather than an interface so that we could implement some default functionality and to make the use of polymorphism throughout the architecture that much easier.

SqlPersistenceContainer

The `SqlPersistenceContainer` is an implementation of a persistence container that is specific to the Microsoft SQL client provided in the `System.Data.SqlClient` namespace. This class provides `INSERT`, `UPDATE`, `DELETE`, and `SELECT` methods that all operate specifically on SQL Server databases. This class uses its internal container mapping to analyze the Object-Relational Mapping and communicate data between the object instance and the data source.

If this particular set of architectural components seems a bit complex, don't worry. The idea here is that the complexity in this portion of the architecture allows nearly all data access by the application to be very quick, very painless, and very easy to read and maintain. A little work up front usually pays for itself many times over by the time the application is done.

Monitoring Services

No matter what kind of application you are making, there will always be certain tasks that your application must perform. One of those tasks is monitoring. By monitoring, we're talking about logging, tracing, error handling, and other tasks related to keeping track of what is going on in the system and who is using it.

The information you need to monitor is probably going to vary based on the application and your needs at the time, but a standard set of services to allow your code to trace valuable information, log errors and other information to various sources, and keep track of who is using the system is essential.

Typically, a formal process involving lots of meetings and dialogue and discussion results in a list of requirements for what monitoring tasks we want our monitor services to perform. In absence of a large number of people, I sat down with myself, and debated for a while. After winning the argument with myself (I often do), I narrowed down the list of monitoring tasks to the following:

- Standardized and Enhanced Tracing
- Obtaining detailed process information for logging during certain events
- Error logging to database and to a file as a backup in case of database failure
- Standardized creation of custom exceptions
- Storage retrieval of custom error message strings in a resource that can be easily globalized.

Now that we have a list of requirements, we can start thinking about the various classes that we're going to put into our monitoring services library. We've taken the list of requirements and come up with the following class diagram:

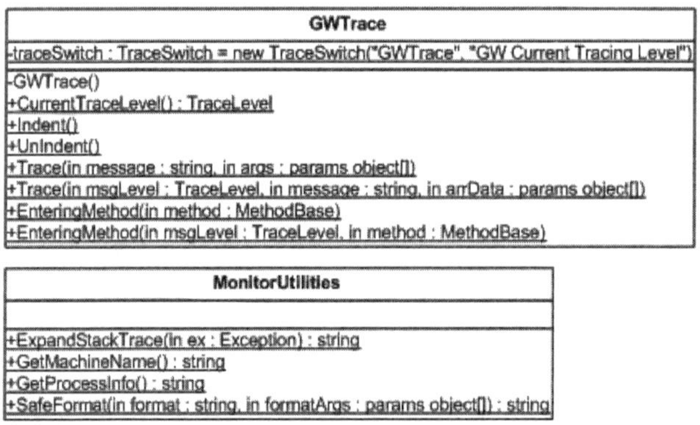

GWTrace

This class is responsible for providing standardized tracing. One of the few annoying things about ASP.NET is that when you use the `Context.Trace` class, you are not actually using the same `Trace` class that an assembly might use. This means that by default, your pages' code-behind classes will write to the page-outputted trace in ASP.NET, but your server controls, business objects, and data (persistable) objects will write their trace information to an entirely different location.

`GWTrace` unifies the location of tracing messages by writing to both locations (if both are available). It is aware of a trace-level switch that exists in the `web.config` file that it will honor when tracing varying degrees of detailed information.

MonitorUtilities

This class contains utility methods that will be found useful by other methods within the monitoring system. For example, it contains methods that retrieve the machine name, an application name (that can actually be set in the `web.config` file), and process information. In addition to providing information gathering methods, it also provides the `SafeFormat` method, which provides a safe, error-free way to map object arguments to format strings. This method also helps to make sure that when formatting strings to log errors, we don't create additional errors by attempting to log bad data.

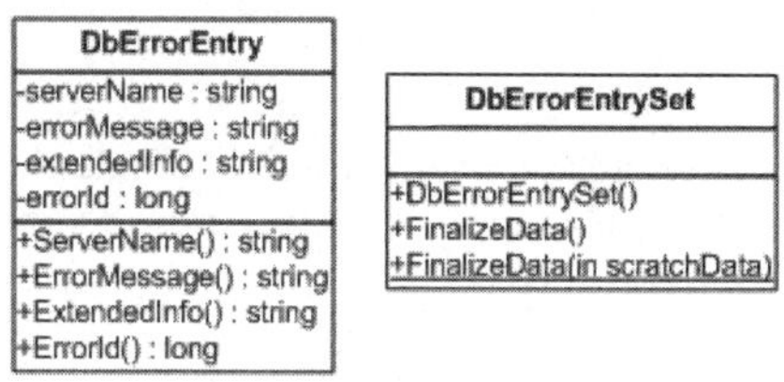

DbErrorEntry

This is a `PersistableObject` that is used for interfacing with the database when storing a single row of error data in the database. It is a simple placeholder for the information that will be written to the database or read when a single error log entry is being queried.

DbErrorEntrySet

`DbErrorEntrySet` is a `PersistableObjectSet` that contains parameter information for retrieving a list of errors within a certain date range. This can be useful for administrative purposes to examine the error log for a particular time frame.

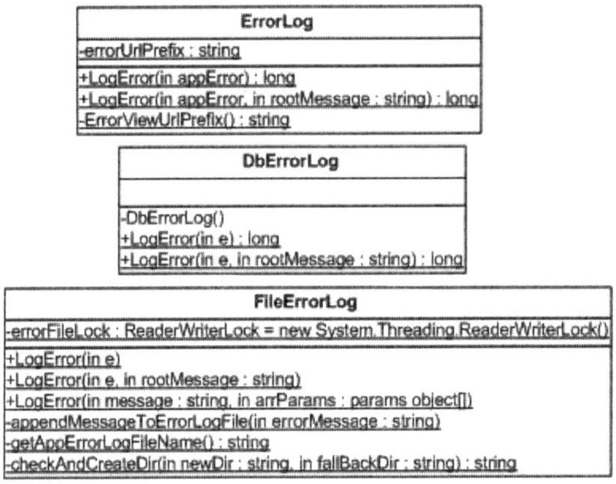

FileErrorLog

This class performs simple error logging to a file. This class can be used on its own, but developers shouldn't be calling this class directly. Instead, they should call the `ErrorLog` class and it will attempt to log the error to the database first, and only use the text file as a backup in case of database failure.

DbErrorLog

This class is responsible for maintaining the error log within the database. This error log contains source information, and detailed information about the process retrieved at run time, as well as the contents of the actual exception itself.

ErrorLog

This class serves as a triage clerk for error logs. It will first attempt to send an error log to the database. If this attempt fails, it will log the error to the file. If the attempt succeeds, it will log information in the file indicating that an error was successfully logged to the database and it will contain the appropriate error ID number.

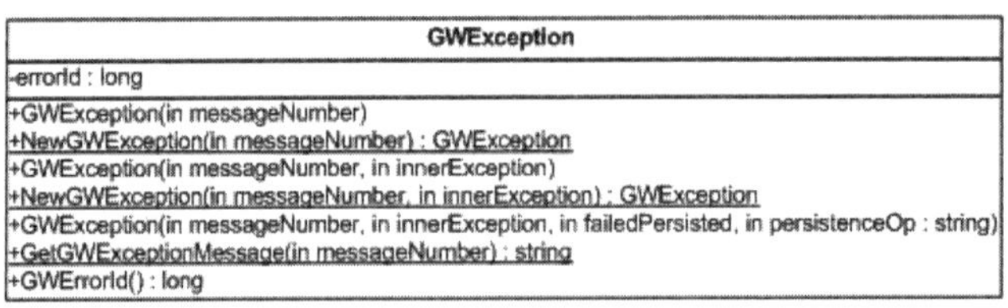

GWException

This class is a custom exception class. When this class is instantiated, the error information available to the class instance is sent to the `ErrorLog` class to be persisted in the database and/or the appropriate text file. This ensures that any time a developer instantiates an exception that is a `GWException` or derives from it, the information about that particular exception will be persisted in some durable format.

Security Services

Security Services are designed to provide, surprisingly enough, security. Our implementation of Security Services is fairly simple: it contains a data class (`PersistableObject`) for communicating authentication requests to and from the database, and it contains a utility class called `Authenticator`, which actually performs the authentication. The following is a class diagram of our security services system:

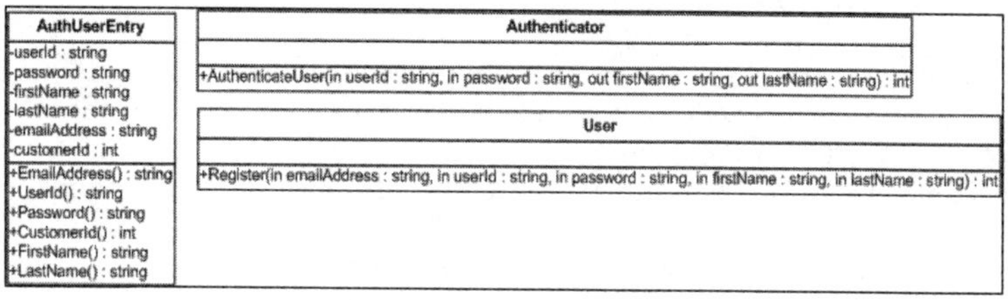

As you can see, the `Authenticator` performs an authentication, `AuthenticateUser`, returning a value that indicates whether the login was valid, and if so the `firstName` and `lastName` parameters are returned. The `User` class has a method called `Register` that allows the creation of new users. The integer return value indicates whether the new user was created or whether the user attempting to register is already in the database. Finally, the `AuthUserEntry` class is a `PersistableObject` that is placed into the container to facilitate the `Authenticator` and `User` classes.

Configuration Services

We need a facility by which we control the configuration options for our website. Configuration Services is one of those places that we think we might need to improve on later, but at this point we can't think of exactly where. So, we're designing the bare minimum set of Configuration Services with the idea that we might need to enhance this section of the architecture as we encounter more complex designs later in our development process. Our implementation of Configuration Services contains only one class: `SiteProfile`. This class contains some static properties that will be available to all object instances running within the application's `AppDomain`. This `SiteProfile` class contains properties like the collection of database type hints that are used to power the CMP data engine and a string that indicates the default data source connection string. These static members are going to be populated during the application's startup event.

The Solution

Unlike other code samples you might see in books, or self-contained applications, the usefulness and benefits of a set of infrastructure code might not be readily apparent. In our case, the code for our architecture might not fully make sense until you actually see the architecture in use in the next few chapters.

Nevertheless, we feel that it is worth taking a look at the complete source code for the foundation on which we will be laying the rest of the book, and the rest of our sample e-commerce application. We'll take a look at the source code, project by project.

If you are following along and typing this in by hand, you are probably a glutton for punishment. The architecture code involves quite a bit of typing. If you do want to type this in yourself, create yourself a blank solution and call it `GadgetsWarehouse` (the name of our fictitious e-commerce website). From there, create a new project (C# Class Library) for each of the projects that we're going to describe.

CMPServices

The CMPServices project is the essential core of the Container-Managed Persistence system. This is, for all intents and purposes, our entire data tier contained in one assembly. To create this by hand, just add a new Class Library (C# of course) to your existing solution and call it CMPServices. Set the default namespace and assembly output filename to GW.CMPServices. What is given below is a listing of each class file in the assembly.

For all of the assemblies that we're going to create in this project, we are going to use a file called SharedAssemblyInfo.cs. This file contains global project information such as version number and a link to the .snk (key) file for strong-naming. To add this file to your project, choose Add Existing Item from your project menu and then find the file. Instead of clicking the Open button, click the down-arrow next to the Open button and choose Link File. This allows you to use this file without copying it to your VS .NET project directory. For a copy of the SharedAssemblyInfo.cs file and the strong-name key you can access the download code for this book on Wrox's website.

For maximum compatibility, I strongly recommend that you download the code as it is from the Wrox website. Typing the code in as you go is an excellent way to learn the new concepts, but there are a myriad of tiny details in configuring the VS .NET environment for this application that are too many to discuss in any one chapter in this book.

CMPConfigurationHandler.cs

This file contains the definition and implementation of the CMPConfigurationHandler class. This class implements the IConfigurationSectionHandler interface, which flags it as being a class that knows how to read and interpret a custom configuration section from a .NET XML configuration file. In our case, that configuration file will be the web.config file. We are using this file to load the CMP metadata required to perform the Object-Relational Mapping that is at the core of our CMP layer.

```
/*
 * Class       : CMPConfigurationHandler
 * Namespace   : GW.CMPServices
 * Assembly    : GW.CMPServices
 * Description : Class provides a custom configuration section
 *               handler to load metadata supply to
 *               populate the in-memory cache of CMP configuration data.
 */

using System;
using System.Xml;
using System.Xml.Serialization;
using System.Configuration;

using System.Reflection;
using System.Diagnostics;

namespace GW.CMPServices
{
/// <summary>
/// CMPConfigurationHandler is a class that provides custom
/// configuration section support for the CMP metadata stored
```

```
/// in the Web.config file.
/// </summary>
public class CMPConfigurationHandler : IConfigurationSectionHandler
{
  private static ContainerMappingSet containerMapSet;

  public CMPConfigurationHandler() { }
  /// <summary>
  /// Create method that is part of the IConfigurationSectionHandler
  /// interface.
  /// </summary>
  /// <param name="parent">parent object</param>
  /// <param name="input">input stream</param>
  /// <param name="section">configuration section root node.</param>
  /// <returns>Object</returns>
```

The `Create` method is part if the `IConfigurationSectionHandler` interface. It is called when the configuration section handler is invoked. We use this method to process the XML in the section and then return `null`.

```
  public object Create( object parent, object input, XmlNode section )
  {
    XmlNode containerMappingRoot =
                     section.SelectSingleNode("//ContainerMappingSet");
    ContainerMappingSet cms = new ContainerMappingSet();
    ContainerMapping cm;
    foreach (XmlNode containerNode in containerMappingRoot.ChildNodes)
    {
      cm = new ContainerMapping( containerNode );
      cms[cm.ContainerMappingId] = cm;
    }
    CMPConfigurationHandler.containerMapSet = cms;

    return null;
  }

  /// <summary>
  /// Exposes arraylist of container mappings read
  /// from the web.config file.
  /// </summary>
  public static ContainerMappingSet ContainerMaps
  {
    get { return containerMapSet; }
    set { containerMapSet = value; }
  }
}
```

CommandMapping.cs

The `CommandMapping` class is a wrapper for a `<CommandMapping>` node in the metadata configuration section. It contains information on a particular command such as `SELECT`, `INSERT`, `UPDATE`, or `DELETE` (CRUD operations). It contains that command's parameters in an `ArrayList`.

```
/*
 * Class       : CommandMapping
 * Namespace   : GW.CMPServices
 * Assembly    : GW.CMPServices
 * Description : Provides a store for information on an individual
 *               object-relational command mapping.
 */

using System;
using System.Collections;
using System.Xml;
using System.Xml.Serialization;

using System.Reflection;

namespace GW.CMPServices
{
  /// <summary>
  /// Summary description for CommandMapping.
  /// </summary>
  public class CommandMapping
  {
    private string commandName;
    private ArrayList commandParameters;
```

All of the constructor overloads for this class eventually call this one method. It is always a good idea to have one entry point for all of your class initialization, regardless of the number of constructors you might have. This makes the class easier to maintain and debug.

```
    private void ConstructCommandMapping( string initCommandName,
                                          ArrayList initCommandParameters )
    {
      commandName = initCommandName;
      commandParameters = initCommandParameters;
    }
```

This method will create an empty command mapping by calling the `ConstructCommandMapping` with the `Not Set` string.

```
    public CommandMapping()
    {
      ArrayList newParams = new ArrayList();
      ConstructCommandMapping( "Not Set", newParams );
    }
```

This method will create a command mapping with the supplied command name by calling `ConstructCommandMapping`.

```
    public CommandMapping( string initCommandName )
    {
      ArrayList newParams = new ArrayList();
      ConstructCommandMapping( initCommandName, newParams );
    }
```

This final method overload will construct a new command mapping with a command-mapping name and an `ArrayList` containing the mapping's parameters which are used to feed the stored procedure parameters when the command mapping is invoked.

```
    public CommandMapping( string initCommandName,
                           ArrayList initCommandParameters )
    {
      ConstructCommandMapping( initCommandName, initCommandParameters );
    }

    public string CommandName
    {
      get { return commandName; }
      set { commandName = value; }
    }

    public ArrayList Parameters
    {
      get { return commandParameters; }
      set { commandParameters = value; }
    }

    public void AddParameter ( CommandParameter newParameter )
    {
      commandParameters.Add( newParameter );
    }
  }
}
```

ContainerMapping.cs

The `ContainerMapping` class represents a single container mapping. As we discussed in the design section, a `ContainerMapping` is a representation of a single type of Object-Relational Mapping as it pertains to a specific container. For example, you might have a container mapping for a `Customer`, which contains enough information to allow the container to perform all four CRUD operations. The container mapping holds up to four command mappings and a unique identifier used to locate the individual mapping within a `ContainerMappingSet`.

The `ContainerMapping` class maps to the root XML node of a container mapping entry in the `web.config` file. The `web.config` file contains data that looks like this:

```
<ContainerMappingSet>
  <ContainerMapping>
    <ContainerMappingId>UserCreate</ContainerMappingId>
    <ContainedClass>AuthUserEntry</ContainedClass>
    <Insert>
        <CommandName>GW_Insert_Customer_Sp</CommandName>
        <Parameter>
          <ClassMember>EmailAddress</ClassMember>
          <ParameterName>@EmailAddress</ParameterName>
          <DbTypeHint>Varchar</DbTypeHint>
          <ParamDirection>Input</ParamDirection>
          <Size>255</Size>
```

```
        </Parameter>
      </Insert>

      ...

    </ContainerMapping>
  </ContainerMappingSet>
```

The following is the source code listing for the ContainerMapping class:

```
/*
 * Class       : ContainerMapping
 * Namespace   : GW.CMPServices
 * Assembly    : GW.CMPServices
 * Description : Class that provides a store for the object-relational
 *               mapping metadata for a container mapping
 */

using System;
using System.Xml;
using System.Xml.Serialization;
using System.Reflection;

namespace GW.CMPServices
{
  /// <summary>
  /// ContainerMapping is a class that maintains data for the containermapping
  /// MetaData.
  /// </summary>
  public class ContainerMapping
  {
    private string containerMappingId;
    private string containedClass;
    private CommandMapping insertCommand;
    private CommandMapping updateCommand;
    private CommandMapping deleteCommand;
    private CommandMapping selectCommand;
```

This method is used by the different constructor overloads to configure a new container mapping. Remember that a container mapping holds four different CommandMapping types, one for each data operation.

```
    private void ConstructContainerMapping( string initContainerMappingId,
                                            string initContainedClass )
    {
      containerMappingId = initContainerMappingId;
      containedClass = initContainedClass;
    }

    public ContainerMapping()
    {
      ConstructContainerMapping( "Not Set", "Not Set" );
```

```
    }

    public ContainerMapping( string initContainerMappingId,
                             string initContainedClass )
    {
      ConstructContainerMapping( initContainerMappingId,
                                 initContainedClass ) ;
    }
```

This next method allows us to build a container mapping based on an XML node. This gives us a shortcut because the metadata information is XML structured. You'll get plenty of opportunity to see the XML for various container mappings throughout this book as they are used for all of our data access methods. This also gives us more control over how the container mapping is to be constructed. If we need to make changes to how it is constructed, most of those changes will be in this one method and we don't have to hunt all over the place to find bits and pieces of construction code.

```
    public ContainerMapping( XmlNode xmlNode )
    {
      containedClass =
        xmlNode.SelectSingleNode( "ContainedClass" ).InnerText;
      containerMappingId =
        xmlNode.SelectSingleNode( "ContainerMappingId" ).InnerText;
      XmlNode commandMappingNode;

      commandMappingNode = xmlNode.SelectSingleNode("Insert");
      if ( commandMappingNode != null )
        insertCommand = CreateCommandMappingFromNode( commandMappingNode );
      commandMappingNode = xmlNode.SelectSingleNode("Update");
      if ( commandMappingNode != null )
        updateCommand = CreateCommandMappingFromNode( commandMappingNode );
      commandMappingNode = xmlNode.SelectSingleNode("Delete");
      if ( commandMappingNode != null )
        deleteCommand = CreateCommandMappingFromNode( commandMappingNode );
      commandMappingNode = xmlNode.SelectSingleNode("Select");
      if ( commandMappingNode != null )
        selectCommand = CreateCommandMappingFromNode( commandMappingNode );
    }
```

The `CreateCommandMappingFromNode` method will take an XML node that contains the root node for `<Insert>`, `<Update>`, `<Delete>`, or `<Select>` and return a new instance of a command mapping.

```
    protected static CommandMapping CreateCommandMappingFromNode(
                                                      XmlNode cmdNode )
    {
      CommandMapping newCmdMap = new CommandMapping();

      newCmdMap.CommandName =
                     cmdNode.SelectSingleNode("CommandName").InnerText;

      CommandParameter newParam;
      foreach (XmlNode cmdParamNode in cmdNode.SelectNodes("Parameter"))
      {
```

```
        newParam = new CommandParameter();
        newParam.ClassMember =
                cmdParamNode.SelectSingleNode("ClassMember").InnerText;
        newParam.DbTypeHint =
                 cmdParamNode.SelectSingleNode("DbTypeHint").InnerText;
        newParam.ParameterName =
               cmdParamNode.SelectSingleNode("ParameterName").InnerText;
        newParam.Size = System.Convert.ToInt32(
                   cmdParamNode.SelectSingleNode("Size").InnerText );
        newParam.ParamDirection =
             cmdParamNode.SelectSingleNode("ParamDirection").InnerText;
        newCmdMap.AddParameter( newParam );
      }

      return newCmdMap;
    }

    public string ContainerMappingId
    {
      get { return containerMappingId; }
      set { containerMappingId = value; }
    }

    public string ContainedClass
    {
      get { return containedClass; }
      set { containedClass = value; }
    }

    public CommandMapping InsertCommand
    {
      get { return insertCommand; }
      set { insertCommand = value; }
    }

    public CommandMapping UpdateCommand
    {
      get { return updateCommand; }
      set { updateCommand = value; }
    }

    public CommandMapping DeleteCommand
    {
      get { return deleteCommand; }
      set { deleteCommand = value; }
    }

    public CommandMapping SelectCommand
    {
      get { return selectCommand; }
      set { selectCommand = value; }
    }
  }
}
```

ContainerMappingSet.cs

The `ContainerMappingSet` is just a placeholder for a list of container mappings. Any time a business object is going to attempt to locate a particular container to perform some kind of database operation, it will be going through an instance of this class to retrieve the container mapping code.

```
/*
 * Class       : ContainerMappingSet
 * Namespace   : GW.CMPServices
 * Assembly    : GW.CMPServices
 * Description : Class that provides a store for the object-relational
 *               mapping metadata for a container mapping set
 */

using System;
using System.Xml;
using System.Xml.Serialization;
using System.Reflection;
using System.Collections;

namespace GW.CMPServices
{
  /// <summary>
  /// Contains a collection of ContainerMappings
  /// </summary>
  public class ContainerMappingSet
  {
    private Hashtable containerMappings;

    public ContainerMappingSet()
    {
      containerMappings = new Hashtable();
    }
```

This next section of code provides the default indexer for instances of this class. It allows us to access the `Hashtable` of cached container mappings with a named index.

```
    public ContainerMapping this [ string key ]
    {
      get
      {
        if ( containerMappings.ContainsKey( key ) )
        {
          return (ContainerMapping) containerMappings[key];
        }
        else
          return null;
      }
      set
      {
        if (containerMappings.ContainsKey( key ) )
        {
          containerMappings.Remove( key );
```

```
            }
            containerMappings.Add(key, value);
          }
        }

        public int Count
        {
          get { return containerMappings.Count; }
        }
      }
    }
```

PersistableObject.cs

All classes that can participate in CMP-based data activity must inherit somehow from this class, either by directly inheriting from it or inheriting from `PersistableObjectSet` (we'll see that class shortly). This class defines the root behavior for all data objects.

```
/*
 * Class       : PersistableObject
 * Namespace   : GW.CMPServices
 * Assembly    : GW.CMPServices
 * Description : Abstract base class for creating an object that is
 *               allowed to take part in container-managed persistance.
 */

using System;
using System.Xml;
using System.Xml.Serialization;
using System.Text;

namespace GW.CMPServices
{
  /// <summary>
  /// Summary description for PersistableObject.
  /// </summary>
  public class PersistableObject
  {
    public PersistableObject()
    {}

    public bool CanPersist ()
    {
      return true;
    }
```

If there were to be some failure in performing a persistence operation using an instance of this object (say, a customer or a product or a shopping cart item, etc.), then we need to know the values contained on that object because we want to know what parameters caused the database to reject the persistence. By providing this `ToXmlString` method, we can serialize the entire instance into a string that can be stored in the database along with the other error information retrieved at the time an exception was thrown. This is an invaluable debugging tool, especially if failures occur in a live, production environment. It does, however, mean that any class deriving from `PersistableObject` will need to abide by the rules that allow class instances to be serializable, such as providing default public constructors and to be marked with the `[Serializable]` attribute.

```
    public string ToXmlString()
    {
      try
      {
        Type objType = this.GetType();
        StringBuilder sb = new StringBuilder();
        System.IO.StringWriter sw = new System.IO.StringWriter( sb );
        XmlSerializer xs = new XmlSerializer( objType );
        xs.Serialize( sw, this );
        return sw.GetStringBuilder().ToString();
      }
      catch
      {
        return "Serialization Failure";
      }
    }
  }
}
```

PersistableObjectSet.cs

A `PersistableObjectSet` is a specialized type of `PersistableObject`. It can send parameters and retrieve output parameter values from a data store just as a `PersistableObject` can. The difference is that when the database retrieves data, that data is placed in a `DataSet` contained within the `PersistableObjectSet` instance. This provides for high-performance retrieval of data while still maintaining the CMP design pattern.

```
/*
 * Class        : PersistableObjectSet
 * Namespace    : GW.CMPServices
 * Assembly     : GW.CMPServices
 * Description  : Base class used for providing base implementation
 *                of persistable object sets
 */

using System;
using System.Data;
using System.Reflection;

namespace GW.CMPServices
{
  /// <summary>
  /// Represents a persistence operation that expects to return
  /// multiple rows of data.
  /// </summary>
  public class PersistableObjectSet : PersistableObject
  {
    protected DataSet internalData;

    public PersistableObjectSet()
    {
      internalData = new DataSet();
    }
```

```
    public virtual void FinalizeData()
    {
      PersistableObjectSet.FinalizeData( internalData );
    }
```

The `FinalizeData` method provides a format for child classes to implement data manipulation methods. If any additional work needs to be done on data retrieved from the database, the class can implement this method as a standard place for data finalization to take place.

```
    public static void FinalizeData(DataSet scratchData )
    {

    }

    public DataSet ResultSet
    {
      get { return internalData; }
      set { internalData = value; }
    }
  }
}
```

StdPersistenceContainer.cs

In order for any persistence operations to take place, they must go through a container. The following class provides the base functionality that must be provided by all containers, regardless of their data source. If containers don't follow a rigid set of standards, then the flexibility benefit of CMP will not be available.

```
/*
 * Class       : StdPersistenceContainer
 * Namespace   : GW.CMPServices
 * Assembly    : GW.CMPServices
 * Description : Standard persistence container prototype base class
 */

using System;

namespace GW.CMPServices
{
  /// <summary>
  /// Base class for all persistence containers
  /// </summary>
  public class StdPersistenceContainer
  {
    protected ContainerMapping currentMap;

    public StdPersistenceContainer( ContainerMapping initCurrentMap )
    {
      currentMap = initCurrentMap;
    }

    public ContainerMapping ContainerMapping
    {
```

```
        get { return currentMap; }
        set { currentMap = value; }
    }
```

Every single container must provide an `Insert`, `Select`, `Update`, and `Delete` method. If someone wants to build a container that doesn't support some of these methods, they should override the methods and throw an exception indicating that the operation is not supported.

```
      public virtual void Insert( PersistableObject insertObject )
      {
      }

      public virtual void Select( PersistableObject selectObject )
      {
      }

      public virtual void Update( PersistableObject updateObject )
      {
      }

      public virtual void Delete( PersistableObject deleteObject )
      {
      }
    }
  }
```

SqlPersistenceContainer.cs

`SqlPersistenceContainer` is a SQL Server-specific implementation of the `StdPersistenceContainer`. All of the data operations dictated by the `StdPersistenceContainer` are performed against a SQL Server database (version 7.0 or above, due to a restriction in the `System.Data.SqlClient` managed provider). This class takes the object-relational metadata provided to it by the `ContainerMapping` instance it maintains as a private member and performs data operations against the database.

```
/*
 * Class       : SqlPersistenceContainer
 * Namespace    : GW.CMPServices
 * Assembly     : GW.CMPServices
 * Description : SQL-based implementation of the StdPersistenceContainer.
 *               Provides persistence functionality for persistable
 *               objects with regard to a MS SQL data store.
 */

using System;
using System.Xml;
using System.Xml.Serialization;
using System.Reflection;
using System.Data;
using System.Data.SqlClient;
```

```
using GW.MonitorServices;
using GW.ConfigurationServices;

using System.Diagnostics;

namespace GW.CMPServices
{
  /// <summary>
  /// SQL-specific implementation of the StdPersistenceContainer
  /// </summary>
  public class SqlPersistenceContainer : StdPersistenceContainer
  {
    public SqlPersistenceContainer() : base() { }

    public SqlPersistenceContainer( ContainerMapping initCurrentMap ) :
                                   base( initCurrentMap )
    {
      // TODO: Add additional code if necessary
    }
```

This next method performs a Select operation, and is the most complex of the four main methods supported by the SqlPersistenceContainer. It will execute a stored procedure and place any return or output values back onto the instance of the PersistableObject that was provided. If, however, the object instance supplied also can be cast to a PersistableObjectSet, then the container will attempt to assign the return value of the stored procedure to a DataSet stored within the PersistableObjectSet.

```
    public override void Select( PersistableObject selectObject )
    {
      GWTrace.EnteringMethod( MethodBase.GetCurrentMethod() );
      try
      {
        CommandMapping cmdMap = currentMap.SelectCommand;
        SqlCommand selectCommand = BuildCommandFromMapping( cmdMap );
        AssignValuesToParameters( cmdMap, ref selectCommand, selectObject );
        selectCommand.Connection.Open();
```

This next line of code will use polymorphism to check if the parameter passed to the method is also a PersistableObjectSet. If it is, then we will be performing operations to select more than one row, and so be populating the DataSet.

```
        if (selectObject is PersistableObjectSet)
        {
          GWTrace.Trace( TraceLevel.Info, "Selecting Plural" );
          AssignReturnValueToDataSet( cmdMap, selectCommand,
                                       ref selectObject );
          AssignOutputValuesToInstance( cmdMap, selectCommand,
                                         ref selectObject );
          selectCommand.Connection.Close();
        }
        else
        {
```

```
            GWTrace.Trace( TraceLevel.Info, "Selecting Singular" );
            selectCommand.ExecuteNonQuery();
            selectCommand.Connection.Close();
            AssignOutputValuesToInstance( cmdMap, selectCommand,
                                          ref selectObject );
          }
          selectCommand.Connection.Dispose();
          selectCommand.Dispose();
        }
        catch (Exception dbException)
        {
          throw new Exception("Persistance (Select) Failed for " +
                              "PersistableObject", dbException );
        }
      }
```

The next method attempts to perform an `Insert` of the supplied object instance based on the current container mapping. It builds a command, assigns values to the stored procedure parameters, and then executes it, assigning return and output values to the object instance. Also worth noting is the fact that the connection is opened and closed quickly. It is closed as soon as it can be closed reasonably. The benefit here is that closing a `SqlConnection` instance automatically disposes it.

You might notice that we're not throwing a `GWException` here. The reason being is that the `GWException` class is designed to log itself to the database first. If we encounter a persistence failure, we can't exactly use persistence to log that failure, can we? The other, more insidious reason is that since our error logging code uses our persistence tier, if our persistence tier were to reference the error logging code, the compiler would complain about a circular reference and reject our attempt. So, the onus is on the business object to catch the error thrown by the persistence tier and re-throw it using our custom `GWException` class to ensure that the error is stored in the database or in the backup file log.

```
      public override void Insert( PersistableObject insertObject)
      {
        GWTrace.EnteringMethod( MethodBase.GetCurrentMethod() );
        try
        {
          CommandMapping cmdMap = currentMap.InsertCommand;
          SqlCommand insertCommand = BuildCommandFromMapping( cmdMap );
          AssignValuesToParameters( cmdMap, ref insertCommand, insertObject);
          insertCommand.Connection.Open();

          insertCommand.ExecuteNonQuery();
          insertCommand.Connection.Close();
          AssignOutputValuesToInstance( cmdMap, insertCommand,
                                        ref insertObject );
          insertCommand.Dispose();
        }
        catch (Exception dbException)
        {
          throw new Exception("Persistance (Insert) Failed for " +
                              "PersistableObject", dbException );
        }
      }
```

The `Update` method will perform a database update based on the data contained in the parameter and the metadata represented by the current container mapping.

```
public override void Update ( PersistableObject updateObject )
{
  try
  {
    CommandMapping cmdMap = currentMap.UpdateCommand;
    SqlCommand updateCommand = BuildCommandFromMapping( cmdMap );
    AssignValuesToParameters( cmdMap, ref updateCommand, updateObject);
    updateCommand.Connection.Open();
    updateCommand.ExecuteNonQuery();
    updateCommand.Connection.Close();
    AssignOutputValuesToInstance( cmdMap, updateCommand,
                                  ref updateObject );

    updateCommand.Dispose();
  }
  catch (Exception dbException)
  {
    throw new Exception("Persistance (Update) Failed for " +
                        "PersistableObject", dbException );
  }
}
```

The `Delete` method performs a similar function to the method above, except that it will use the metadata information contained in the current mapping to perform a `Delete` operation.

```
public override void Delete( PersistableObject deleteObject )
{
  try
  {
    CommandMapping cmdMap = currentMap.DeleteCommand;
    SqlCommand deleteCommand = BuildCommandFromMapping( cmdMap );
    AssignValuesToParameters( cmdMap, ref deleteCommand, deleteObject);
    deleteCommand.Connection.Open();
    deleteCommand.ExecuteNonQuery();
    deleteCommand.Connection.Close();
    AssignOutputValuesToInstance( cmdMap, deleteCommand,
                                  ref deleteObject );

    deleteCommand.Dispose();
  }
  catch (Exception dbException)
  {
    throw new Exception("Persistance (Delete) Failed for " +
                        "PersistableObject", dbException );
  }
}
```

This next method takes the output of the stored procedure and assigns that output to the internal `DataSet` stored within the `PersistableObjectSet` that was passed to the container. It does this by using a `DataAdapter` on the command that was passed to it.

```
private void AssignReturnValueToDataSet( CommandMapping
            SqlCommand currentCmd,
            ref PersistableObject persistObjectSet )
{
  DataSet internalData =
              ((PersistableObjectSet)persistObjectSet).ResultSet;
  SqlDataAdapter sqlDa = new SqlDataAdapter( currentCmd );
  sqlDa.Fill( internalData );
}
```

This next method uses Reflection to take the output values returned from the stored procedure execution and assigns them to the corresponding properties on the object instance as indicated by the Object-Relational Mapping metadata. The small amount of Reflection being used here is so minute compared to the execution time of the stored procedure itself that the performance impact is too small to notice under normal system load, so we think the solution should be acceptable.

```
private void AssignOutputValuesToInstance( CommandMapping cmdMap,
                SqlCommand currentCmd,
                ref PersistableObject persistObject )
{
  Type objType;
  PropertyInfo prop;

  objType = persistObject.GetType();
  SqlParameter curParam;
  foreach (CommandParameter cmdParameter in cmdMap.Parameters )
  {
    if ( (cmdParameter.RealParameterDirection ==
                        ParameterDirection.InputOutput ) ||
    (cmdParameter.RealParameterDirection ==
                        ParameterDirection.ReturnValue ) ||
    (cmdParameter.RealParameterDirection == ParameterDirection.Output))
    {
      curParam = currentCmd.Parameters[ cmdParameter.ParameterName ];
      prop = objType.GetProperty( cmdParameter.ClassMember );
      if ( curParam.Value != DBNull.Value )
        prop.SetValue( persistObject, curParam.Value, null );
    }
  }
}
```

This next method performs the opposite of the previous method. It takes the values stored in public fields or properties on the object and places them in the appropriate stored procedure parameters.

```
private void AssignValuesToParameters( CommandMapping cmdMap,
                ref SqlCommand currentCmd,
                PersistableObject persistObject )
{
  Type objType;
  PropertyInfo prop;

  objType = persistObject.GetType();
```

```
foreach (CommandParameter cmdParameter in cmdMap.Parameters )
{
  if ( (cmdParameter.RealParameterDirection ==
                                    ParameterDirection.Input ) ||
    (cmdParameter.RealParameterDirection ==
                                 ParameterDirection.InputOutput ) )
  {
    prop = objType.GetProperty( cmdParameter.ClassMember );
    currentCmd.Parameters[ cmdParameter.ParameterName ].Value =
                              prop.GetValue( persistObject, null );
```

This trace method is handy and can easily be removed (it might be removed in our final code build). The idea here is that if we're watching the page output tracing information when looking at a rendered page, we can use this line of code to examine the values sent to various stored procedures for quick and easy debugging without having to use breakpoints.

```
        GWTrace.Trace( TraceLevel.Verbose,
          "Value Set for Parameter {0} is {1}",
          cmdParameter.ParameterName,
          currentCmd.Parameters[ cmdParameter.ParameterName ].Value );
      }
    }
  }
```

This next method takes a `CommandMapping` object (remember that a `CommandMapping` is just a representation of the mapping between a class and a stored procedure) and uses the information contained within it to create a valid instance of a `SqlCommand` stored procedure.

```
private SqlCommand BuildCommandFromMapping( CommandMapping cmdMap )
{
  SqlConnection conn = new
                    SqlConnection(SiteProfile.DefaultDataSource);

  SqlCommand sqlCommand = conn.CreateCommand();
  sqlCommand.CommandText = cmdMap.CommandName;
  sqlCommand.CommandType = CommandType.StoredProcedure;
```

This next block of code creates `SqlParameter` instances for all of the parameters found in the metadata definition for a command mapping. We use a `SiteProfile` object to map the string representation of a parameter's data type to an actual `SqlDbType`.

```
  foreach ( CommandParameter cmdParameter in cmdMap.Parameters )
  {
    SqlParameter newParam = new SqlParameter();
    newParam.ParameterName = cmdParameter.ParameterName;
    newParam.Direction = cmdParameter.RealParameterDirection;
    newParam.SqlDbType =
        (SqlDbType)SiteProfile.DbTypeHints[cmdParameter.DbTypeHint];
    newParam.Size = cmdParameter.Size;

    sqlCommand.Parameters.Add( newParam );
```

```
        GWTrace.Trace( TraceLevel.Verbose,
          "Command Parameter Added for SQL Persistence: {0}",
          newParam.ParameterName );
      }

      return sqlCommand;
    }
  }
}
```

ConfigurationServices

`ConfigurationServices` is a project that contains tools for automating access to the configuration subsystem of an application. At the moment it contains nothing more than a class that maintains some static properties that can be queried by any code in the application, essentially providing a few global variables. An entire project was created for this because each application has unique configuration needs, and we may come back to this project before we are done and add more enhanced functionality.

The SiteProfile Class

This class is simply a placeholder for static values relating to the website's configuration.

```
/*
 * Class       : SqlPersistenceContainer
 * Namespace   : GW.ConfigurationServices
 * Assembly    : GW.ConfigurationServices
 * Description : Provides static member accessibility for information
 *               obtained from web.config
 */

using System;
using System.Collections;

namespace GW.ConfigurationServices
{
  /// <summary>
  /// SiteProfile class provides various globally accessible
  /// data.
  /// </summary>
  public class SiteProfile
  {
    private static Hashtable dbTypeHints;
    private static string defaultDataSource;

    static SiteProfile()
    {
      dbTypeHints = new Hashtable();
    }

    public static Hashtable DbTypeHints
    {
      get { return dbTypeHints; }
```

```
        set { dbTypeHints = value; }
      }

      public static string DefaultDataSource
      {
        get { return defaultDataSource; }
        set { defaultDataSource = value; }
      }
    }
  }
```

MonitorServices

There are two monitoring projects in our core architecture: `MonitorServices` and `MonitorServicesLogging`. `MonitorServices` contains tracing tools and utilities, while `MonitorServicesLogging` contains all of the code necessary for throwing and creating errors and logging information to various sources.

GWTrace.cs

This class provides a standard facility for tracing information. Its main use is to consolidate tracing messages traced by standard assemblies and by ASP.NET code, which normally trace to two different locations. We have sealed the class so that developers cannot override any of its tracing functionality.

```
/*
 * Class       : GWTrace
 * Namespace   : GW.MonitorServices
 * Assembly    : GW.MonitorServices
 * Description : Enhanced tracing functionality to consolidate system
 *               and http tracing log and provide support for trace
 *               switches.
 */

using System;
using System.Diagnostics;
using System.Reflection;
using System.Runtime.Remoting.Messaging;

namespace GW.MonitorServices
{
  /// <summary>
  /// Trace consolidation class
  /// </summary>
  public sealed class GWTrace
  {
    private GWTrace() { } // prevent instantiation.
```

This `TraceSwitch` to which the next line of code refers is stored in the `web.config` file. For more information on Trace Switches and how they work, you can look for Trace Switch in the MSDN documentation. Essentially, they provide configurable levels of monitoring detail for the .NET Framework's built-in tracing mechanisms.

```
private static readonly TraceSwitch traceSwitch =
           new TraceSwitch("GWTrace", "GW Current Tracing Level");

public static TraceLevel CurrentTraceLevel
{
  get { return traceSwitch.Level; }
}

[Conditional("TRACE")]
public static void Trace( string message, params Object[] args )
{
  Trace( TraceLevel.Info, message, args );
}
```

This next method performs the actual trace. It takes as arguments a configurable trace level, a message to log, and an array of objects to map to the formatted message string.

```
[Conditional("TRACE")]
public static void Trace( TraceLevel msgLevel,
                          string message,
                          params Object[] arrData )
{
  if ( msgLevel <= traceSwitch.Level )
  {
    // current trace level is more than level at which
    // message occurred, a trace should be written.
    // Always protect against bad data...
    message = ( message == null ? string.Empty : message.Trim() );
    message = MonitorUtilities.SafeFormat( message, arrData );
```

This next code block will log the trace message to the standard tracing mechanism. If there is an available HTTP context (the code is running under a website), it will attempt to log that same message to the `HttpContext`'s trace. The `Warn` method will log trace information to the web trace log so that it will be displayed in red text.

```
    try
    {
      System.Diagnostics.Trace.WriteLine( message );
      System.Web.HttpContext httpContext =
                                  System.Web.HttpContext.Current;
      if ( httpContext != null )
      {
        if ( msgLevel == TraceLevel.Error )
          httpContext.Trace.Warn( message );
        else
          httpContext.Trace.Write( message );
      }
    }
    catch
    {
      // Do nothing: do not corrupt the current error
```

```
            // with a failure to trace an error
          }
        }
      }
```

This next method is an overload for `EnteringMethod`. It provides detailed information to the tracing system about the method that is currently being executed. This provides invaluable information in tracking down where your application is going and how long it is spending there.

```
      [Conditional("TRACE")]
      public static void EnteringMethod( MethodBase method )
      {
        EnteringMethod( TraceLevel.Info, method );
      }
```

The `EnteringMethod` method will first check the trace level. If we are configured to log enough detail information, then we will trace the method signature that was passed to the method as an argument. We use a little bit of Intermediate Language knowledge here because the name of a constructor is called `.ctor` as far as Reflection is concerned.

```
      [Conditional("TRACE")]
      public static void EnteringMethod( TraceLevel msgLevel,
        MethodBase method )
      {
        try
        {
          if ( traceSwitch.Level >= TraceLevel.Error )
          {
            string methodName =
              ( method.Name.Equals(".ctor")? "Constructor" : method.Name );
            Trace ( msgLevel,
              "Entering {0}.{1}() [Signature: {2}]",
              method.DeclaringType.Name, methodName, method.ToString() );
          }
        }
        catch
        {
          // Again, do nothing here. The failure to trace should not create
          // another failure.
        }
      }

    }
  }
```

If you're curious about Intermediate Language, you can find a very readable introduction to this subject in Simon Robinson's *Advanced .NET Programming*, (Wrox Press, ISBN 1-86100-629-2).

The MonitorUtilities Class

`MonitorUtilities` is a class that provides utility routines for querying system information such as process and thread data that can be logged to the database (or file backup) at the time an error is logged.

```
/*
 * Class        : MonitorUtilities
 * Namespace    : GW.MonitorServices
 * Assembly     : GW.MonitorServices
 * Description : Utility class (static methods only) for us in logging
 *               information about important events.
 */
using System;
using System.Text;
using System.Runtime.Remoting.Messaging;

namespace GW.MonitorServices
{
  /// <summary>
  /// Utility class to aid in obtaining and logging detailed information.
  /// </summary>
  public class MonitorUtilities
  {
```

This next method turns a nested exception into a user-readable string listing out the entire chain of nested `Exception` objects thrown.

```
    public static string ExpandStackTrace( Exception ex )
    {
      StringBuilder buffer = new StringBuilder(1024);
      while (ex != null)
      {
        if (buffer.Length > 0)
          buffer.Insert(0, ex.StackTrace + "\nRe-Thrown (" + ex.Message +
                                                                  ")\n");
        else
          buffer.Insert(0, ex.StackTrace + "\n");

        ex = ex.InnerException;
      }
      buffer.Replace(" in ", "\n\tin\n");
      return buffer.ToString();
    }

    public static string GetMachineName()
    {
      return System.Environment.MachineName;
    }
```

In this next block we obtain process information for purposes of tracing. We found out the hard way that by default, .NET applications are not allowed to access this information. There are instructions included in the code that illustrate how we can enable access to process information from our application.

```
    /// <summary>
    /// In order to use the GetProcessInfo method, the ASP.NET account
    /// must have access to the performance information registry keys.
    /// To accomplish this, do the following:
```

```
/// <pre>
/// Open REGEDT32.EXE
/// Navigate to HKEY_LOCAL_MACHINE\Software\Microsoft\
///                              Windows NT\CurrentVersion\PerfLib
/// Navigate to the Security Menu
/// Click Permissions
/// Select the local machine account under which ASP.NET is running
/// (default is ASPNET)
/// Click Add
/// Now this application and all ASP.NET apps on the machine have
///  access to this data.
/// This function should NOT EVER be called if your application is
/// running on a third-party hosting company.
/// </pre>
/// </summary>
/// <returns>string containing process info</returns>
public static string GetProcessInfo()
{
  try
  {
  System.Diagnostics.Process curProcess =
                 System.Diagnostics.Process.GetCurrentProcess();

  return string.Format(
    "[Process:{0}, {1}][Thread: {2}][AppDomain:{3}]",
    curProcess.Id, curProcess.ProcessName,
    AppDomain.GetCurrentThreadId(),
    AppDomain.CurrentDomain.FriendlyName );
 }
 catch
 {
     return "Process Information Unavailable.";
 }
}
```

The `SafeFormat` method is responsible for wrapping the call to `string.Format` in a `try...catch` block.

```
    public static string SafeFormat(string format,
                               params Object[] formatArgs )
    {
      format = ( format == null ? string.Empty : format.Trim() );
      try
      {
        return string.Format(format, formatArgs );
      }
      catch
      {
        return format + " (Error binding arguments)";
      }
    }
  }
}
```

MonitorServicesLogging

The `MonitorServicesLogging` project contains classes responsible for logging error information to the database and to file locations. It also contains a custom `Exception` class and code that allows error messages to be read from an embedded resource file (`ErrorMessages.resx`). This file contains error messages in the format `E*`. This means that if the code wanted to retrieve the error message that has the value 1000 for its message number, the key within the string table in the resource file would be `E1000`. You will see all the error strings if you download the book code from the Wrox website.

The DbErrorEntry Class

`DbErrorEntry` is a `PersistableObject` that represents a single entry in the error log table.

```
/*
 * Class        : DbErrorEntry
 * Namespace    : GW.MonitorServices.Logging
 * Assembly     : GW.MonitorServices.Logging
 * Description  : PersistableObject to carry error information to the
 *                system error table in the database.
 */

using System;
using System.Data;
using System.Xml.Serialization;

using GW.CMPServices;

namespace GW.MonitorServices.Logging
{
  /// <summary>
  /// Single entry in the error table
  /// </summary>
  [Serializable()]
  public class DbErrorEntry : PersistableObject
  {
    private string serverName;
    private string errorMessage;
    private string extendedInfo;
    private long errorId;

    [XmlAttribute("servername")]
    public string ServerName
    {
      get { return serverName; }
      set { serverName = value; }
    }

    [XmlAttribute("errormessage")]
    public string ErrorMessage
    {
      get { return errorMessage; }
      set { errorMessage = value; }
    }
```

```
    [XmlAttribute("extendedinfo")]
    public string ExtendedInfo
    {
      get { return extendedInfo; }
      set { extendedInfo = value; }
    }

    [XmlAttribute("errorid")]
    public long ErrorId
    {
      get { return errorId; }
      set { errorId = value; }
    }
  }
}
```

The DbErrorEntrySet Class

This class represents a result set containing many error entries. Those entries are stored in the internal `DataSet` provided by the parent `PersistableObjectSet` class.

```
/*
 * Class       : DbErrorEntrySet
 * Namespace   : GW.MonitorServices.Logging
 * Assembly    : GW.MonitorServices.Logging
 * Description : PersistableObjectSet derivative for holding the results
 *               of selecting db errors from the database.
 */

using System;
using System.Data;

using GW.CMPServices;

namespace GW.MonitorServices.Logging
{
  /// <summary>
  /// Collection of error entries.
  /// </summary>
  public class DbErrorEntrySet : PersistableObjectSet
  {
    public DbErrorEntrySet() : base() { }

    override public void FinalizeData()
    {
      DbErrorEntrySet.FinalizeData( internalData );
    }

    new public static void FinalizeData( DataSet scratchData )
    {
      scratchData.Tables[0].TableName = "SystemErrors";
    }
  }
}
```

The DbErrorLog Class

The DbErrorLog class is responsible for writing error information to the database. If it fails to write that information to the database, it throws an exception so that the calling code can recover from that and write the error information to a backup file.

```
/*
 * Class        : DbErrorLog
 * Namespace    : GW.MonitorServices.Logging
 * Assembly     : GW.MonitorServices.Logging
 * Description  : Class that is responsible for logging system errors to
 *                the database.
 */

using System;
using System.Text;
using System.Reflection;
using System.Diagnostics;

using GW.CMPServices;
using GW.MonitorServices;

namespace GW.MonitorServices.Logging
{
  /// <summary>
  /// Error logging (DB) class
  /// </summary>
  public class DbErrorLog
  {
    private DbErrorLog() { }

    public static long LogError( Exception e )
    {
      return LogError( e, string.Empty );
    }
```

The LogError method here is responsible for logging an error to the database. We use the ExpandStackTrace method covered earlier to provide detailed information on all errors in the error stack to aid developers in debugging an application.

```
    public static long LogError( Exception e, string rootMessage )
    {
      GWTrace.EnteringMethod( MethodBase.GetCurrentMethod() );
      StringBuilder buffer = new StringBuilder(2048);
      try
      {
        if (rootMessage.Length > 0)
          buffer.AppendFormat( "{0}\n\n", rootMessage );
        buffer.Append( MonitorUtilities.ExpandStackTrace( e ));

        DbErrorEntry dbEntry = new DbErrorEntry();
        dbEntry.ErrorMessage = buffer.ToString();
        dbEntry.ExtendedInfo = MonitorUtilities.GetProcessInfo();
        dbEntry.ServerName = MonitorUtilities.GetMachineName();
```

```
            SqlPersistenceContainer sqlPC = new SqlPersistenceContainer(
              CMPServices.CMPConfigurationHandler.ContainerMaps["ERROR_LOG"] );
            sqlPC.Insert( dbEntry );
            return dbEntry.ErrorId;
          }
          catch (Exception ex )
          {
            // this must be thrown so the generic log front-end can
            // tell that there was a db error log failure and write the
            // error to a disk file instead.
            GWTrace.Trace( TraceLevel.Error, "LogError Failed [{0}]",
                           ex.ToString() );
            throw new Exception("Database log failure", ex );
          }
        }
      }
    }
```

The FileErrorLog Class

This class performs the same function as `DbErrorLog`, only the destination for errors sent to this class a text file that stores errors wrapped up in minimal HTML for easy viewing in a browser.

```
/*
 * Class       : FileErrorLog
 * Namespace   : GW.MonitorServices.Logging
 * Assembly    : GW.MonitorServices.Logging
 * Description : Class responsible for logging error information to HTML
 *               text files as backup/alternate to DB error logging.
 */

using System;
using System.Configuration;
using System.Diagnostics;
using System.Reflection;

namespace GW.MonitorServices.Logging
{
  /// <summary>
  /// FileErrorLog performs error logging operations on text files.
  /// </summary>
  public class FileErrorLog
  {
```

In this next line of code, we are declaring a `ReaderWriterLock` so that we have exclusive, thread-safe access to this file while we're writing information to it. All other attempts to access this file while we're using it will be queued up and have to wait until the file operation is complete.

```
    private static readonly System.Threading.ReaderWriterLock
                 errorFileLock = new System.Threading.ReaderWriterLock();

    public static void LogError( Exception e )
```

```
    {
      LogError( e, string.Empty );
    }
```

This next overload of `LogError` will log the error message contained in the parameters.

```
    public static void LogError( Exception e, string rootMessage )
    {
      GWTrace.EnteringMethod( MethodBase.GetCurrentMethod() );
      rootMessage = ( rootMessage == null ? string.Empty :
                                                rootMessage.Trim() );
      Exception originalException = e;

      System.Text.StringBuilder buffer = new
                                              System.Text.StringBuilder(4096);
      if ( rootMessage.Length > 0)  buffer.AppendFormat(
                        "<font color='RED' size=2><b>{0}</b></font><br/>",
                        rootMessage );
```

This next section of code will loop through all nested exceptions and concatenate them so that every last drop of error information will be logged to the text/HTML file.

```
      while (e != null )
      {
        buffer.AppendFormat(
            "<font color='RED' size=2><b>{0}</b></font><br/>", e.Message );
        if (e.TargetSite != null )
        {
          buffer.Append("<font size=1>");
          buffer.AppendFormat( "at method {0}.{1}(...)<br/>",
                               e.TargetSite.DeclaringType.Name,
                               e.TargetSite.Name );
        }
        e = e.InnerException;
      }

      e = originalException;
      buffer.Append(
           "<br><font size=2 color=red><b>Stack Trace:</b></font><br/>\n");
      buffer.Append("<font size=1>\n");
      buffer.Append(MonitorUtilities.ExpandStackTrace(e).Replace(
                                                     "\n", "<br>\n"));
      buffer.Append("</font>");

      appendMessageToErrorLogFile( buffer.ToString() );
    }

    public static void LogError( string message, params Object[] arrParams)
    {
      message = ( message == null ? string.Empty : message.Trim() );
      message = MonitorUtilities.SafeFormat( message, arrParams );
      appendMessageToErrorLogFile( message );
    }
```

This next method performs the actual file I/O for logging the exception to the HTML text file. The file that is used as the error log file is indicated by configuration properties in the `web.config` file.

```
private static void appendMessageToErrorLogFile ( string errorMessage )
{
  // Note that if the ASPNET account does not have write privileges
  // in the directory that you are planning on storing the file-based
  // error log, that file will never be created.
  System.IO.StreamWriter errLog = null;
  errorFileLock.AcquireWriterLock(10000);
  try
  {
    errLog = System.IO.File.AppendText( getAppErrorLogFileName() );
    errLog.WriteLine("<span style='font-family:Verdana'>" +
                                                  "<font size=2>");
    errLog.WriteLine("<br/><hr/>\n");
    errLog.WriteLine(
            "The following error occurred in the application on {0}",
            System.DateTime.Now);
    errLog.WriteLine("<hr/>\n");
    errLog.WriteLine( errorMessage );
    errLog.Flush();
    errLog.Close();
  }
  catch (Exception ex)
  {
    GWTrace.Trace(
      TraceLevel.Error, "An error occurred when saving an error to " +
                                        "disk: {0}", ex.ToString() );
  }
  finally
  {
    errorFileLock.ReleaseLock();
    try
    {
      if (errLog != null )
      {
        errLog.Flush();
        errLog.Close();
      }
    }
    catch { }
  }
}
```

This next method is responsible for obtaining the filename of the error log to which all of the error information will be written. It uses the `checkAndCreateDir` helper method to check and see if the indicated directory exists. If anything goes wrong, then we will default the directory to `C:\`.

```
private static string getAppErrorLogFileName()
{
  string errorLogBaseDir =
```

```
System.Configuration.ConfigurationSettings.AppSettings["ErrorLogBaseDir"];
      string errorLogDir = checkAndCreateDir( errorLogBaseDir, "C:\\");

      string errorFileName = string.Format( "Error-{0}.htm",
                             System.DateTime.Now.ToString("yyyyMMdd"));

      return errorLogDir + errorFileName;
    }

    private static string checkAndCreateDir( string newDir,
                                             string fallBackDir )
    {
      GWTrace.EnteringMethod( MethodBase.GetCurrentMethod() );
      if (System.IO.Directory.Exists( newDir ) ) return newDir;

      try
      {
        System.IO.Directory.CreateDirectory( newDir );
        if (System.IO.Directory.Exists( newDir ) )
          return newDir;
        else
          return fallBackDir;
      }
      catch (Exception ex )
      {
        GWTrace.Trace( TraceLevel.Error,
          "There was an error creating the directory {0} : {1}",
          newDir,
          ex.ToString() );
        return fallBackDir;
      }
    }
  }
}
```

The ErrorLog Class

The `ErrorLog` class performs a triage function for logging errors. It will take an error, attempt to log it to the database (via the `DbErrorLog` class), and if that fails, it will attempt to log the error to a backup file (via the `FileErrorLog` class).

```
/*
 * Class       : ErrorLog
 * Namespace   : GW.MonitorServices.Logging
 * Assembly    : GW.MonitorServices.Logging
 * Description : Class for handling all forms of error logging.
 */

using System;
using System.Configuration;
using System.Reflection;
using System.Diagnostics;
```

```
namespace GW.MonitorServices.Logging
{
  /// <summary>
  /// Triage component for sending errors to database and file
  /// with file as backup
  /// </summary>
  public class ErrorLog
  {
    private static string errorUrlPrefix;

    public static long LogError( Exception appError )
    {
      return LogError( appError, string.Empty );
    }
```

The `LogError` method performs the main triage for logging errors. It will first attempt to log the error to the database, and then log a reference to that error to the text file. If this fails for any reason, it will attempt to log that failure to the text/HTML file. If *that* fails, then it will log the fact that the backup error logging mechanism failed to the runtime tracing system.

```
    public static long LogError( Exception appError, string rootMessage )
    {
      GWTrace.EnteringMethod( MethodBase.GetCurrentMethod() );
      rootMessage = ( rootMessage == null ? string.Empty :
                                            rootMessage.Trim() );
      try
      {
        long errorId = DbErrorLog.LogError( appError, rootMessage );
        FileErrorLog.LogError( GWException.GetGWExceptionMessage(
                               GWExceptionMessages.SeeDatabase ),
                               ErrorViewUrlPrefix, errorId );
        return errorId;
      }
      catch (Exception dbError )
      {
        GWTrace.Trace( TraceLevel.Error, "DB Error Log Attempt Failed" );
        try
        {
          FileErrorLog.LogError( appError, rootMessage );
          FileErrorLog.LogError( dbError,
                                 GWException.GetGWExceptionMessage(
                                       GWExceptionMessages.DbLogFailed ) );
          return -1;
        }
        catch
        {
          GWTrace.Trace( TraceLevel.Error,
                         "Backup File Error Log Attempt Failed");
          return -2;
        }
      }
    }
```

```
    private static string ErrorViewUrlPrefix
    {
      get
      {
        if ( errorUrlPrefix != null) return errorUrlPrefix;

        string prefix =
             ConfigurationSettings.AppSettings["ErrorViewUrlPrefix"];
        prefix = ( prefix == null ? string.Empty : prefix.Trim() );

        if (prefix.Length == 0 )
          prefix = "/GadgetsWarehouse/ErrorLog/";

        errorUrlPrefix = prefix;
        return errorUrlPrefix;
      }
    }
  }
}
```

The GWException Class

The `GWException` class is a custom exception class that has built-in knowledge of the persistence system and monitoring utilities so that any time anyone throws an exception of this type, that exception will automatically be persisted in some durable location such as a database or a text file.

```
/*
 * Class       : GWException
 * Namespace   : GW.MonitorServices.Logging
 * Assembly    : GW.MonitorServices.Logging
 * Description : Custom application exception class that handles logging
 *      of all GW errors
 */

using System;
using System.Resources;
using System.Reflection;
using System.Runtime.Serialization;

using GW.CMPServices;

namespace GW.MonitorServices.Logging
{
  /// <summary>
  /// Custom exception class for the Gadgets Warehouse
  /// </summary>
  public class GWException : System.ApplicationException
  {
    private long errorId;

    public GWException( GWExceptionMessages messageNumber ) :
           base ( GWException.GetGWExceptionMessage( messageNumber ) )
    {
```

```
    string message = this.Message;
    errorId = ErrorLog.LogError( this, message );
  }

  public static GWException NewGWException(
                                  GWExceptionMessages messageNumber )
  {
    return new GWException( messageNumber );
  }

  public GWException( GWExceptionMessages messageNumber,
                      Exception innerException) :
    base( GWException.GetGWExceptionMessage( messageNumber ),
          innerException )
  {
    string message = this.Message;
    errorId = ErrorLog.LogError( this, message );
  }

  public static GWException NewGWException(
          GWExceptionMessages messageNumber, Exception innerException )
  {
    return new GWException( messageNumber, innerException );
  }
```

In this next method, you can see that this exception class knows how to persist failures on a `PersistableObject` by calling its `ToXmlString` method. As we saw earlier, that method provides an XML serialized copy of the instance so that we can see both in the trace and in the database what actually caused the database to reject the persistence operation.

```
  public GWException( GWExceptionMessages messageNumber,
                      Exception innerException,
                      PersistableObject failedPersisted,
                      string persistenceOp ) :
    base( GWException.GetGWExceptionMessage( messageNumber ),
          innerException )
  {
    string message = this.Message;
    message += " Persistence Failed: {0} on [{1}]";
    message = MonitorUtilities.SafeFormat(message, persistenceOp,
                                    failedPersisted.ToXmlString());
    errorId = ErrorLog.LogError( this, message );
  }
```

This next method retrieves an exception message from the internal resource file based on a numeric key that is supplied by the `GWExceptionMessages` enumeration. You can tell from the format string we're using that the error messages are stored in the resource file with keys in the form `E####` where `####` is the integer value of the enumeration member, as we mentioned earlier.

```
  internal static string GetGWExceptionMessage(
                                  GWExceptionMessages messageNumber )
  {
```

```
        ResourceManager rm = new ResourceManager(
                                "GW.MonitorServices.Logging.ErrorMessages",
                                Assembly.GetExecutingAssembly() );
        return rm.GetString( string.Format("E{0}", (int)messageNumber) );
      }

      public long GWErrorId
      {
        get { return errorId; }
      }
    }
  }
```

The GWExceptionMessages Class

This is the enumeration that contains the integer values that function as keys in the resource file for loading error strings.

```
/*
 * Enumeration : GWExceptionMessages
 * Namespace   : GW.MonitorServices.Logging
 * Assembly    : GW.MonitorServices.Logging
 * Description : Enumeration containing index values into the string
 *               resource containing the standardized error messages
 */

using System;

namespace GW.MonitorServices.Logging
{
  public enum GWExceptionMessages
  {
    DefaultMessage = 1000,
    DbLogFailed = 1001,
    SeeDatabase = 1002,
    PersistenceFailure = 1003
  }
}
```

SecurityServices

The `SecurityServices` project currently is fairly limited. All it does at the moment is perform simple authentication of users. As the project progresses, we may encounter issues that our design did not quite cover, such as things involving Web Services, and so we may revisit this project and see if anything needs to be added.

The AuthUserEntry Class

`AuthUserEntry` is a `PersistableObject` that represents a single user within the database and it is used to communicate with the authentication stored procedure.

```
using System;
using GW.CMPServices;

namespace GW.SecurityServices
{
  /// <summary>
  /// Persistable Object for user entries communicating to the DB.
  /// </summary>
  [Serializable()]
  public class AuthUserEntry : PersistableObject
  {
    private string userId;
    private string password;
    private string firstName;
    private string lastName;
    private string emailAddress;
    private int customerId;


    public string EmailAddress
    {
      get { return emailAddress; }
      set { emailAddress = value; }
    }

    public string UserId
    {
      get { return userId; }
      set { userId = value; }
    }

    public string Password
    {
      get { return password; }
      set { password = value; }
    }

    public int CustomerId
    {
      get { return customerId; }
      set { customerId = value; }
    }

    public string FirstName
    {
      get { return firstName; }
      set { firstName = value; }
    }

    public string LastName
    {
      get { return lastName; }
      set { lastName = value; }
    }
  }
}
```

The Authenticator Class

Authenticator is a class that performs authentication of users based on usernames and passwords being supplied. If the user is authenticated, more detailed information about that user is returned in the form of `out` parameters to the authentication method.

```
/*
 * Class       : Authenticator
 * Namespace   : GW.SecurityServices
 * Assembly    : GW.SecurityServices
 * Description : Responsible for authenticating a site user
 */

using System;

using GW.CMPServices;
using GW.MonitorServices;

namespace GW.SecurityServices
{
  /// <summary>
  /// Authenticates GW users
  /// </summary>
  public class Authenticator
  {
    public int AuthenticateUser( string userId, string password,
                                 out string firstName, out string lastName )
    {
      SqlPersistenceContainer spc = new SqlPersistenceContainer(
                 CMPConfigurationHandler.ContainerMaps["UserValidate"] );
      AuthUserEntry authUser = new AuthUserEntry();
      authUser.UserId = userId;
      authUser.Password = password;

      spc.Select( authUser );
      firstName = authUser.FirstName;
      lastName = authUser.LastName;
      return authUser.CustomerId;
    }
  }
}
```

Summary

This chapter covered quite a bit of ground. The first thing we did was take a look at the needs we had in terms of architecture, and then we took a fairly generic look at what it is that a good set of architecture code needs to provide to an application. This turned into a detailed design where we developed the class diagrams for all of the projects we built. Finally, we took a look at the code for the architecture.

Any architecture must solve the problems of data access, monitoring, security, and configuration if that architecture is to provide standardized services to a web application. All data-driven applications need to access data, and we definitely need to be able to monitor the internals of our applications. Security and configuration are things that we know we're going to need as we get further into the development of our application.

As I said earlier in the chapter, the architecture might not appear to be all that impressive standing on its own; it is really nothing more than a collection of utility assemblies. However, the true usefulness of this architecture will become readily apparent when we move further into the project and start creating user interface code and business objects that will utilize this architecture.

CHAPTER 3

3

Product Catalog

In the last chapter we had a look at the core architectural services for our application – these will ensure that everything we build starts from a solid foundation. In this chapter, we're going to take a look at the product catalog.

The product catalog presents a unique challenge. It doesn't make any difference what you are selling, or what kind of e-commerce website you have; if you are selling something, you need a product catalog. This chapter is going to take you through some of the challenges of creating a product catalog that is fast, efficient, and flexible enough to support a fully functioning e-commerce website. We'll walk through the problems involved in creating product catalogs, the design of GadgetsWarehouse.com's product catalog, and how we implemented it.

The Problem

You might be wondering what problems could you have with a product catalog? It's pretty straightforward, right? You've got products, you've got prices, maybe you've got some categories, but ultimately, it's pretty simple. Unfortunately for most of us, the products we're trying to sell aren't so easily pigeon-holed.

There are quite a few things that we need to think about when we're building the product catalog. The following is a quick list of some aspects of the product catalog that we need to be concerned about:

- Speed
- Flexibility
- Scalability
- Reliability

Speed

The product catalog is the central core around which the rest of the e-commerce website revolves. If the product catalog is creating bottlenecks or slowing the customer down, you are going to notice customers leaving your site in droves. The product catalog needs to be engineered in such a way that queries against it are fast and efficient, and retrieving product information should ideally be faster than the rendering time of the page.

Flexibility

One thing that can kill your website quickly is a rigid product-catalog structure. If your catalog cannot expand and shift with the demands of your customers, then you will be spending an extremely large amount of time both re-writing your website and redesigning your database. There is always one motto that all website designers and developers need to keep in mind:

> **No matter what you intended your site to do, your customers will use it in a way you didn't intend.**

What you need to be able to do is roll with the punches and grow, expand, and change your product catalog quickly and with minimal impact or pain on your customers. Imagine that you have just opened a commerce site and you're selling widgets. After selling widgets happily for months, you notice that customers have been demanding mountains of widget accessories from your site. They are buying widgets from your site, and accessories from your competitors. If you want to keep your customers, you'll need to expand to pick up the new accessories. If your product catalog is designed to be too inflexible to handle that, it might take months of development time to rebuild your application from the ground up to handle the shift.

Scalability

Here we're not talking about scaling hardware, or scaling out your database by using a cluster. What we're talking about here is scaling the size and content of your database without losing performance. After your company adjusts to selling both widgets and widget accessories, you need to expand. Your customers are demanding more and more variety in their widgets. If your product catalog starts to lose efficiency or simply can't handle a large increase in product volume, you will again be put between a rock and a hard place. Your catalog needs to be ready to handle a lot of products. A good plan is to design your product catalog to handle far more products than you can conceive of selling. That should get you into a good starting place, but don't rely on that estimate. After all, Bill Gates did say that no one would ever need more than 640k of RAM, and I've had to reboot twice to reclaim more of my 256MB.

Reliability

This point cannot be stressed enough. Your product catalog absolutely and without a doubt, must be 100% reliable. You must design for 100% reliability and you need to program for it. The database that holds your product catalog needs to follow the "5 9s" rule, which essentially means 99.999% availability. If you can't get that kind of guarantee from your database, you need to look elsewhere for a data solution, or be able to justify the lack of availability to your satisfaction. You might be able to make exceptions or cut corners in other places of your application, but if your product catalog slows down or disappears because the database goes down or a query runs away, you won't be doing much selling until that gets fixed. Before you take your e-commerce site live, make sure that nothing short of a natural disaster can take out your product catalog. In fact, many e-commerce sites have entire copies of their site (including mirrors of their databases) running in different geographic locations so that they can maintain a running site even if something disastrous does happen to the main data center.

The Design

Now that we've talked about the things that we need to keep in mind when we're building the design for a product catalog, let's roll up our sleeves and build one. Designing our product catalog actually involves quite a bit, but we'll separate it into three main sections.

- The Database
- The Presentation Tier
- The Business and Data Tier

The first thing we're going to do is create the design for our database. We need a clear, solid, and approved database design before we can work out any of the details of the code we're going to write.

The Database

Before we get into the actual database diagrams and start listing off the various tables we think we need, we should start at a higher level and work down. It is frequently a good exercise when building a database design to identify the basic constructs or "units of data" that you think you are going to need to keep track of without worrying about keys, relationships, indexes, constraints, etc. Often worrying about those details too soon can inhibit you from thinking about what you really need for your design. For our product catalog, this is the list of the things we're going to want:

- Products
- Categories
- Lists of Products
- Customizable Product Attributes (sales/marketing data)
- SKUs and Price
- Image URLs and Links

Products

This is pretty straightforward. We know that we're going to need to track product information such as name, description, and so on.

Categories

From the design meetings for our fictitious website we know that we want to at least be able to support the notion of departments and categories. By category, we're talking about a top-level category. We'll be enforcing a business rule where we won't have any products within these categories. Second-level categories, or categories within a top-level category, are going to be referred to as departments in terms of the UI. However, to us, they're still just nested or 'sub' categories. Even though we're only using two category levels, we are going to try to structure the product catalog itself to support an infinite amount of category nesting in case we need to utilize more levels in the future.

Lists of Products

One of our favorite features of some of the e-commerce sites that we like to use is product lists. We want to be able to have the site administrators (not to be confused with the site programmers) be able to enter in arbitrary product lists such as Top 10s, Bestsellers, Gift Ideas, Seasonal Lists, and so on. These lists should be easy to use and easy to maintain through an administration tool.

Product Attributes

One thing that we know is that we don't know everything. It is not only possible, but very likely that we will learn more about our own business as the site grows and customers use it. We will probably need to add more custom information to a product in a uniform fashion that allows sales managers to define what attributes can be added to products. This will allow people who might not have familiarity with the products or even with the code to pick up notes, magazines, or Internet articles and attach useful pieces of information to products in a format defined by the people who know the products best, rather than the programmers.

For example, let's say one of the product types that we're planning on selling is Radio Controlled cars. Customers who buy RC cars generally want to know things like the frequency of the controller crystal so they can tell if they can race against other cars. How do you store that? You can't add it to the product table, since you'd be wasting a field for all but a small portion of your products.

Instead, what we're going to do is make it so that a sales manager can create an attribute called "Frequency" with a drop-down list of available choices. Then, data entry clerks can simply punch in the frequency of the product and it will be added to only those products where that attribute is applicable. It requires using some complex joins to pull back out of the database, but, as we'll see, the end result is an amazing amount of flexibility and scalability, two of the main requirements of our product catalog.

SKUs and Prices

SKU is an acronym for *Stock-Keeping Unit.* In essence, all it really means is that it is *your* own private identifier for that particular product. It should not be confused with a UPC, which stands for *Universal Product Code.* These codes are global. An SKU is really whatever you want it to be; it is what your store and your warehouse use to refer to your stock. We need to be able to keep track of SKUs and prices.

One feature that we want our application to be able to support is the fact that a product might actually have multiple SKUs. This gives us the ability to present one single product page for products that come in multiple colors, or movies that might come in more than one format. For example, the red version of something and the blue version of something will have different SKUs. However, we want our site to still be able to treat them as the same product, since they only differ by color. Also, movies often have multiple releases in VHS, and even more varieties of DVD. We want to be able to group these together so customers can look at a single title and see all the variations (SKUs) associated with it. The main reason we want this feature is that we're not sure exactly of all the different reasons why we might use this feature, but to make our product catalog as flexible as possible, we want to be able to support it out of the box rather than having to code it in later.

Image Links

For the most part, we know that we can easily get away with naming our picture files with the product identifier in order to get product pictures to show up. However, we want to be able to support more than just thumbnails and blow-up shots. For example, if we want to sell some software for some reason (maybe it goes along with a really cool GPS gadget) then we might want to be able to provide a list of screenshots of that software in action. Our product catalog should be able to support the notion of an unlimited number of pictures being associated with any given product.

Database Tables

So, now that we've talked about the various different things that we want our product catalog to be able to keep track of, let's take a look at the design we came up with for all of the various tables involved in the product catalog:

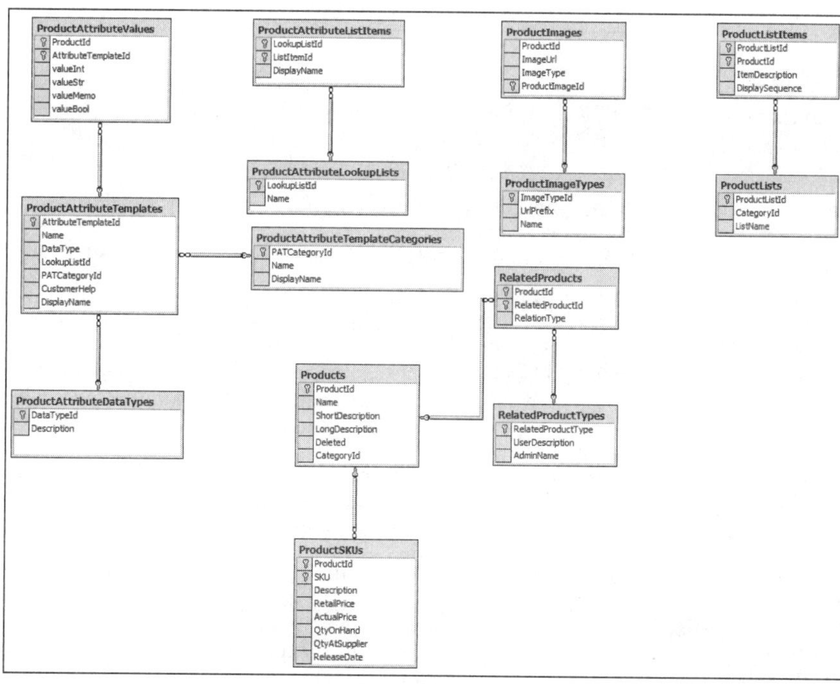

The diagram is useful, to a point. It shows what tables we're going to make and how they're related, but it doesn't have any information on data types or *why* we're designing the tables this way. Let's take a look at some table definitions to get a clearer picture of the tables we're using and why.

Products Table

This is the main product table. It contains information on individual products. Keep in mind that each product can have one or more SKUs associated with it.

Column	Data Type	Description
`ProductId`	`Int`	Unique (autoincrement) ID for the product.
`Name`	`Varchar(50)`	The short name of the product. This appears in browse lists and in the shopping cart and orders.
`ShortDescription`	`Varchar(100)`	Short description this appears in browse lists.
`LongDescription`	`Varchar(4000)`	The long description, which can contain HTML, is displayed on the product detail page.
`Deleted`	`Bit`	A flag indicating whether or not the product has been deleted. This is here for future expansion and our product doesn't currently use it.
`CategoryId`	`Int`	The ID of the category to which this product belongs. A product can belong to one and only one category.

ProductSKU Table

This table contains the list of all SKUs in the database. Each SKU is associated to one and only one product ID.

Column	Data Type	Description
`ProductId*`	`Int`	ID of the product to which the SKU is linked.
`SKU*`	`Varchar(11)`	The actual Stock Keeping Unit, an 11-character string.
`Description`	`Varchar(50)`	The description of the SKU. This is to support naming individual SKUs to provide color or other distinctions.
`RetailPrice`	`Money`	This price is to be displayed with a slash through it so the customer sees what a discount they're getting by using our site to purchase their gadgets.
`ActualPrice`	`Money`	This is the price the customer will be charged for purchasing this SKU.
`QtyOnHand`	`Int`	For future expansion – used to track availability of product.

Column	Data Type	Description
QtyAtSupplier	Int	For future expansion – used to track availability of product at the supplier. These two Qty fields are what most sites use to determine the "Ships Within" time, for example, 24 hours if there is QtyOnHand > 0, 48 if QtyAtSupplier > 0, or 2-3 weeks if they're out of stock.
ReleaseDate	DateTime	For future expansion, by setting this to a time in the future, the site can be coded to allow customers to pre-order items.

ProductImages Table

A cross-reference table that contains a list of images and/or screenshots associated with a particular product. Note that all of these tables revolve around the product and not the SKU.

Column	Data Type	Description
ProductId	Int	ID of the product to which the image belongs
ImageUrl	Varchar(255)	URL pointing to the image itself
ImageType	Int	ID foreign key pointing at an ID in the ProductImageTypes table
ProductImageId*	Int	Unique ID/Key for this table

ProductImageTypes Table

This is the reference table containing a list of different image types. It provides a URL prefix that allows images of different types to be stored either on different servers or in different folders, and so on.

Column	Data Type	Description
ImageTypeId*	Int	Key for the table, used by ProductImages table
UrlPrefix	Varchar(50)	Prefix for the URL, such as /screenshots or /views
Name	Varchar(50)	Name of the image type used to distinguish screenshots from product views, etc.

RelatedProducts Table

Rather than creating tables for product accessories, upsells, and cross-sells, we decided to use a single table with a relation type that allows us to store all the product relations we need in one table. This lets us create accessories, cross-sells, up-sells, or anything else we can think of to link one product to another without having to create a new table each time we think of a new use for linking products.

Column	Data Type	Description
ProductId*	Int	"Source" product ID
RelatedProductId*	Int	"Destination" or "related" product ID
RelationType	Int	ID of the RelationType in the RelatedProductTypes table

RelatedProductTypes Table

This is the reference table that contains the list of relation types and their user and administrative descriptions.

Column	Data Type	Description
RelatedProductType*	Int	ID of this relation type
UserDescription	Varchar(255)	What the user sees when displayed related products of this type, such as "If you like this product you might also like..."
AdminName	Varchar(50)	Administrative name for this relation type, like "Cross Sell", "Upsell" or "Accessory" etc.

Categories Table

This table contains the list of all of the product categories in the database.

Column	Data Type	Description
CategoryId*	Int	Unique ID for the category.
Description	Varchar(50)	Description of the category.
Notes	Text	In case the UI needs to make use of a large amount of text for a category (say for some promotion).
ParentCategoryId	Int	ID of the parent category. Used to establish the category hierarchy. Top-level categories have NULL as their parent category.

ProductAttributeTemplates Table

These are the meta-definitions for product attribute values. Administrators or marketers set up these templates to create attributes that can be added to products that supply additional information such as batteries required, electronics information like audio attributes or video details, or even things like the length of the manufacturer's warranty. Remember that the templates are just definitions of the data that can be added to products, not the data itself.

Column	Data Type	Description
AttributeTemplateId*	Int	The unique ID for the template.
Name	Varchar(50)	The name of the template. This is used for administrative purposes and not displayed to the users.
DataType	Int	Data type of the template. Reference to ProductAttributeDataTypes table.
LookupListId	Int	If the DataType is a lookup list, then this column indicates the lookup list that restricts the domain of values that can be added to a product for this template. This gives the effect of administrators having a drop-down box of available values when adding attribute values.
PATCategoryId	Int	Category to which this attribute belongs. This serves to further organize the display of product attribute categories.
CustomerHelp	Varchar(4000)	If the UI is coded to support this in the future, we can add lengthy text here to be displayed in a pop-up window to tell the customer exactly what the attribute means and what impact it has on the product.
DisplayName	Varchar(255)	The name of the attribute template as displayed to the user.

ProductAttributeValues Table

This is a cross-reference table that maps attribute templates to individual products while supplying data values. When administrators add attribute values to a product, the values appear in this table.

Column	Data Type	Description
ProductId*	Int	ID of the product to which the data value is mapped.
AttributeTemplateId*	Int	ID of the template for which the value is supplied.
valueInt	Int	Integer value. If the data type of the template is an integer, the data value is stored in this column. If the data type is a lookup list, the ID of the lookup list item is also stored in this column.

Table continued on following page

Column	Data Type	Description
valueStr	Varchar(255)	If the data type of the template is a string, the data value is stored in this column.
valueMemo	Text	If the data type of the template is a memo (Text), the value is stored in this column.
valueBool	Bit	If the data type of the template is Boolean, then the value of the attribute is stored in this column.

ProductAttributeLookupLists Table

This table contains the names and IDs of all of the various lookup lists. For future expansion we could add a column to this table to let us know who created the list and when.

Column	Data Type	Description
LookupListId*	Int	Unique ID of the lookup list.
Name	Varchar(80)	Name of the lookup list. For administrative use; users don't see this name.

ProductAttributeListItems Table

This table contains all of the individual list items that belong to the lookup lists. Each list item has its own unique ID.

Column	Data Type	Description
LookupListId	Int	ID of the lookup list to which this item belongs
ListItemId*	Int	Auto-incrementing ID column
DisplayName	Varchar(50)	The name of the lookup list item displayed in drop-down lists to administrators and displayed as an attribute value to customers

ProductAttributeTemplateCategories Table

This table contains the definitions for the attribute template categories.

Column	Data Type	Description
PATCategoryId*	Int	Unique ID for the attribute template category.
Name	Varchar(50)	Administrative name for the category.
DisplayName	Varchar(255)	User/Customer-displayed category name.

The ProductCatalog Assembly Design

In the previous chapter we built quite a few projects that contained the various pieces of the core architecture code. In this chapter, we're going to build one assembly that will perform about 90% of the work for the product catalog features we plan on implementing. We are going to create some user controls that will go in our web project and we'll create some web pages that perform the activities we want performed on the product catalog.

Let's take a look at the class diagrams for the classes that will interact with the data structures we have outlined above. After that, we'll go into detail on what each of those classes does.

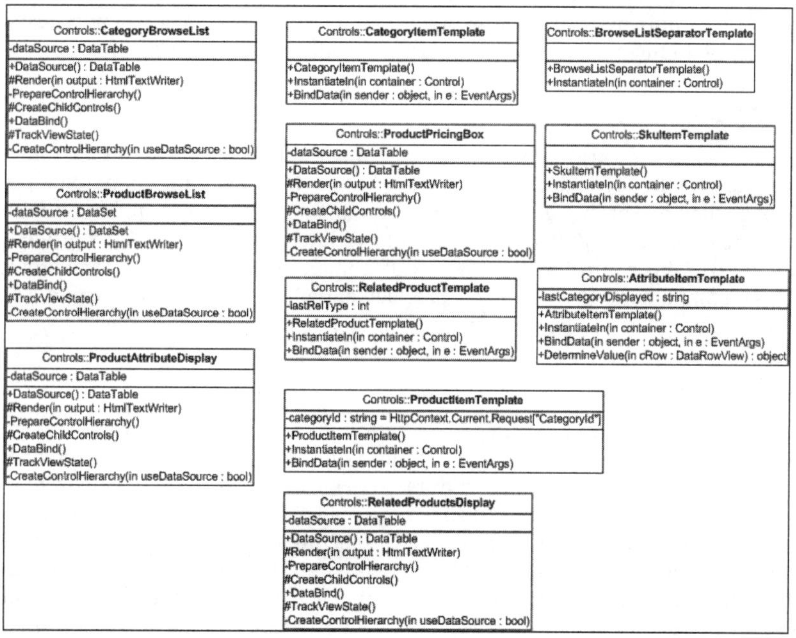

CategoryBrowseList

The `CategoryBrowseList` is a composite server control. Its job will be to display a list of categories in the main content portion of the page in a nice, graphical manner. It should allow people to click on the thumbnail icon for a particular category. The main user interface will allow you to choose a department (top-level category) via a user control. This will bring up the list of categories or sub-categories within that particular department. Clicking that category will bring you to a page that contains the product browse list control.

ProductBrowseList

This is also a composite server control. It will be responsible for displaying a list of products. Each time a user clicks into a sub-category, (a category beneath a department as far as the user is concerned) that user will see a list of products within that category. The list will contain product names, descriptions, thumbnails, and all of the pricing information belonging to the various SKUs associated with those products. Neither browse list control will use the `DataGrid`, as they both have fairly complex displays that don't lend themselves to a columnar display. Instead, they will be using a `DataList` to accomplish the display.

ProductAttributeDisplay

When a user clicks into a particular product page, they will be presented with the product details by default. There will be a navigation strip allowing them to view other aspects of the product, such as attributes, related products, etc. The attributes display will display the additional data that was supplied by administrators in the form of attributes.

The control will first display the attribute category. Underneath those category displays, the product attribute value will be displayed. This list will allow values like the frequency of radio controlled cars, the sound system support of a DVD player, or the battery life of other rechargeable gadgets to be entered, all without the involvement of a single programmer. In this way, the sales, marketing, and publishing staff can supply detailed information about the product through an administration tool, which is then visible to the user through the attribute display and other screens.

ProductPricingBox

When looking at any of the various detail pages belonging to a product, one of the things that the marketing people keep saying is that the user should never lose the ability to purchase the product, no matter what page they're working on. So, we want some way to provide a highly reusable way of displaying pricing information that also includes the various purchase links for a product, like adding it to the shopping cart. This control will display a box containing the pricing information and purchase links for all SKUs that belong to a particular product, allowing you to buy any color, shape, variation, or format of a single product from the same page.

RelatedProductsDisplay

Another essential tool for marketing and getting customers to buy things is to provide cross-sells and up-sells, which are really just ways of moving a customer's interest from one product to another by getting them to buy a similarly priced product with different features, or by getting them to buy a product with more features. We could have easily just decided to create tables for cross-sells and up-sells. However, there are other ways in which you can relate one product to another, so we decided to generalize that somewhat. We have the ability to create an unlimited number of relation types, and when an administrator relates a product to another, they simply choose *how* that product is related to the other from a drop-down box. This gives us the ability to support cross-sell, up-sell, accessories, and the famous "customers who bought this also liked..." type of functionality without having to re-write anything in our database. Again, this goes back to the scalability and flexibility requirements of our product catalog.

The next diagram contains the business classes and the data classes that provide the underlying framework on which the above UI elements are built:

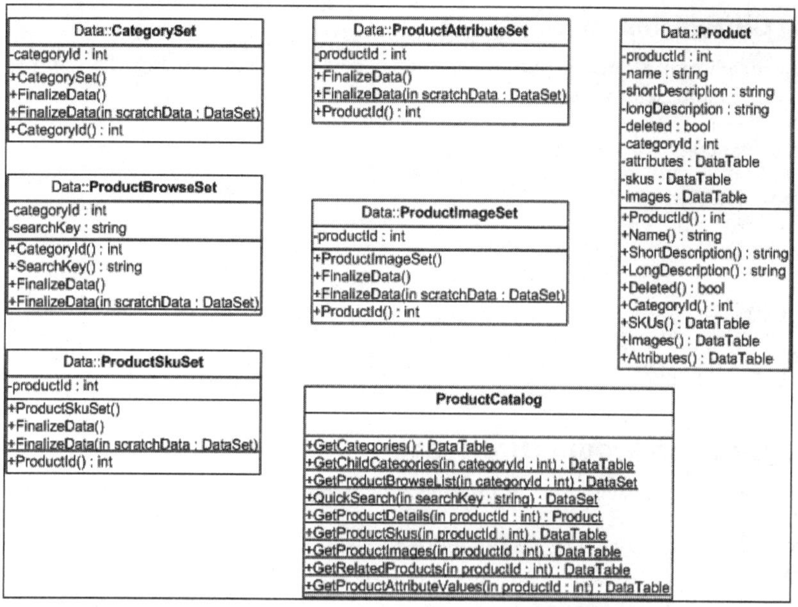

What we don't have listed here are the user controls that won't actually make it into the ProductCatalog assembly. Remember that VS.NET creates user controls in such a way that the codebehind for them resides in the web application's main assembly. You can see the source code to those in the UserControls folder of the downloadable code: LeftCategories.ascx, ProductDetailNavStrip.ascx, and TopCategoryDropDown.ascx.

The Solution

At this point we should have a fairly clear understanding of what it is we're trying to implement. We've seen the tables in the database that we're going to work with, and we've seen the class diagrams that will eventually be the classes we code for our product catalog. This next section will take you through the source code for most of our product catalog elements. As we develop the components we'll show them to you in action.

Stored Procedures

All of our database design won't do us much good if we can't access the data. As we mentioned in the previous chapter when discussing Container Managed Persistence, all of our data access is going to be through stored procedures. This gives us the maximum amount of performance and flexibility from our database, and makes the code easier to maintain.

The following is a list of the stored procedures we created to drive the product catalog portion of our website.

Gw_Select_Categories

This stored procedure is a simple routine that selects a list of categories. It will either obtain all categories in the database or all categories with a supplied parent category ID:

```
CREATE PROCEDURE Gw_Select_Categories
@CategoryId int
AS
  IF @CategoryID = -1
    SELECT CategoryId, Description, Notes, ParentCategoryId
    FROM Categories Order by Description
  ELSE
    SELECT CategoryId, Description, Notes, ParentCategoryId
    FROM Categories
    WHERE ParentCategoryId = @CategoryId ORDER BY Description
GO
```

Gw_Select_CategoryProductBrowseList

This stored procedure retrieves a list of products belonging to a certain category:

```
CREATE PROCEDURE Gw_Select_Category_ProductBrowseList
@CategoryId int
AS
  SELECT Products.ProductId, Products.Name, ShortDescription,
         LongDescription, Deleted, CategoryId,
         ProductSkus.RetailPrice, ProductSkus.ActualPrice,
         ProductSkus.Description SkuDesc, ProductSkus.SKU,
         Products.CategoryId
  FROM Products
  INNER JOIN ProductSKUs ON Products.ProductId = ProductSKUs.ProductId
  WHERE Products.CategoryId = @CategoryId
  ORDER BY Name ASC, ProductSkus.ActualPrice DESC
GO
```

Gw_Select_Product

This stored procedure retrieves details about a single product from the database:

```
CREATE PROCEDURE Gw_Select_Product
@ProductId int,
@Name varchar(50) output,
@ShortDescription varchar(100) output,
@LongDescription varchar(4000) output,
@Deleted bit output,
@CategoryId int output
AS
  SELECT @ProductId = ProductId,
         @Name = Name,
         @ShortDescription = ShortDescription,
         @LongDescription = LongDescription,
         @Deleted = Deleted,
        @CategoryId = CategoryId
  FROM Products WHERE ProductId = @ProductId
GO
```

Gw_Select_ProductAttributeValues

The following stored procedure is one of the more complex ones that we have for the product catalog. It retrieves a list of all of the product attribute values assigned to a product. The complexity comes from retrieving the lookup display value and we have to use the SQL `CASE` statement:

```
CREATE PROCEDURE Gw_Select_Product_AttributeValues
@ProductId int
AS
SELECT pav.ProductId, pav.AttributeTemplateId, pav.valueInt, pav.valueStr,
       pav.valueMemo, pav.valueBool, pat.Name TemplateName,
       pat.DataType, pat.LookupListId, pat.PATCategoryId,
       pat.DisplayName TemplateDisplayName, patc.Name CategoryName,
  CASE
  WHEN pat.LookupListId > 0 THEN (
    SELECT DisplayName FROM ProductAttributeListItems
    WHERE
      LookupListId = pat.LookupListId AND ListItemId = pav.valueInt )
  WHEN pat.LookupListId = 0 THEN ''
    END as LookupDisplayValue
  FROM ProductAttributeValues pav INNER JOIN
      ProductAttributeTemplates pat ON pav.AttributeTemplateId =
      pat.AttributeTemplateId
  INNER JOIN ProductAttributeTemplateCategories patc
    ON pat.PATCategoryID = patc.PATCategoryID
  WHERE pav.ProductId = @ProductId ORDER BY patc.Name, pat.DisplayName
GO
```

Gw_Select_Product_Skus

The following stored procedure retrieves all of the SKUs and pricing information for a particular product:

```
CREATE PROCEDURE Gw_Select_Product_Skus
@ProductID int
AS
  SELECT ProductId, SKU, Description, RetailPrice, ActualPrice,
         QtyOnHand, QtyAtSupplier, ReleaseDate
  FROM ProductSKUs WHERE ProductId = @ProductId
GO
```

CMP Metadata

Now that we have defined our stored procedures, we need to add their metadata to the `web.config` file for the CMP architecture to make use of them. The pattern of *Stored Procedures* followed by *CMP Metadata* is one that we'll see throughout subsequent chapters. We won't show all of the CMP metadata that goes into the `web.config` file as there is a lot of it, and it's all quite similar. The remainder can be inspected from looking at the `web.config` file itself in the complete code download.

Here we'll have a look at the metadata for the `Gw_Select_Product` stored procedure:

```
<GWConfig>
  <ContainerMappingSet>
    ...
    <ContainerMapping>
      <ContainerMappingId>SingleProduct</ContainerMappingId>
      <ContainedClass>Product</ContainedClass>
        <Select>
          <CommandName>Gw_Select_Product</CommandName>
          <Parameter>
            <ClassMember>ProductId</ClassMember>
            <ParameterName>@ProductId</ParameterName>
            <DbTypeHint>Int</DbTypeHint>
            <ParamDirection>Input</ParamDirection>
            <Size>4</Size>
          </Parameter>
          <Parameter>
            <ClassMember>Name</ClassMember>
            <ParameterName>@Name</ParameterName>
            <DbTypeHint>Varchar</DbTypeHint>
            <ParamDirection>Output</ParamDirection>
            <Size>50</Size>
          </Parameter>
          <Parameter>
            <ClassMember>ShortDescription</ClassMember>
            <ParameterName>@ShortDescription</ParameterName>
            <DbTypeHint>Varchar</DbTypeHint>
            <ParamDirection>Output</ParamDirection>
            <Size>100</Size>
          </Parameter>
          <Parameter>
            <ClassMember>LongDescription</ClassMember>
            <ParameterName>@LongDescription</ParameterName>
            <DbTypeHint>Varchar</DbTypeHint>
            <ParamDirection>Output</ParamDirection>
            <Size>4000</Size>
          </Parameter>
          <Parameter>
            <ClassMember>Deleted</ClassMember>
            <ParameterName>@Deleted</ParameterName>
            <DbTypeHint>Bit</DbTypeHint>
            <ParamDirection>Output</ParamDirection>
            <Size>1</Size>
          </Parameter>
          <Parameter>
            <ClassMember>CategoryId</ClassMember>
            <ParameterName>@CategoryId</ParameterName>
            <DbTypeHint>Int</DbTypeHint>
            <ParamDirection>Output</ParamDirection>
            <Size>4</Size>
          </Parameter>
        </Select>
    </ContainerMapping>
    ...
  </ContainerMappingSet>
</GWConfig>
```

In this snippet, we can see the container mapping ID, which we'll use later to identify this particular container mapping, the `<Select>` node that contains the information for selecting data, such as the `<CommandName>` that contains the name of the stored procedure to be used, and a `<Parameter>` element for each parameter of the stored procedure. The beauty of this whole set up as we mentioned in the previous chapter, is that any changes to the stored procedures themselves simply require a change in the `web.config` file, but our application code need not be touched.

Again, this metadata only works because, if you remember from Chapter 2, we have defined a custom configuration handler. Custom configuration handlers allow you to put non-standard data formats into the `web.config` file and specify which class is responsible for loading that data. In our case, we add the following to the top of our `web.config` file to tell it how it should load our configuration section:

```
<configSections>
  <section name="GWConfig"
```

The Presentation Layer – Server Controls

This next section is devoted entirely to the server controls. The way our application architecture is structured means most of the hard work is done by the data tier and by the presentation layer, with the business layer forming a thin layer of communication and interpretation between the two. As such, we have quite a few reusable interface elements that are worth discussing. We will be skipping over a few of the user controls (such as the category browsing control, the product detail navigation strip, etc.) in the interest of keeping this chapter short enough to avoid becoming a cure for insomnia.

If you are following along and entering the code as you go, you need to create a new C# Class Library at this point called `ProductCatalog`. Set the default namespace and output filename to `GW.Web.ProductCatalog`. Each of the classes listed below is its own C# file within the project.

CategoryBrowseList

As we said in our design discussion, the `CategoryBrowseList` class is responsible for displaying a list of categories and allowing a user to click on one to be taken to the product browse listing page.

One thing that you'll notice with almost all of our server controls is that they look very similar. This is because they are mainly adapted from the MSDN sample "Templated Databound Control". I removed the templating portion because we don't need it, but this template we're using is the basic template for creating a composite server control that can have its child members restore their state from `ViewState` on postback.

```
using System;
using System.Web.UI;
using System.Web.UI.WebControls;
using System.ComponentModel;
using System.Collections;
using System.Diagnostics;
using System.Data;
using System.Drawing;

namespace GW.Web.ProductCatalog.Controls
{
  /// <summary>
  /// Category browse list display control
  /// </summary>
```

The ToolboxDataAttribute lets us define the format of the string that will be used when this control is dragged from the toolbox onto the designer surface.

```
[ToolboxData(
     "<{0}:CategoryBrowseList runat=server></{0}:CategoryBrowseList>")]
public class CategoryBrowseList : System.Web.UI.WebControls.WebControl,
                                  INamingContainer
{
  private DataTable dataSource;

  [Bindable(true),
  Category("Data"),
  DefaultValue(null),
  Description(
    "The data source from which to display the browse listing"),
```

The following attribute makes the DataSource property invisible to the IDE at design-time to reinforce the concept that this property needs to be set at run time.

```
  DesignerSerializationVisibility(DesignerSerializationVisibility.Hidden)]
  public DataTable DataSource
  {
    get
    { return dataSource; }
    set { dataSource = value; }
  }
  /// <summary>
  /// Render this control to the output parameter specified.
  /// </summary>
  /// <param name="output"> The HTML writer to write out to </param>
  protected override void Render(HtmlTextWriter output)
  {
    PrepareControlHierarchy();
    RenderContents(output);
  }
```

PrepareControlHierarchy is a placeholder method. If we need to do any preparation on the control hierarchy before the controls are actually rendered, we would do it in this method. For our purposes, this method almost always looks exactly like this. However, if you expand on our solution in your own code, you may end up expanding on this method.

```
  private void PrepareControlHierarchy()
  {
    if (HasControls() == false)
      return;
  }
```

CreateChildControls is called by the ASP.NET control rendering process. If the page on which the control resides is in a PostBack state, then it will call CreateControlHierarchy, indicating to not bind data.

```
protected override void CreateChildControls()
{
  Controls.Clear();
  if (Page.IsPostBack)
    CreateControlHierarchy(false);
}

public override void DataBind()
{
  base.OnDataBinding(EventArgs.Empty);
  Controls.Clear();
  ClearChildViewState();

  CreateControlHierarchy(true);
  ChildControlsCreated = true;
}
```

The following method is probably not necessary, but we leave it here to remind us that we can override it. The idea is that if we need to specifically invoke the `TrackViewState` method on any of our child controls, we need to override this method to accomplish that. The code template that we use to create all of our server controls therefore overrides this method so we don't forget about it.

```
protected override void TrackViewState()
{
  base.TrackViewState();
}
```

As with any composite server control, the real guts of the control are going to be found in the `CreateControlHierarchy()` method. This method creates instances of the nested controls and optionally binds them to the data source if the control was created on the first-run through a page (for example, it is not a `PostBack` display). You can see from the listing below that we're going to be displaying a three column list of categories, and each category will be rendered using the `CategoryItemTemplate` class.

```
private void CreateControlHierarchy( bool useDataSource )
{
  DataList dl = new DataList();
  dl.RepeatColumns = 3;
  dl.RepeatDirection = RepeatDirection.Horizontal;
  dl.ID = "categoryList";
```

In this next line, we're creating an instance of an item template for our `DataList`. This item template contains all of the logic and code necessary to render a single item within our list. You can see all of that code in the `CategoryItemTemplate` class.

```
  dl.ItemTemplate = new CategoryItemTemplate();
  dl.ItemStyle.Width = new Unit(33, UnitType.Percentage);
  dl.ItemStyle.HorizontalAlign = HorizontalAlign.Center;
  dl.ItemStyle.VerticalAlign = VerticalAlign.Top;

  Controls.Add( dl );
```

```
        if (useDataSource == true )
        {
          dl.DataSource = dataSource;
          dl.DataBind();
        }
      }
    }
  }
```

CategoryItemTemplate

This is a template class that is responsible for rendering a single category display within a category browse listing. When an instance of the template is bound to a row of data, the result is a piece of renderable HTML. It allows the user to click on the category to open up the product listing page for that category.

```
using System;
using System.Web;
using System.Web.UI;
using System.Web.UI.WebControls;
using System.ComponentModel;
using System.Collections;
using System.Diagnostics;
using System.Data;
using System.Drawing;
using System.Text;

namespace GW.Web.ProductCatalog.Controls
{
  /// <summary>
  /// Displayable item template for category browse list control.
  /// </summary>
  public class CategoryItemTemplate : ITemplate
  {
    public CategoryItemTemplate() { }
```

The `InstantiateIn` method is invoked each time an instance of this template is instantiated within a rendering container. In our case, the container is the data list. Because we're just going to be rendering raw HTML and not creating additional server controls, we'll use a literal control and set up an event handler that is invoked each time that literal control is bound to a row of data.

```
    public void InstantiateIn( Control container )
    {
      Literal l = new Literal();
      l.DataBinding += new EventHandler(this.BindData);
      container.Controls.Add( l );
    }
```

The following method is called each time a row is bound to the literal control. We retrieve the row of data to which this item is bound and use the data contained in that row to construct the HTML that we're going to be rendering.

```
      public void BindData( object sender, EventArgs e)
      {
        Literal l = (Literal)sender;
        DataListItem container = (DataListItem)l.NamingContainer;
        DataRowView currentRowView = (DataRowView) container.DataItem;

        HttpContext ht = HttpContext.Current;
```

The next thing that we're going to do is construct a string of HTML that will be placed into the literal control directly. To do this in the most efficient way possible we're going to use a `StringBuilder`. The HTML we're rendering is a table containing a link to the subcategory for each row in the data source.

```
        StringBuilder sb = new StringBuilder();
        sb.Append("<table >");
        sb.Append("<tr><td align=\"center\">");
        sb.AppendFormat(
          "<a href=\"Subcategory.aspx?categoryId={0}&subCategoryId={1}\">",
          ht.Request["categoryId"],
          currentRowView["CategoryId"]);

        sb.AppendFormat (
          "<img src=\"images/Categories/{0}.jpg\" alt=\"{1}\" border=\"0\" " +
          height=\"50\" width=\"50\"></a><br>",
          (int)currentRowView["CategoryId"],
          currentRowView["Description"]);
        sb.AppendFormat("<b>{0}</b><br><font size=\"1\">{1}</font>",
          currentRowView["Description"],
          currentRowView["Notes"]);
        sb.Append("</td>");
        sb.Append("</tr></table>\n");
        l.Text = sb.ToString();
      }
    }

  }
```

Let's see what the category browse list looks like on our preliminary site with some sample data:

In the above screenshot we've taken a clip of the category browse list control. We'll see what it all looks like in a full, complete page after we've taken a look at the rest of the code for the product catalog.

ProductBrowseList

The product browse list control is responsible for displaying a list of products in a vertical fashion. This list of products will contain description, name, and SKU information as well as pricing data and buttons for adding the product to the shopping cart. Because we know we will eventually be supporting a wish list, we will create a placeholder button just to make sure the layout looks right with all of the buttons in place.

```
using System;
using System.Web.UI;
using System.Web.UI.WebControls;
using System.ComponentModel;
using System.Collections;
using System.Diagnostics;
using System.Data;
using System.Drawing;

namespace GW.Web.ProductCatalog.Controls
{
  /// <summary>
  /// List of products, can come from any query, search or whatever.
  /// </summary>
  [ToolboxData(
      "<{0}:ProductBrowseList runat=server></{0}:ProductBrowseList>")]
  public class ProductBrowseList : System.Web.UI.WebControls.WebControl,
                                   INamingContainer
  {
    private DataSet dataSource;
    [Bindable(true),
    Category("Data"),
    DefaultValue(null),
    Description(
        "The data source from which to display the product listing"),
    DesignerSerializationVisibility(DesignerSerializationVisibility.Hidden)
    ]
    public DataSet DataSource
    {
      get { return dataSource; }
      set { dataSource = value; }
    }
```

To keep things short and simple, I've hidden the implementation of the `TrackViewState`, `PrepareControlHierarchy`, etc. methods and skipped to the important one:

```
    private void CreateControlHierarchy(bool useDataSource )
    {
      DataList dl = new DataList();
      dl.RepeatColumns = 1;
      dl.RepeatDirection = RepeatDirection.Vertical;
      dl.ID = "productList";
      dl.ItemTemplate = new ProductItemTemplate();
      dl.ItemStyle.Width = new Unit(700, UnitType.Pixel);
      dl.Width = new Unit(650, UnitType.Pixel);
      dl.SeparatorTemplate = new BrowseListSeparatorTemplate();
```

```
        Controls.Add( dl );

        if (useDataSource == true )
        {
          dl.DataSource = dataSource.Tables[0];
          dl.DataBind();
        }
      }
    }
  }
```

BrowseListSeparatorTemplate

This is a simple control used by the `ProductBrowseList` control that essentially draws a horizontal line between products. We've used an entire class so that if we want to modify the separation code later it should be easy to locate and enhance.

```
using System;
using System.Web;
using System.Web.UI;
using System.Web.UI.WebControls;
using System.ComponentModel;
using System.Collections;
using System.Diagnostics;
using System.Data;
using System.Drawing;
using System.Text;
namespace GW.Web.ProductCatalog.Controls
{
  /// <summary>
  /// Category item template display
  /// </summary>
  public class BrowseListSeparatorTemplate : ITemplate
  {
    public BrowseListSeparatorTemplate() { }

    public void InstantiateIn( Control container )
    {
      Literal l = new Literal();
      l.Text = "<hr color=\"#000066\" size=\"1\" width=\"100%\">";
      container.Controls.Add( l );
    }
  }
}
```

ProductItemTemplate

The `ProductItemTemplate` class is a bound template control that is responsible for displaying a single product as it should be displayed within a product browse list. It accomplishes this by creating a `DataBinding` event handler and producing a string of rendered HTML output in response to that event.

```
using System;
using System.Web;
```

```
using System.Web.UI;
using System.Web.UI.WebControls;
using System.ComponentModel;
using System.Collections;
using System.Diagnostics;
using System.Data;
using System.Drawing;
using System.Text;

namespace GW.Web.ProductCatalog.Controls
{
  /// <summary>
  /// Item template display rendering code for an individual product
  /// within a product browse list.
  /// </summary>
  public class ProductItemTemplate : ITemplate
  {
    private string categoryId = HttpContext.Current.Request["CategoryId"];

    public ProductItemTemplate() { }

    public void InstantiateIn( Control container )
    {
      Literal l = new Literal();
      l.DataBinding += new EventHandler(this.BindData);
      container.Controls.Add( l );
    }
```

This method is invoked whenever the template instance is bound to a particular row of data. We can get at this row of data by first obtaining a reference to the container. The container, in our case, is a `DataListItem` (because our main control is a `DataList`). Once we have a reference to the container, we can obtain a reference to the row of data itself by accessing the container's `DataItem` property.

```
    public void BindData( object sender, EventArgs e)
    {
      Literal l = (Literal)sender;
      DataListItem container = (DataListItem)l.NamingContainer;
      DataRowView currentRowView = (DataRowView) container.DataItem;

      StringBuilder sb = new StringBuilder();

      if ((categoryId == null) || (categoryId == ""))
        categoryId = currentRowView["ParentCategoryId"].ToString();
```

What we want to do with the `StringBuilder` is create a table that displays a product. Within this table, we're going to display the product's pricing information, name, and short description, and we're going to render links that will allow us to add the product to the shopping cart or add it to the wish list, or view details. The main effort of this section of code is in constructing the various URLs to perform functions on the product in the browse list.

As always, a major design goal with our server controls is that they should be bindable, but they shouldn't actually perform the call that retrieves the data. This allows them to be as reusable as possible. As such, the calling page will have invoked a business object that, through CMP, called the `Gw_Select_Category_ProductBrowseList` stored procedure. The result is that each time this template is bound to a row, it is bound to a row of results from that stored procedure, so the columns we're referring to below are the columns created in that stored procedure's SQL query.

```
      sb.Append("<table width=\"650\" border=\"0\" cellspacing=2 cellpadding=0>");
      sb.Append("<tr>");
      sb.Append("<td vAlign=\"center\" width=\"80\" align=\"center\">\n");
      sb.AppendFormat("<img src=\"products/images/tn/{0}.jpg\" alt=\"{1}\" " +
        width=\"80\" height=\"80\" border=\"0\"><br>",
        currentRowView["ProductId"], currentRowView["Name"]);
      sb.AppendFormat("<font color=\"red\"><b>${0}</b></font>",
        currentRowView["ActualPrice"]);
      sb.Append("</td>");
      sb.Append("<td colspan=\"3\" vAlign=\"center\" width=\"550\">");
      sb.AppendFormat("Gadgets Warehouse # {0}\n<br>", currentRowView["SKU"]);
      sb.AppendFormat("<b>{0}</b><br>\n", currentRowView["SkuDesc"]);
      sb.Append(currentRowView["ShortDescription"]);
      sb.Append("<br>");
      sb.Append("</td>");
      sb.Append("</tr><tr>");
      sb.Append("<td><Br></td>");
      sb.AppendFormat("<td><a href=\"ShoppingCart.aspx?AddToCart={0}\">" +
     "<img align=\"absmiddle\" src=\"images/gad_arrow.gif\" border=\"0\">" +
     "</a> Add to Cart</td>",
        currentRowView["SKU"]);
      sb.Append("<td><img align=\"absmiddle\" " +
                "src=\"images/gad_arrow.gif\"> Add to Wishlist</td>");
      sb.Append("<td>");
      sb.AppendFormat("<a href=\"" +
    "ProductDetail.aspx?productId={0}&categoryId={1}&SubcategoryId={2}\">",
        currentRowView["ProductId"], categoryId,
        currentRowView["CategoryId"]);
      sb.Append("<img align=\"absmiddle\" src=\"images/gad_arrow.gif\" " +
                "border=\"0\"></a>View Details</td>");

      sb.Append("</tr>");
      sb.Append("</table>\n");
      l.Text = sb.ToString();
    }
  }
}
```

Let's take a look at what the product browse list looks like on its own when rendered on a page:

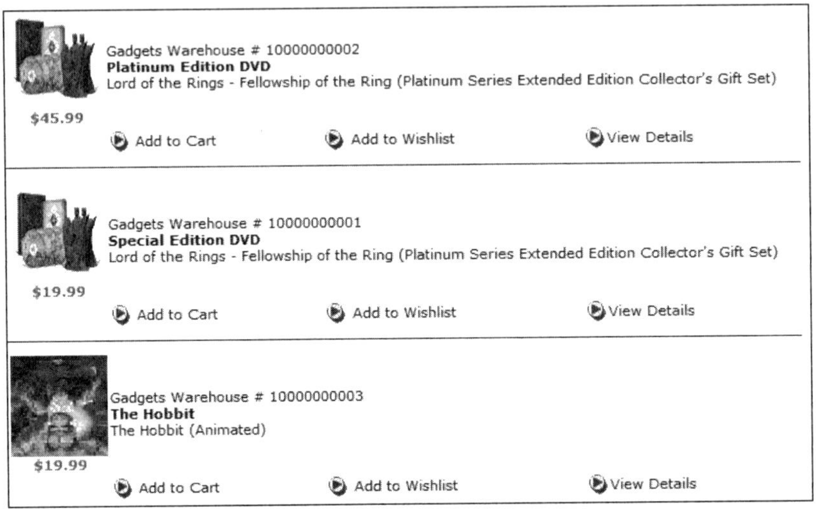

ProductAttributeDisplay

The `ProductAttributeDisplay` control is responsible for rendering all of the custom attributes that have been assigned to a single product, including the category to which those attributes belong. This control will be found on the Details portion of the product detail navigation.

If you'll recall from our database design, we have attribute templates that dictate the name and data type of an attribute value. When a template is mapped to a product and given a value, we have a "product attribute value". The following server control is responsible for displaying a list of such values. It does this by creating child controls and utilizing the `AttributeItemTemplate` class, which implements `ITemplate` so it can be bound to a row of data.

All of the results bound to this control will have been retrieved by a business object that selected the results through our CMP layer from the `Gw_Select_Product_AttributeValues` stored procedure.

```
using System;
using System.Web.UI;
using System.Web.UI.WebControls;
using System.ComponentModel;
using System.Collections;
using System.Diagnostics;
using System.Data;
using System.Drawing;

namespace GW.Web.ProductCatalog.Controls
{
  /// <summary>
  /// Product attribute display control
  /// </summary>
  [ToolboxData(
 "<{0}:ProductAttributeDisplay runat=server></{0}:ProductAttributeDisplay>")]
  public class ProductAttributeDisplay :
         System.Web.UI.WebControls.WebControl, INamingContainer
  {
    private DataTable dataSource;
```

```
    [Bindable(true),
    Category("Data"),
    DefaultValue(null),
    Description(
    "The data source from which to display the attribute listing"),
    DesignerSerializationVisibility(DesignerSerializationVisibility.Hidden)]
    public DataTable DataSource
    {
      get { return dataSource; }
      set { dataSource = value; }
    }
```

Again, I've taken out the method implementations common to our template and thus common to all of the server controls that we're building for this site. If you need to refer to those methods, you can get them from code we included earlier in the chapter.

```
    private void CreateControlHierarchy( bool useDataSource )
    {
      DataList dl = new DataList();
      dl.RepeatColumns = 1;
      dl.RepeatDirection = RepeatDirection.Vertical;
      dl.ID = "productAttributeList";
      dl.ItemTemplate = new AttributeItemTemplate();
      dl.Width = new Unit(100, UnitType.Percentage);

      Controls.Add( dl );

      if (useDataSource == true )
      {
        dl.DataSource = dataSource;
        dl.DataBind();
      }
    }
  }
}
```

AttributeItemTemplate

In order to render a single attribute for a product, a template needs to be created that will display the data-bound contents of a single product attribute as queried from the database. The attribute item template is a little bit more complex than some of the other templates we've created so far. The main reason is that there is a private member that we're using to store some information. This is because of a key fact that we needed to know in order to accomplish this template: a template is instantiated once per page, but is bound many times. Therefore, you can keep instance-scope members around between binding calls. This enables us to keep track of the last attribute category that was displayed so we can perform a display grouping on attribute groups. This also relies on the fact that the results coming back from the database are *sorted* by category.

The following is the code listing for this template:

```
using System;
using System.Web;
using System.Web.UI;
using System.Web.UI.WebControls;
using System.ComponentModel;
```

```
using System.Collections;
using System.Diagnostics;
using System.Data;
using System.Drawing;
using System.Text;

namespace GW.Web.ProductCatalog.Controls
{
  /// <summary>
  /// Attribute item display template
  /// </summary>
  public class AttributeItemTemplate : ITemplate
  {
    private string lastCategoryDisplayed;

    public AttributeItemTemplate()
    {
      lastCategoryDisplayed = "";
    }

    public void InstantiateIn( Control container )
    {
      Literal l = new Literal();
      l.DataBinding += new EventHandler(this.BindData);
      container.Controls.Add( l );
    }
```

The `BindData` method, when bound to a row of data, is going to render an attribute value in HTML. The additional bit of code here conditionally renders a "group header" that displays the attribute category name above the attribute. This header is displayed each time we switch from one category to the other. To make sure that the first category is also displayed as a header, the constructor for this template sets the last category displayed to "", so the first category will be considered a change from the original.

```
    public void BindData( object sender, EventArgs e)
    {
      Literal l = (Literal)sender;
      DataListItem container = (DataListItem)l.NamingContainer;
      DataRowView currentRowView = (DataRowView) container.DataItem;
      StringBuilder sb = new StringBuilder();

      string currentCategoryName =
                              currentRowView["CategoryName"].ToString();
      if (currentCategoryName != lastCategoryDisplayed)
      {
        // display the group heading
        sb.Append("<table width=\"100%\" border=\"0\" cellspacing=\"0\" "+
                  "cellpadding=\"3\" bgcolor=\"#E6DFBB\">");
        sb.Append("<tr><td width=\"100%\">");
        sb.AppendFormat("<b><font size=\"2\" face=\"Tahoma\" " +
                        "color=\"Maroon\">{0}</font></b>",
          currentRowView["CategoryName"]);
        sb.Append("</td></tr></table><br>");
      }
```

```
        sb.Append("<table width=\"100%\" border=\"0\" cellspacing=\"2\" " +
                  "cellpadding=\"0\">");
        sb.Append("<tr><td width=\"150\" align=\"right\" valign=\"top\">");
        sb.AppendFormat("<b>{0}</b>: </td>\n",
                        currentRowView["TemplateDisplayName"]);
        sb.AppendFormat("<td valign=\"top\">{0}</td></tr></table>\n",
                        DetermineValue( currentRowView ) );

        l.Text = sb.ToString();
        lastCategoryDisplayed = currentCategoryName;
      }
```

One of the key things that we need to do is figure out how to display the attribute value. If you'll remember from our database design, we can have attribute values with data types of strings, integers, Booleans, and strings that are retrieved from a lookup list. The `DetermineValue` method returns the appropriate column in the result set that represents the current value based on the data type of the attribute template of the value assigned to the product.

```
      public object DetermineValue( DataRowView cRow )
      {
        int dataType = (int)cRow["DataType"];
        switch (dataType)
        {
          case 0:
            // integer
            return (int)cRow["valueInt"];
            // break;
          case 1:
            // lookup list item
            return (string)cRow["LookupDisplayValue"];
            // break;
          case 2:
            // string
            return (string)cRow["valueStr"];
            // break;
          case 3:
            // bool
            return (bool)cRow["valueBool"];
            // break;
          case 4:
            // memo
            return (string)cRow["valueMemo"];
            // break;
          default:
            return "(no value)";
        }
      }
    }
  }
```

Now that we've seen the code to display product attributes, let's take a look at this control in action. As usual, we're cutting out the page navigation and headers and footers to keep things clearer for now:

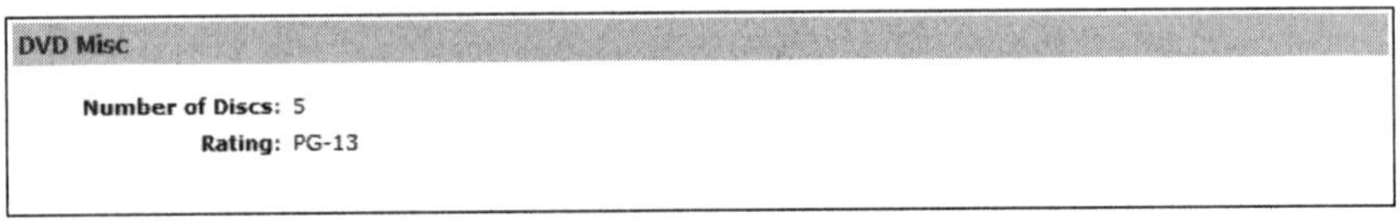

Again, keep in mind that we're using dummy data, so some things might not be accurate in the screenshots. The final version of the application is likely to look slightly different from the shots we're displaying here. As you can see, the category for the attributes displayed is called DVD Misc and there are two attributes assigned to the DVD we're looking at (which happens to be the special edition DVD for Lord of the Rings).

ProductPricingBox

Each time we display one of the navigation tabs belonging to a particular product, such as details, overview, images, and so on, we want to be able to place a pricing box at the top of that display. Doing this means that no matter what view of a product the customer is looking at, they can still add the SKU to their shopping cart or add it to their wish list and get real pricing data as well. By now the sight of a server control should be pretty familiar, so as usual we're going to cut to the important method:

```
      private void CreateControlHierarchy( bool useDataSource )
      {
        DataList dl = new DataList();
        dl.CellPadding = 2;
        dl.CellSpacing = 2;
        dl.RepeatColumns = 1;
        dl.RepeatDirection = RepeatDirection.Vertical;
        dl.ID = "skuList";
        dl.ItemTemplate = new SkuItemTemplate();
        //e6dfbb
        dl.AlternatingItemStyle.BackColor = Color.FromArgb(230, 223, 187);
        dl.Width = new Unit(100, UnitType.Percentage);
        Controls.Add( dl );

        if (useDataSource == true )
        {
          dl.DataSource = dataSource;
          dl.DataBind();
        }
      }
    }
  }
```

SkuItemTemplate

This is the source code to the template used to display a single SKU within a product pricing box. Its main function is to allow the customer to click on the SKU in order to purchase it as well as displaying the price and description.

```
using System;
using System.Web;
using System.Web.UI;
using System.Web.UI.WebControls;
```

```
using System.ComponentModel;
using System.Collections;
using System.Diagnostics;
using System.Data;
using System.Drawing;
using System.Text;

namespace GW.Web.ProductCatalog.Controls
{
  /// <summary>
  /// Template for displaying a single SKU within a pricing
  /// environment, displays name, price, and add to cart buttons.
  /// </summary>
  public class SkuItemTemplate : ITemplate
  {
    public SkuItemTemplate() { }

    public void InstantiateIn( Control container )
    {
      Literal l = new Literal();
      l.DataBinding += new EventHandler(this.BindData);
      container.Controls.Add( l );
    }
```

Here we are with the `BindData` method again. This time, we are creating a small HTML table that will contain a single product SKU, as well as its pricing information. At the bottom of the table we also have a link to add the item to the shopping cart.

```
    public void BindData( object sender, EventArgs e)
    {
      Literal l = (Literal)sender;
      DataListItem container = (DataListItem)l.NamingContainer;
      DataRowView currentRowView = (DataRowView) container.DataItem;

      HttpContext ht = HttpContext.Current;

      StringBuilder sb = new StringBuilder();
      sb.Append("<table width=\"100%\" border=\"0\" cellspacing=0 "+
                "cellpadding=0>");
      sb.Append("<tr><td valign=\"top\" width=\"65%\">");
      sb.AppendFormat("<B>{0}</B>",
        currentRowView["Description"]);
      sb.Append("<br>");
      sb.AppendFormat("<a href=\"ShoppingCart.aspx?AddToCart={0}\">" +
     "<img border=\"0\" src=\"images/gad_arrow.gif\" align=\"absmiddle\">" +
     "</a> Add to Cart ",
        currentRowView["SKU"]);
      sb.Append("<img src=\"images/gad_arrow.gif\" align=\"absmiddle\"> " +
                "Add to Wishlist");
      sb.Append("</td>");
      sb.Append("<td width=\"35%\" align=\"right\" valign=\"top\">");
      sb.AppendFormat("<b>Our Price: <font color=\"red\">${0}</font></b>",
                     currentRowView["ActualPrice"]);
```

```
            sb.AppendFormat("<br>Retail: <s>${0}</s>",
                            currentRowView["RetailPrice"]);
            sb.Append("</td></tr></table><br>");
            l.Text = sb.ToString();
        }
    }
}
```

This is the end result of the `ProductPricingBox` and `SkuItemTemplate` classes:

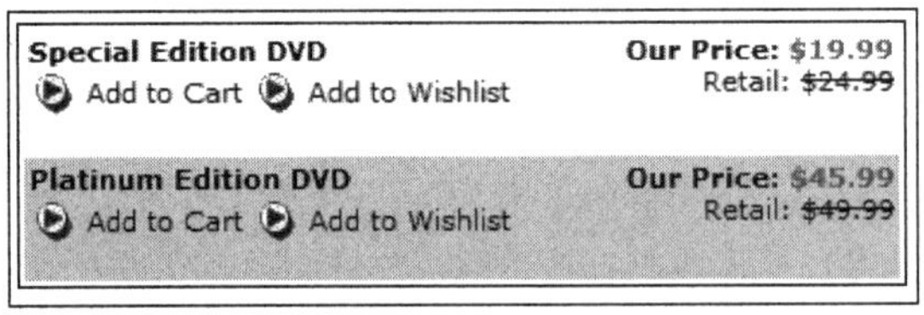

RelatedProductDisplay

Another one of the navigation tabs available to the customer when looking at an individual product is the Related Products tab. This tab will display all of the different kinds of relations associated with the current product, including up-sells, cross-sells, and even accessories like batteries. Again, we'll cut straight to the main `CreateControlHierarchy` method:

```
        private void CreateControlHierarchy( bool useDataSource )
        {
          DataList dl = new DataList();
          dl.RepeatColumns = 1;
          dl.RepeatDirection = RepeatDirection.Vertical;
          dl.ID = "relatedProductList";
          dl.ItemTemplate = new RelatedProductTemplate();
          dl.Width = new Unit(100, UnitType.Percentage);

          Controls.Add( dl );

          if (useDataSource == true )
          {
            dl.DataSource = dataSource;
            dl.DataBind();
          }
        }
    }
}
```

RelatedProductTemplate

As I'm sure you're used to seeing by now, each composite server control that uses a `DataList` also has to have a template to display a single item within the context of the control. This is the source code to display a single related product:

```
using System;
using System.Web;
using System.Web.UI;
using System.Web.UI.WebControls;
using System.ComponentModel;
using System.Collections;
using System.Diagnostics;
using System.Data;
using System.Drawing;
using System.Text;

namespace GW.Web.ProductCatalog.Controls
{
  /// <summary>
  /// Related product single item display template
  /// </summary>
  public class RelatedProductTemplate : ITemplate
  {
    private int lastRelType;

    public RelatedProductTemplate()
    {
      lastRelType= -1;
    }

    public void InstantiateIn( Control container )
    {
      Literal l = new Literal();
      l.DataBinding += new EventHandler(this.BindData);
      container.Controls.Add( l );
    }
```

This control is using the same "visible grouping" technique that we used when displaying product attributes above. It keeps track of the last relation type displayed, and if it changes, it will add a relation type description header to the output. This allows us to group all of the up-sells (price/feature increase), cross-sells (similar product), accessories, etc. together.

```
    public void BindData( object sender, EventArgs e)
    {
      Literal l = (Literal)sender;
      DataListItem container = (DataListItem)l.NamingContainer;
      DataRowView currentRowView = (DataRowView) container.DataItem;
      StringBuilder sb = new StringBuilder();

      int currentRelType = (int)currentRowView["RelationType"];
      if (currentRelType != lastRelType)
      {
        // display rel type description header
        sb.Append("<table width=\"100%\" border=\"0\" cellspacing=\"0\" " +
                  "cellpadding=\"3\" bgcolor=\"#E6DFBB\">");
        sb.Append("<tr><td width=\"100%\">");
        sb.AppendFormat("<B><font size=\"2\" face=\"Tahoma\" "+
                        "color=\"Maroon\">{0}</font></b>\n",
```

```
            currentRowView["RelationDesc"]);
          sb.Append("</td></tr></table><br>");
        }
        sb.Append("<table width=\"100%\" border=\"0\" cellspacing=\"2\" "+
                  "cellpadding=\"0\">");
        sb.Append("<tr><td width=\"100%\">");
        sb.AppendFormat("<a href=\"ProductDetail.aspx?" +
         "categoryId={0}&subCategoryId={1}&productId={2}\">",
          currentRowView["ParentCategoryId"], currentRowView["CategoryId"],
          currentRowView["ProductId"]);
        sb.AppendFormat("{0}</a> - <font color=\"Red\">" +
          "<b>{1:C}</b></font><br>\n", currentRowView["Name"],
          currentRowView["ActualPrice"]);
        sb.AppendFormat("{0}", currentRowView["ShortDescription"]);
        sb.Append("</td></tr></table>");

        l.Text = sb.ToString();

        lastRelType = currentRelType;
      }
    }
  }
```

Here's the output of the related products display control and template:

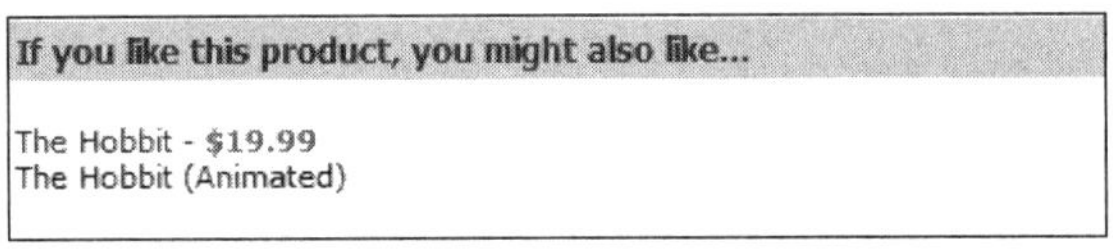

It might not all seem like much, but when you put it all together into the nice graphical framework for the rest of the site, you get pages that look like this:

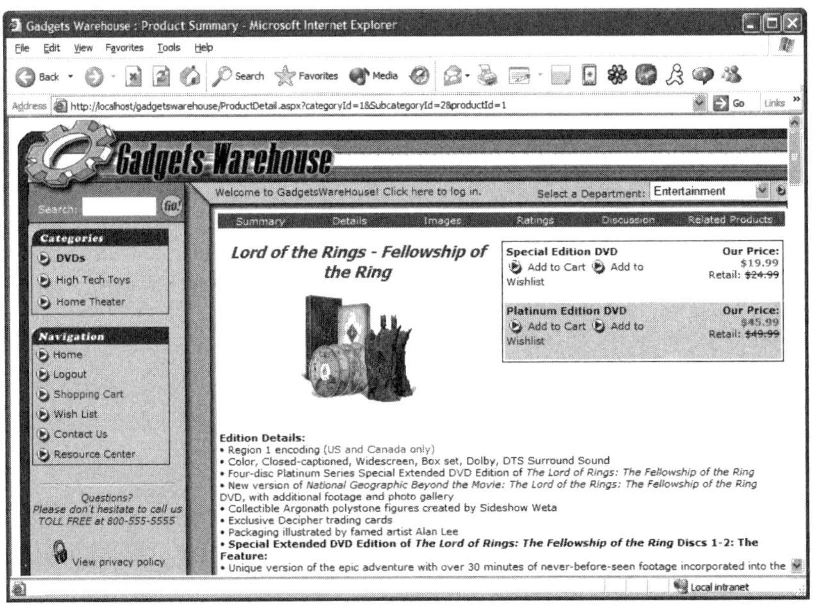

Don't panic. A lot of the code used to generate the controls, navigation, and graphic framework surrounding our product information will be explained later in the book and is available in the downloadable code. Below is another example of what the finished product looks like with the UI controls in place:

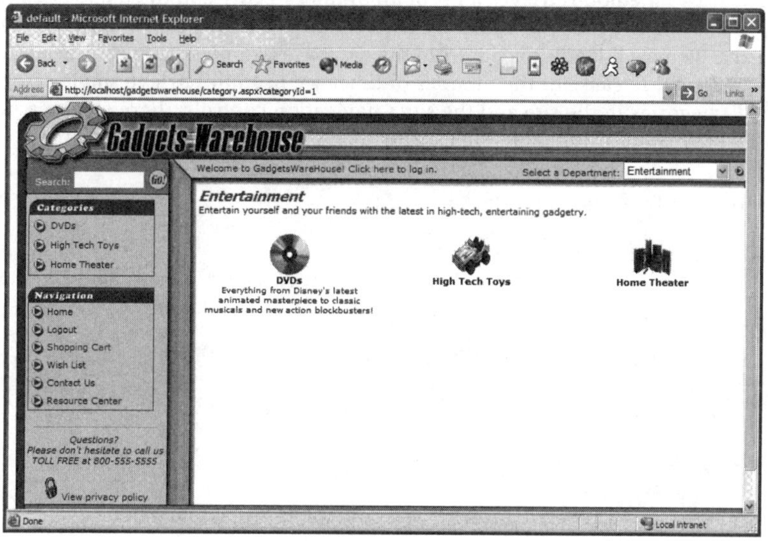

Business and Data Classes

While looking at the user interface screenshots might be nice, that information contained in those screenshots didn't just magically arrive. There is an entire suite of business and data components that combined to produce the output for those controls. We won't go into the detail on every single `PersistableObject` control because most of them are fairly straightforward placeholders for stored procedure parameters.

ProductCatalog

The main workhorse of the product catalog subsystem is, interestingly enough, the `ProductCatalog` class. It is through this class that all operations on the product catalog itself take place. It manages all of the associated data objects and container persistence information and provides the presentation layer with suitable and reliable data.

```
using System;
using System.Data;

using GW.CMPServices;
using GW.Web.ProductCatalog.Data;

namespace GW.Web.ProductCatalog
{
  /// <summary>
  /// Class responsible for performing product catalog related
  /// business functions.
```

```
/// </summary>
public class ProductCatalog
{
```

The `GetCategories` method retrieves a list of all of the categories in the database. There is an added twist in that we're using the cache to speed up performance. First we check the cache to see if the data is cached. If it isn't, then we'll load the data from the database and place it in the cache. If it is, we simply return the cached data. Because of the number of times we need to retrieve single categories and scan through lists of categories in the site and the site's navigation controls, there will be a noticeable performance improvement by caching the categories.

```
  public static DataTable GetCategories()
  {
    DataTable categoryTable =
          (DataTable)System.Web.HttpContext.Current.Cache["categories"];
    if (categoryTable  == null )
    {
      categoryTable = GetChildCategories(-1);

      System.Web.HttpContext.Current.Cache["categories"] = categoryTable;
    }

    return categoryTable;
  }
```

This is the first time we're seeing our CMP architecture in action. The first thing we do is instantiate a persistence container. Once we have the persistence container, and it knows what container map it is working against (in this case `Categories`), we can create an instance of a `PersistableObject` (or `PersistableObjectSet`) and proceed to select data from the database.

```
  public static DataTable GetChildCategories( int categoryId )
  {

    SqlPersistenceContainer spc = new SqlPersistenceContainer(
               CMPConfigurationHandler.ContainerMaps["Categories"] );
    CategorySet catSet = new CategorySet();
    catSet.CategoryId = categoryId;
    spc.Select( catSet );
    catSet.FinalizeData();

    return catSet.ResultSet.Tables[0];
  }
```

In the same way, we use the CMP architecture to get more product details:

```
  public static DataSet GetProductBrowseList( int categoryId )
  {
    SqlPersistenceContainer spc = new SqlPersistenceContainer(
          CMPConfigurationHandler.ContainerMaps["ProductBrowseList"] );
    ProductBrowseSet pbs = new ProductBrowseSet();
    pbs.CategoryId = categoryId;
```

```
    spc.Select( pbs );
    pbs.FinalizeData();
    return pbs.ResultSet;
  }

  public static Product GetProductDetails( int productId )
  {
    SqlPersistenceContainer spc = new SqlPersistenceContainer(
            CMPConfigurationHandler.ContainerMaps["SingleProduct"] );
    Product loadedProduct = new Product();
    loadedProduct.ProductId = productId;
    spc.Select( loadedProduct );

    // now load product images
    loadedProduct.Images = GetProductImages( productId );

    // load product SKUs
    loadedProduct.SKUs = GetProductSkus( productId );

    // load product attributes
    loadedProduct.Attributes = GetProductAttributeValues( productId );
    return loadedProduct;
  }

  public static DataTable GetProductSkus(int productId )
  {
    SqlPersistenceContainer spc = new SqlPersistenceContainer(
               CMPConfigurationHandler.ContainerMaps["ProductSkus"] );
    ProductSkuSet prodSkus = new ProductSkuSet();
    prodSkus.ProductId = productId;
    spc.Select( prodSkus );
    prodSkus.FinalizeData();
    return prodSkus.ResultSet.Tables[0];
  }


  public static DataTable GetProductImages(int productId )
  {
    SqlPersistenceContainer spc = new SqlPersistenceContainer(
             CMPConfigurationHandler.ContainerMaps["ProductImages"] );
    ProductImageSet prodImages = new ProductImageSet();
    prodImages.ProductId = productId;
    spc.Select( prodImages );
    prodImages.FinalizeData();
    return prodImages.ResultSet.Tables[0];
  }

  public static DataTable GetRelatedProducts( int productId )
  {
    SqlPersistenceContainer spc = new SqlPersistenceContainer(
        CMPConfigurationHandler.ContainerMaps["RelatedProducts"] );
    ProductAttributeSet relatedProducts = new ProductAttributeSet();
    relatedProducts.ProductId = productId;
    spc.Select( relatedProducts );
```

```
      relatedProducts.FinalizeData();
      return relatedProducts.ResultSet.Tables[0];
    }

    public static DataTable GetProductAttributeValues( int productId )
    {
      SqlPersistenceContainer spc = new SqlPersistenceContainer(
            CMPConfigurationHandler.ContainerMaps["ProductAttributes"] );
      ProductAttributeSet prodAttributes = new ProductAttributeSet();
      prodAttributes.ProductId = productId;
      spc.Select( prodAttributes );
      prodAttributes.FinalizeData();
      return prodAttributes.ResultSet.Tables[0];
    }
  }
}
```

You'll have seen a button for **Search** functionality in the main navigation bar in some of the earlier screenshots. We'll be adding a method called `QuickSearch` to this class, which is used to drive the results from the search button in the next chapter when we come to implement the **Search** functionality.

Product

The `Product` class represents a single product within the database. It not only contains the information specific to a single product, but also contains `DataTable` fields that hold the product attributes, SKUs, and images.

```
using System;
using System.Data;

using GW.CMPServices;

namespace GW.Web.ProductCatalog.Data
{
  /// <summary>
  /// Persistable object that contains a product and associated
  /// information such as attributes, SKUs, and images.
  /// </summary>
  public class Product : PersistableObject
  {
    private int productId;
    private string name;
    private string shortDescription;
    private string longDescription;
    private bool deleted;
    private int categoryId;

    private DataTable attributes;
    private DataTable skus;
    private DataTable images;

    public int ProductId
    {
```

```
      get { return productId; }
      set { productId = value; }
    }

    public string Name
    {
      get { return name; }
      set { name = value; }
    }

    public string ShortDescription
    {
      get { return shortDescription; }
      set { shortDescription = value; }
    }

    public string LongDescription
    {
      get { return longDescription; }
      set { longDescription = value; }
    }

    public bool Deleted
    {
      get { return deleted; }
      set { deleted = value; }
    }
    public int CategoryID
    {
      get { return categoryID; }
      set { categoryID = value; }
    }

    public DataTable SKUs
    {
      get { return skus; }
      set { skus = value; }
    }

    public DataTable Images
    {
      get { return images; }
      set { images = value; }
    }
    public DataTable Attributes
    {
      get { return attributes; }
      set { attributes = value; }
    }
  }
}
```

Summary

This chapter has been all about the product. The point to take away from this chapter is that the product is everything. Getting the customer *to* your product quickly and efficiently is imperative:

- If they can't find what they're looking for, they'll go elsewhere.
- If they find it, and it's hard to buy it, they won't buy it.

There are many things to think about when developing your product catalog. When building your own catalog, figure out what you want to sell and how you think you should sell it. Then, put yourself in the position of a consumer of that product. Give them an experience that takes them to what you want them to buy in the least number of key clicks, with little frustration, no hassle, and without preventing them from doing what they want to do on your site. If you keep those goals in mind, you will have a successful product catalog.

In this chapter we learned some useful techniques – we learned how to create the database design for the product catalog, and the composite server controls used in the presentation layer of our product catalog, and we learned about creating a business class that communicates with the database using our Container Managed Persistence layer. The next chapter is about searching for products, another important aspect of ensuring that your customers can find what you want them to buy.

CHAPTER 4

4

Product Searching

As we mentioned in the product catalog chapter, one of the most important things to consider when designing your website is the ease with which of your customers can find your products. This may sound like a simple task, but there are many different aspects of it that need to be considered when developing a good product searching design and solution.

This chapter will take you through an analysis of the common problems found in developing product search solutions. Then, we will have a look at the product search design for Gadgets Warehouse and finally we'll walk you through the source code involved in building our particular product searching solution.

By the time the chapter is complete, you should have a firm grasp of the decisions that need to be made when building a search solution as well as how to implement whatever solution you decide upon.

The Problem

Developing a good product searching solution is crucial to the success of your application. In fact, the ability of your customers to locate your products should always be at the top of your list of priorities. Before we talk about how to do it right, let's have a look at a couple of examples of product searching and location gone wrong.

There are two main ways to ruin your product location. You can provide too much information or you can provide too little. If a customer clicks into a category of your products, and there are 150 pages of products to sift through with no way of filtering and sorting that down into something more manageable, the customer will become frustrated and go somewhere else to buy their products. The other way is by not providing enough information. If your product search has 30 different search criteria that you can specify, and is so restrictive that even customers who know exactly what they're looking for can't find anything, those customers will leave and take their business elsewhere.

> **The job of marketing and advertising people is to draw people to your website. The job of programmers and site designers is to ensure that the site experience is pleasant enough so that they come back.**

When building a search engine for your site, you need to make sure that it is easy to use, and gives the user the option to use more detailed or advanced searching if they want. If the user wants to do a quick keyword search, they shouldn't have to fill out a huge form, and if the user wants to search for a particular **Stock Keeping Unit** (SKU) or give a price range, they should be able to do that as well, and the system should respond quickly and with an appealing user interface. If you're going to cut corners in your website, don't do it anywhere near your product catalog or your product search.

The Design

We're going to split the design of our search functionality into two parts: Quick Search and Advanced Search. We are going on the assumption that the advanced search can potentially cause more resource usage on the server, so we want to make sure that it is called less frequently, but we don't want to restrict the users either.

After some debating, we decided that the majority of the users hitting the site that are looking to buy something in particular will probably just use a keyword search and browse the results to find what they're looking for. Therefore, we decided to make the quick search functionality a part of the main navigation strip on the left side of the site. Once the user performs a quick search, they will then have a link at the top of those results if they want to use the advanced search. This way, the user can find what they are looking for, but they are still following a flow that we feel provides the most efficient use of resources on our server.

Another advantage we have is that a lot of our work has already been done for us, so we are under the impression that the development effort for product searching should be fairly easy. We don't have to design the product catalog database, or any of the tables, and we already have a bunch of reusable controls that we built for the previous chapter that we don't have to rewrite this time around.

There are dozens of different ways to accomplish searching. There are tools you can use like Index Server that will give you robust searching functionality. My goal here for this chapter isn't to show you how to use third-party tools to accomplish the search. By doing it the "hard way", we can build a good framework for searching and viewing results. The results should be easy enough to plug into a third-party engine if you want to expand on what we create here for this chapter.

Quick Search

The quick search is going to be a quick simple substring search – it won't be handling things like AND or OR. It just does a simple substring search. As I said, we'll be building a framework that you can use, and expand on as you see fit for your own website. The user will have the option to perform a quick search from any page on the site. As such, it will be a part of the left-side navigation strip. You might remember seeing its placeholder from the previous chapter, but here is a cutout of what the quick search query interface looks like:

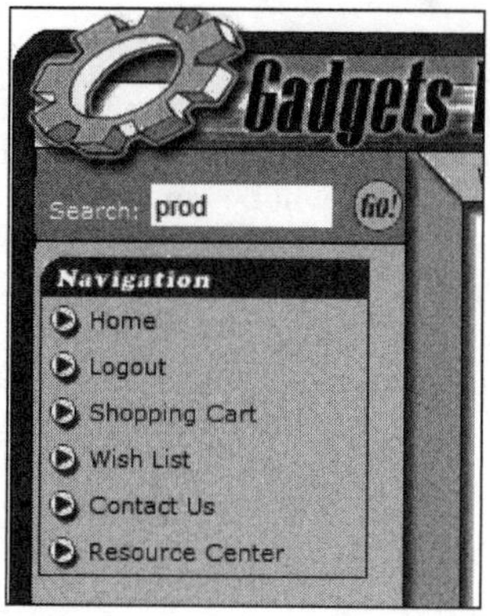

This search box is part of a user control that allows users to click the Go! button and perform a quick search.

Users will be able to type in their search query and click the Go! button, and they will be brought to the Quick Search results page. That results page is going to reuse the product browse list control we developed in the previous chapter. The results of the quick search will come from a substring comparison of the product name, short description, long description, and the SKU description.

The advantage we have here is that we have most of the groundwork already laid in place for our user interface for displaying lists of products, so we can almost leave that out of our design for now. The main thing we need to do is take a look at what information we want returned and how we want the query to work. All of that is part of the solution and we'll take a look at the stored procedure and related metadata in the solution section of this chapter.

Advanced Search

After the user performs a quick search, they will be presented with a link to perform an advanced search even if the quick search returned results. This search will be an entirely new search with new criteria. By following this link, the user will be presented with a somewhat more advanced data entry form for search criteria. By submitting that form with valid criteria, they will then be taken to the listing of search results. Conveniently enough, we already have a control in place that displays product listings so we will be able to leverage that work without too much additional effort.

Let's take a look at the criteria that we want the user to be able to enter into the data entry form and how we're going to use that to perform the search:

SKU

This might seem odd to have in the product search. After all, as we discussed before, the Stock Keeping Unit is a value that really only makes sense to your website and your fulfillment backend. The reason you might want this is because the SKU is the single most uniquely identifying feature that any product might have. It will take you directly to a product without having to do any additional work. Users looking for an SKU might be using your advanced search in response to an advertisement they saw (which included the SKUs for the sale items) or they might be responding to a targeted e-mail or a note they jotted down the last time they were looking at your site.

Name

This is pretty obvious. This will allow users of the site to search on the product name. This is a substring search, so if the user supplies the word "ring", and they are searching for "Lord of the Rings" or something with the word "Fringe" in it, both will be considered valid results on this type of search. We thought about making it a pure keyword search where the user had to match full, valid words against words in our database, but we decided that might restrict the results too much and discourage users. The other thing to consider is that if you want to make the SQL query a bit more complex, you could present the user with a radio button that allows them to choose to which of the "name" fields they want their substring to apply. This might give them finer-grained results and use less resources doing searches on your system.

Description

This functions the same way as the Name search, but the search is performed against the description field. If any of the SKU, Name, or Description values match, the search engine will consider that product a match until it rules out price range and category.

Price Range

If a product is still considered a match (SKU, Name, or Description matched the user's criteria) it will have to match the price range. By default, the price range is from 0 to 100,000. If the user performing the search supplies their own range, it will be used to further narrow the results.

Category

Another way the user can further narrow the results of the advanced search is by supplying a department (top-level category in our GadgetsWarehouse.com implementation of the product catalog). In fact, the user interface will require the user to choose at least one department in which to search, though they can choose as many as they like. The search on a department will be a "deep" search. This means that if the user searches within a department, all categories that belong to that department will be included in the search.

The Solution

At this point, we have looked at some of the problems presented by product searching and making sure that customers have a quick and easy way of reaching whatever product they are looking for. Now its time to get on with stored procedures and C# code that will provide the customers with that search functionality. Just as we split up the design work into Quick and Advanced searching, we will split up the solution the same way.

Quick Search

The quick search is a simple substring search. Our main goal is that we want the data *output* to conform to the same rules that the output of the product browse list uses. By doing this, we can guarantee that we can reuse the product browse list control to display both quick and advanced search results. After all, the whole point of creating those composite server controls was to get the most out of code reuse possible.

We're going to step through the code in the order in which we created it. One thing that is almost as important as the final product is the process you use to get there. We'll take a look at the development of the stored procedure, then putting the Container Managed Persistence (CMP) metadata into the `web.config` file, modifying the business code, and then finally creating the user interface.

Stored Procedure

To ensure that our stored procedure for performing a quick search produces the same column output as the product browse list, we basically took the top half of the select statement from the browse list stored procedure `Gw_Select_Category_ProductBrowseList` that we saw in the previous chapter, and pasted it into ours. The only thing we changed here is the `WHERE` clause. As you can see, we are comparing the user's input against the product name, short description, long description, and even the individual SKU description.

The following is a copy of what our stored procedure looks like from inside SQL Server 2000:

```
CREATE PROCEDURE Gw_Product_QuickSearch
@SearchKey varchar (200)
AS
  SELECT Products.ProductId, Name, ShortDescription, LongDescription,
         Deleted,  ProductSkus.RetailPrice, ProductSkus.ActualPrice,
         ProductSkus.Description SkuDesc, ProductSkus.SKU,
         Products.CategoryId,
         ParentCategoryId = (
           SELECT ParentCategoryId FROM Categories cats
           WHERE cats.CategoryId = Products.CategoryId )
  FROM Products
  INNER JOIN ProductSKUs ON Products.ProductId = ProductSKUs.ProductId
  WHERE NAME LIKE '%' + @SearchKey+ '%'
     OR ShortDescription LIKE '%'+@SearchKey+'%'
     OR LongDescription LIKE '%'+@SearchKey+'%'
     OR ProductSkus.Description LIKE '%'+@SearchKey+'%'
  ORDER BY Name ASC, ProductSkus.ActualPrice DESC
GO
```

CMP Metadata

The following is the CMP metadata that allows us to invoke the Quick Search stored procedure we developed above. When we access this metadata stored in `web.config`, we will do so by using a key into the list of container mappings that corresponds to the `<ContainerMappingId>` element.

```
<ContainerMapping>
  <ContainerMappingId>QuickSearch</ContainerMappingId>
  <ContainedClass>ProductBrowseSet</ContainedClass>
  <Select>
    <CommandName>Gw_Product_QuickSearch</CommandName>
    <Parameter>
      <ClassMember>SearchKey</ClassMember>
      <ParameterName>@searchKey</ParameterName>
      <DbTypeHint>Varchar</DbTypeHint>
      <ParamDirection>Input</ParamDirection>
      <Size>200</Size>
```

```
      </Parameter>
    </Select>
  </ContainerMapping>
```

Change to ProductCatalog

The next thing we're going to do is modify the `ProductCatalog` class in our `ProductCatalog` assembly that we built in the previous chapter. We're going to add a method called `QuickSearch` that accepts a single search key, performs the search, and returns a `DataSet` containing the results of that search. The following is the code listing for the `QuickSearch` method:

```
public static DataSet QuickSearch( string searchKey)
{
  SqlPersistenceContainer spc = new SqlPersistenceContainer(
       CMPConfigurationHandler.ContainerMaps["QuickSearch"]);
  ProductBrowseSet pbs = new ProductBrowseSet();
  pbs.SearchKey = searchKey;
  spc.Select( pbs );
  pbs.FinalizeData();
  return pbs.ResultSet;
}
```

One thing to note is that we reused the `ProductBrowseSet` class. We didn't feel the need to create a new class just for containing the quick search parameter (search key), so we simply added a property called `SearchKey` to the `ProductBrowseSet` class and reused that as our `PersistableObjectSet` for this operation.

Quicksearch.aspx

Here is a view of `QuickSearch.apsx` from the design view, showing the important user controls:

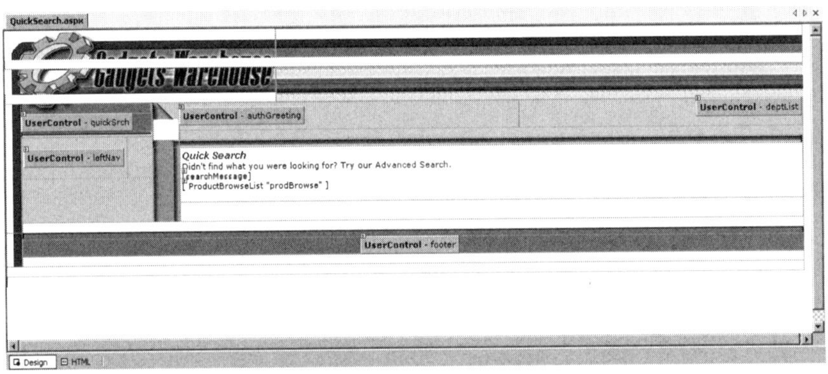

This next bit of code might seem a little daunting and hard to read, but everyone has to do it at some point. I wanted to make sure that you saw an entire page from start to finish that included all of the user controls that we use for the standard UI look and, feel, and navigation strips as well as the code that contains the composite server controls and other things.

```
<%@ Register TagPrefix="GWU" TagName="QuickSearch"
Src="UserControls/QuickSearch.ascx" %>
<%@ Register TagPrefix="GWU" TagName="LeftNavigator"
Src="UserControls/LeftNavigator.ascx" %>
<%@ Register Tagprefix="GWU" TagName="AuthGreeting"
Src="UserControls/AuthGreeting.ascx" %>
<%@ Register TagPrefix="GWU" TagName="Footer" Src="UserControls/Footer.ascx" %>
<%@ Register TagPrefix="GWU" TagName="TopCategoryDropDown"
Src="UserControls/TopCategoryDropDown.ascx" %>
<%@ Register TagPrefix="GW" Namespace="GW.Web.ProductCatalog.Controls"
Assembly="GW.Web.ProductCatalog" %>
<%@ Page language="c#" Codebehind="QuickSearch.aspx.cs" AutoEventWireup="false"
Inherits="GW.Web.QuickSearch" %>
<!DOCTYPE HTML PUBLIC "-//W3C//DTD HTML 4.0 Transitional//EN" >
<HTML>
 <HEAD>
  <title>Gadgets Warehouse - Quick Search</title>
  <meta name="GENERATOR" Content="Microsoft Visual Studio 7.0">
  <meta name="CODE_LANGUAGE" Content="C#">
  <meta name="vs_defaultClientScript" content="JavaScript">
  <meta name="vs_targetSchema"
       content="http://schemas.microsoft.com/intellisense/ie5">
  <LINK href="Styles/main.css" type="text/css" rel="stylesheet">
 </HEAD>
 <BODY text="#000000" vLink="#000000" aLink="#000000" link="#000000"
      leftMargin="0" topMargin="0">
  <form id="default" method="post" runat="server">
   <TABLE cellSpacing="0" cellPadding="0" width="100%" bgColor="#ffffff">
    <TBODY>
     <TR>
      <TD vAlign="top" width="100%">
       <TABLE cellSpacing="0" cellPadding="0" width="100%">
        <TBODY>
         <TR>
          <TD vAlign="top" width="375" height="39"><IMG height="39"
              src="Images/gad_head01.jpg" width="375" border="0"></TD>
          <TD vAlign="top" width="100%" background="Images/gad_head_bg2.jpg"
              height="39"> </TD>
         </TR>
        </TBODY>
       </TABLE>
      </TD>
     </TR>
     <TR>
      <TD vAlign="top" width="100%" height="100%">
       <TABLE height="100%" cellSpacing="0" cellPadding="0" width="100%">
        <TBODY>
         <TR>
          <TD vAlign="top" width="375" height="33"><IMG height="33"
               src="Images/gad_head02.jpg" width="375" border="0"></TD>
          <TD vAlign="top" width="100%" background="Images/gad_head_bg1.jpg"
              height="33"> </TD>
         </TR>
        </TBODY>
```

```
  </TABLE>
 </TD>
</TR>
<TR>
 <TD vAlign="top" width="100%">
  <TABLE cellSpacing="0" cellPadding="0" width="100%">
   <TBODY>
    <TR>
     <TD vAlign="top" width="21" background="Images/gad_farleft_bg.jpg"
       height="100%"><IMG height="1" src="Images/gad_farleft_bg.jpg"
       width="21" border="0"></TD>
     <TD vAlign="top" width="100%">
      <TABLE cellSpacing="0" cellPadding="0" width="100%">
       <TBODY>
        <TR>
         <TD vAlign="top" bgColor="#e6dfbb">
          <TABLE cellSpacing="0" cellPadding="0">
           <TBODY>
            <TR>
             <TD vAlign="top"><IMG src="Images/gad_head06.jpg"></TD>
            </TR>
            <TR>
             <TD vAlign="top" bgColor="#ab951e">
              <GWU:QuickSearch id="quickSrch" runat="Server" />
             </TD>
            </TR>
            <TR>
             <TD vAlign="top" bgColor="#e6dfbb" height="100%">
              <TABLE height="100%" cellSpacing="0" cellPadding="0"
                     width="100%" bgColor="#e6dfbb">
               <TBODY>
                <TR>
                 <TD vAlign="top"><IMG src="Images/gad_left_divide.jpg">
                 </TD>
                </TR>
                <TR>
                 <TD vAlign="top" height="100%">
                  <TABLE height="100%" cellSpacing="0" cellPadding="3">
                   <TBODY>
                    <TR>
                     <TD><!--------- LEFT COLUMN start --------->
                      <GWU:LeftNavigator id="leftNav" runat="Server"
                       /></TD>
                    </TR>
                   </TBODY>
                  </TABLE>
                 </TD>
                </TR>
               </TBODY>
              </TABLE>
             </TD>
            </TR>
           </TBODY>
          </TABLE>
```

```
</TD>
<TD vAlign="top" width="100%" height="100%">
 <TABLE height="100%" cellSpacing="0" cellPadding="0">
  <TBODY>
   <TR>
    <TD vAlign="top"><IMG height="22"
        src="Images/gad_head03.jpg" width="35" border="0"></TD>
    <TD width="100%" bgColor="#e6dfbb">
     <TABLE cellSpacing="0" cellPadding="0" width="100%">
      <TBODY>
       <TR>
        <TD><GWU:AuthGreeting id="authGreeting" runat="Server"/>
        </TD>
        <TD align="right">
         <GWU:TopCategoryDropDown id="deptList" runat="Server"/>
         <br>
        </TD>
       </TR>
      </TBODY>
     </TABLE>
    </TD>
   </TR>
   <TR>
    <TD vAlign="top"><IMG height="9" src="Images/gad_head04.jpg"
      width="35" border="0"></TD>
    <TD vAlign="top"><IMG height="9" src="Images/gad_head05.jpg"
      width="100%" border="0"></TD>
   </TR>
   <TR>
    <TD vAlign="top" width="35"
        background="Images/gad_head04a.jpg" height="100%"
    > </TD>
    <TD vAlign="top" width="100%">
```

This next part is the section of the page that we're actually concerned with. Everything above was copied from a template that was graciously provided to us by the graphic talent at 3-Spark Studios (once they saw my artistic ability, they refused to let me use my own graphics). This section below contains the code that places the `ProductBrowseList` control and a label control that will display the results of the search in a user-friendly fashion:

```
     <TABLE cellSpacing="0" cellPadding="3" width="100%">
      <TBODY>
       <TR>
        <TD vAlign="top">
         <font color="Maroon" size="2">
         <b><i>Quick Search</i></b></font><br>
         Didn't find what you were looking for? Try our
         <a href="AdvancedSearch.aspx">Advanced Search</a>.<br>
         <asp:Label ID="searchMessage" Runat="server">
         </asp:Label>
         <br>
         <GW:ProductBrowseList id="prodBrowse" runat="server" />
         <!---------- CENTER BODY stop ----------><BR>
```

The remainder of the code for this page is also part of the template, and simply closes the various navigation strips. Also included is the standard footer control:

```
                                </TD>
                              </TR>
                            </TBODY>
                          </TABLE>
                        </TD>
                      </TR>
                    </TBODY>
                  </TABLE>
                </TD>
              </TR>
            </TBODY>
          </TABLE>
        </TD>
      </TR>
      <TR>
        <TD vAlign="top" width="21" background="Images/gad_farleft_bg.jpg"
            height="100%"><IMG height="1" src="Images/gad_farleft_bg.jpg"
            width="21" border="0"></TD>
        <TD vAlign="top">
          <TABLE cellSpacing="0" cellPadding="0" width="100%">
            <TBODY>
              <TR>
                <TD><IMG height="8" src="Images/gad_foot01.jpg"
                          width="100%"></TD>
              </TR>
              <TR>
                <TD align="middle" width="100%" bgColor="#ab951e">
                <!--------- FOOTER start --------->
                  <GWU:Footer id="footer" runat="Server" />
                </TD>
              </TR>
            </TBODY>
          </TABLE>
        </TD>
      </TR>
    </TBODY>
  </TABLE>
  </TD>
 </TR>
 </TBODY>
</TABLE>
</TD></TR></TBODY></TABLE>
</form>
</BODY>
</HTML>
```

QuickSearch.aspx.cs

Now that we've seen the HTML portion of our web page, let's have a look at the code-behind class. This class is responsible for performing the actual query against the database to execute the quick search and binding those results to the product browse list control.

```
using System;
using System.Collections;
using System.ComponentModel;
using System.Data;
using System.Drawing;
using System.Web;
using System.Web.SessionState;
using System.Web.UI;
using System.Web.UI.WebControls;
using System.Web.UI.HtmlControls;

using GW.Web.ProductCatalog;

namespace GW.Web
{
  /// <summary>
  /// Summary description for QuickSearch.
  /// </summary>
  public class QuickSearch : System.Web.UI.Page
  {
    protected GW.Web.ProductCatalog.Controls.ProductBrowseList prodBrowse;
    protected System.Web.UI.WebControls.Label searchMessage;
    protected GW.Web.UserControls.QuickSearch qs;

    private void Page_Load(object sender, System.EventArgs e)
    {
      // Put user code to initialize the page here
      if (!Page.IsPostBack)
      {
        LoadData();
      }
    }

    private void LoadData()
    {
      DataSet products =
             ProductCatalog.ProductCatalog.QuickSearch(Request["searchKey"]);
      if (products.Tables[0].Rows.Count == 0)
      {
        searchMessage.Text =
                          "There were no products that matched your query.";
      }
      else
      {
        searchMessage.Text =
                 "Your search returned <b><font color=\"Maroon\">" +
                 products.Tables[0].Rows.Count.ToString() +
                 "</font></b> results.<br><br>";
        prodBrowse.DataSource = products;
        prodBrowse.DataBind();
      }
    }
```

```
    #region Web Form Designer generated code
    override protected void OnInit(EventArgs e)
    {
      //
      // CODEGEN: This call is required by the ASP.NET Web Form Designer.
      //
      InitializeComponent();
      base.OnInit(e);
    }

    /// <summary>
    /// Required method for Designer support - do not modify
    /// the contents of this method with the code editor.
    /// </summary>
    private void InitializeComponent()
    {
      this.Load += new System.EventHandler(this.Page_Load);

    }
    #endregion
  }
}
```

Quick Search in Action

The change to the stored procedure, the inclusion of the CMP metadata, the modification to the business class and finally the creation of the new `.aspx` page combine to produce a clean, quick, easy-to-use interface that customers can use to quickly retrieve product listings. The following screenshot shows a search on the word ring in our small sample database:

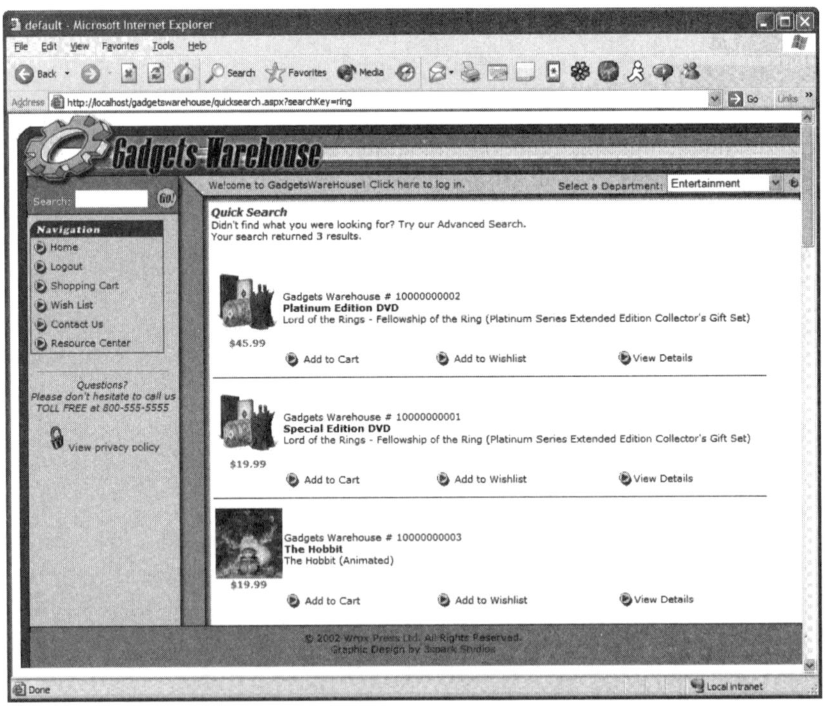

Advanced Search

The Advanced Search facility is, naturally enough, slightly more advanced than the Quick Search facility. The style of solution is still similar, however. The first thing we are going to do is write a stored procedure that performs the advanced search. Then we'll put down the metadata for that procedure into our `web.config` file. After that, we modify the code in the `ProductCatalog` class to provide a method that performs an advanced search. Finally, we'll take a look at the ASP.NET and code-behind class for the advanced search and what it all looks like when it's done.

Stored Procedure

We ran into a bit of a problem when developing the stored procedure. We wanted the user to be able to select a list of departments (parent categories) that they would use to filter their search results. The problem is that the parent category is a calculated column based on a sub-query. You can't actually get SQL Server to perform any logic in the `WHERE` clause based on the value of the calculated column. As a result, we decided that we would perform the advanced search in its entirety in the stored procedure, and do the category filtering in the `FinalizeData` method of the `AdvancedSearchSet` class.

The following is the listing for the advanced search stored procedure:

```
CREATE PROCEDURE Gw_Product_AdvancedSearch
@SKU varchar(11),
@Name varchar(50),
@Description varchar(100),
@MinPrice money,
@MaxPrice money
AS
  SELECT Products.ProductId, Name, ShortDescription, LongDescription,
         Deleted,  ProductSkus.RetailPrice, ProductSkus.ActualPrice,
         ProductSkus.Description SkuDesc, ProductSkus.SKU,
         Products.CategoryId,
         ParentCategoryId = (
            SELECT ParentCategoryId FROM Categories cats
            WHERE cats.CategoryId = Products.CategoryId )
  FROM Products
  INNER JOIN ProductSKUs ON Products.ProductId = ProductSKUs.ProductId
  WHERE (
        (SKU = @SKU) OR
        ( Products.Name LIKE @Name ) OR
        ( Products.ShortDescription LIKE  @Description ) ) AND
            ( (ProductSkus.ActualPrice >= @MinPrice) AND
              (ProductSkus.ActualPrice <= @MaxPrice) )
  ORDER BY Name ASC, ProductSkus.ActualPrice DESC
GO
```

One other thing worth noting is that we are not using wildcard symbols in this stored procedure. The reason for this is that the customer might quite often be sending blank values to the procedure. The way the logic is structured, if they sent a blank to the product name or short description, and we wrapped that in `%`s for wildcard, we would be comparing fields against `%%`, which we found out matches *all* patterns, making our search worthless. As such, we're going to decide at run time which values should be wrapped in wildcards.

CMP Metadata

Now that we know what our stored procedure looks like and we know the profile of all of the parameters, we can define our CMP metadata and place it into the `web.config` file as follows:

```
<ContainerMapping>
  <ContainerMappingId>AdvancedSearch</ContainerMappingId>
  <ContainedClass>AdvancedSearchSet</ContainedClass>
  <Select>
    <CommandName>Gw_Product_AdvancedSearch</CommandName>
    <Parameter>
      <ClassMember>SKU</ClassMember>
      <ParameterName>@SKU</ParameterName>
      <DbTypeHint>Varchar</DbTypeHint>
      <ParamDirection>Input</ParamDirection>
      <Size>11</Size>
    </Parameter>
    <Parameter>
      <ClassMember>Name</ClassMember>
      <ParameterName>@Name</ParameterName>
      <DbTypeHint>Varchar</DbTypeHint>
      <ParamDirection>Input</ParamDirection>
      <Size>50</Size>
    </Parameter>
    <Parameter>
      <ClassMember>Description</ClassMember>
      <ParameterName>@Description</ParameterName>
      <DbTypeHint>Varchar</DbTypeHint>
      <ParamDirection>Input</ParamDirection>
      <Size>100</Size>
    </Parameter>
    <Parameter>
      <ClassMember>MinPrice</ClassMember>
      <ParameterName>@MinPrice</ParameterName>
      <DbTypeHint>Money</DbTypeHint>
      <ParamDirection>Input</ParamDirection>
      <Size>8</Size>
    </Parameter>
    <Parameter>
      <ClassMember>MaxPrice</ClassMember>
      <ParameterName>@MaxPrice</ParameterName>
      <DbTypeHint>Money</DbTypeHint>
      <ParamDirection>Input</ParamDirection>
      <Size>8</Size>
    </Parameter>
  </Select>
</ContainerMapping>
type="GW.CMPServices.CMPConfigurationHandler, GW.CMPServices"/>
</configSections>
```

AdvancedSearch.aspx

With our data all taken care of in the stored procedure and the metadata placed snugly in the `web.config` file, we're all set and ready to create our Advanced Search page.

Here's a picture of `AdvancedSearch.aspx` from the design view, again showing the important user controls:

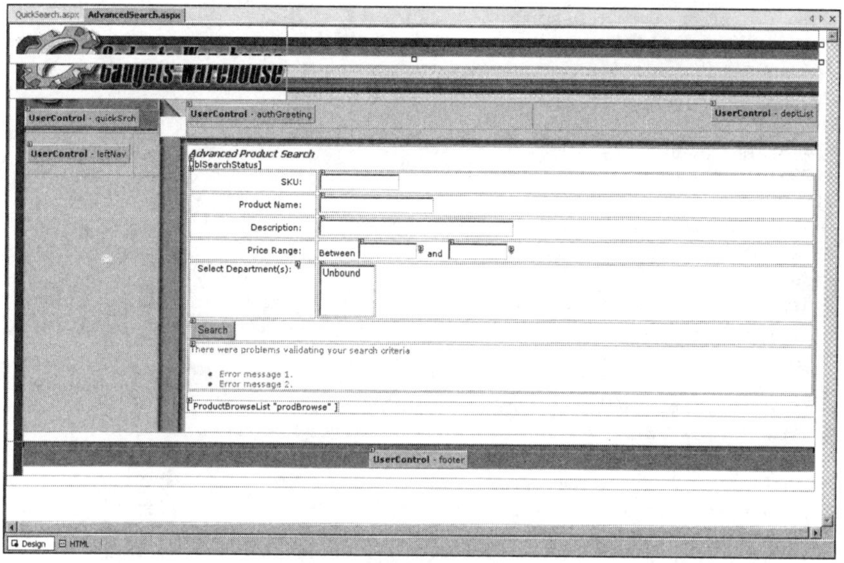

Let's go straight into the main section of our page. The important thing here is that we're using two panels. The first panel contains all of the search criteria user input code, and the second panel contains a product browse list composite server control. The first time the user sees the page, the criteria panel is visible. When they post back to perform the actual search, the `criteriaPanel` panel will be hidden and the `resultsPanel` panel will be made visible.

```
<asp:Panel ID="criteriaPanel" Runat="Server">
  <TABLE cellSpacing="2" cellPadding="2" width="100%"
        border="0">
   <TR>
    <TD align="right" width="150">SKU:</TD>
    <TD width="600">
     <asp:TextBox id="txtSKU" Runat="server"
       MaxLength="11" Width="108px">
     </asp:TextBox></TD>
   </TR>
   <TR>
    <TD align="right" width="150">Product Name:</TD>
```

```
<TD>
  <asp:TextBox id="txtName" Runat="server"
    MaxLength="50"></asp:TextBox></TD>
</TR>
<TR>
 <TD align="right" width="150">Description:
 </TD>
 <TD>
  <asp:TextBox id="txtDescription" Runat="server"
    MaxLength="100" Width="263px">
  </asp:TextBox></TD>
</TR>
<TR>
 <TD align="right" width="150">Price Range:
 </TD>
 <TD>Between
  <asp:TextBox id="txtMinPrice" Runat="server"
    MaxLength="10" Width="80px">
  </asp:TextBox>
  <asp:RangeValidator id="vldPriceMin" Runat="server"
    ErrorMessage="Valid range for minimum price is between 0 and 100,000"
    MaximumValue="100000" MinimumValue="0"
    ControlToValidate="txtMinPrice" Type="Currency"
    >*</asp:RangeValidator> and 
  <asp:TextBox id="txtMaxPrice" Runat="server" MaxLength="10"
              Width="80px"></asp:TextBox>
  <asp:RangeValidator id="vldMaxPrice" runat="server"
 ErrorMessage="Valid range for the Maximum Price is between 0 and 100000."
 MaximumValue="100000" MinimumValue="0" ControlToValidate="txtMaxPrice"
 Display="Dynamic" Type="Currency">*</asp:RangeValidator></TD>
</TR>
<TR>
 <TD vAlign="top" align="right" width="150">Select Department(s):
  <asp:RequiredFieldValidator id="vldDepartments" Runat="server"
      ErrorMessage="You must select at least one category from the list."
      ControlToValidate="lbDepartments"
      Display="Dynamic">*</asp:RequiredFieldValidator></TD>
 <TD>
  <asp:ListBox id="lbDepartments" Runat="server"
              SelectionMode="Multiple"></asp:ListBox></TD>
</TR>
<TR>
 <TD colSpan="2">
  <asp:Button id="btnSubmit" Runat="server"
             Text="Search"></asp:Button></TD>
</TR>
<TR>
 <TD colSpan="2">
  <asp:ValidationSummary id="vldSummary" Runat="server"
      HeaderText="There were problems validating your search criteria"
      DisplayMode="BulletList"></asp:ValidationSummary></TD>
</TR>
</TABLE>
</asp:Panel>
```

```
  <asp:Panel ID="resultsPanel" Runat="server">
   <GW:ProductBrowseList id="prodBrowse" runat="server"></GW:ProductBrowseList>
  </asp:Panel>
</TD>
```

AdvancedSearch.aspx.cs

This is the source listing for the advanced search code-behind class:

```
using System;
using System.Collections;
using System.ComponentModel;
using System.Data;
using System.Drawing;
using System.Web;
using System.Web.SessionState;
using System.Web.UI;
using System.Web.UI.WebControls;
using System.Web.UI.HtmlControls;

using GW.MonitorServices;
using GW.MonitorServices.Logging;
using System.Reflection;
using System.Diagnostics;

namespace GW.Web
{
  /// <summary>
  /// Summary description for AdvancedSearch.
  /// </summary>
  public class AdvancedSearch : System.Web.UI.Page
  {
    protected System.Web.UI.WebControls.TextBox txtSKU;
    protected System.Web.UI.WebControls.TextBox txtName;
    protected System.Web.UI.WebControls.TextBox txtMinPrice;
    protected System.Web.UI.WebControls.TextBox txtMaxPrice;
    protected System.Web.UI.WebControls.TextBox txtDescription;
    protected System.Web.UI.WebControls.ListBox lbDepartments;
    protected System.Web.UI.WebControls.Button btnSubmit;
    protected System.Web.UI.WebControls.RangeValidator vldPriceMin;
    protected System.Web.UI.WebControls.RequiredFieldValidator vldDepartments;
    protected System.Web.UI.WebControls.ValidationSummary vldSummary;
    protected System.Web.UI.WebControls.RangeValidator vldMaxPrice;
    protected System.Web.UI.WebControls.Panel resultsPanel;
    protected System.Web.UI.WebControls.Panel criteriaPanel;
    protected GW.Web.ProductCatalog.Controls.ProductBrowseList prodBrowse;
    protected System.Web.UI.WebControls.Label lblSearchStatus;

    private void Page_Load(object sender, System.EventArgs e)
    {
      // Put user code to initialize the page here
      if (!Page.IsPostBack)
      {
        BindSearchCriteria();
      }
    }
```

If the user has hit the page without doing a post back, then we know that they haven't entered any search criteria, so we will make sure that the results panel is hidden, and present the user with the search input form:

```
private void BindSearchCriteria()
{
  resultsPanel.Visible = false;
  lblSearchStatus.Text = "Please supply your criteria. Any of the " +
        "description fields may match, while all of the price range " +
        "and department criteria must match.<br>";
  DataTable categories = ProductCatalog.ProductCatalog.GetCategories();
  DataView dvTopLevel = new DataView( categories );
  dvTopLevel.RowFilter = "ParentCategoryId IS NULL";
  lbDepartments.DataSource = dvTopLevel;
  lbDepartments.DataTextField = "Description";
  lbDepartments.DataValueField = "CategoryId";
  lbDepartments.DataBind();
}
```

I've clipped out the code generated by the web forms designer.

This next method is called when the customer has supplied the search criteria and requests the results. It will hide the search criteria panel, and display the results panel and then bind the results of the advanced search to the product browse list control.

```
private void btnSubmit_Click(object sender, System.EventArgs e)
{
  GWTrace.EnteringMethod( MethodBase.GetCurrentMethod());

  criteriaPanel.Visible = false;
  resultsPanel.Visible = true;

  string selCatList = string.Empty;
```

The next few lines of code will build a comma-delimited list of selected top-level categories in which to perform the advanced search:

```
  for (int i=0; i< lbDepartments.Items.Count; i++)
  {
    if (lbDepartments.Items[i].Selected == true)
    {
      if (selCatList == string.Empty)
        selCatList = lbDepartments.Items[i].Value;
      else
        selCatList += "," + lbDepartments.Items[i].Value;
    }
  }
```

Next we pass our search parameters to the advanced search facility – note we use the ternary operator (`?`) to ensure that blank fields for the name and description are not wrapped in wildcard characters (`%`) as we mentioned earlier when looking at the `Gw_Product_AdvancedSearch` stored procedure. Also, we ensure that default values are passed from the minimum and maximum price if none has been specified.

```
        DataSet dsResults = ProductCatalog.ProductCatalog.AdvancedSearch (
          txtSKU.Text,
          ( txtName.Text == "" ? "" : "%" + txtName.Text + "%"),
          ( txtDescription.Text == "" ? "" : "%" + txtDescription.Text + "%" ),
          selCatList,
          ( txtMaxPrice.Text == ""
                      ? 100000 : System.Convert.ToDecimal( txtMaxPrice.Text ) ),
          ( txtMinPrice.Text == ""
                      ? 0 : System.Convert.ToDecimal( txtMinPrice.Text ) ) );

        if (dsResults.Tables[0].Rows.Count == 0)
          lblSearchStatus.Text = "Your advanced product search did not return "+
            "any results. Try using a broader selection of criteria next time.";
        else
          lblSearchStatus.Text = "Your advanced product search returned " +
                                 "<font color=\"Maroon\"><b>"+
                                 dsResults.Tables[0].Rows.Count.ToString() +
                                 "</b></font> results.";

        prodBrowse.DataSource = dsResults;
        prodBrowse.DataBind();
      }
    }
  }
```

Product Catalog Addition

In order to be able to run the new stored procedure, we need to modify our `ProductCatalog` business class so that it can invoke the persistence container with the right metadata and process the results.

```
public static DataSet AdvancedSearch( string sku,
                                      string name,
                                      string description,
                                      string deptList,
                                      decimal maxPrice,
                                      decimal minPrice)
{
  SqlPersistenceContainer spc = new SqlPersistenceContainer(
                  CMPConfigurationHandler.ContainerMaps["AdvancedSearch"]);
  AdvancedSearchSet advSet = new AdvancedSearchSet();
  advSet.SKU = sku;
  advSet.Description = description;
  advSet.Name = name;
  advSet.CategoryFilter = deptList;
  advSet.MaxPrice = maxPrice;
  advSet.MinPrice = minPrice;
  spc.Select( advSet );
  advSet.FinalizeData();
  GWTrace.Trace( TraceLevel.Info,
    "After finalizedata, advSet.table0 rowcount {0}",
    advSet.ResultSet.Tables[0].Rows.Count);
  return advSet.ResultSet;
}
```

AdvancedSearchSet

The following source listing is from the `AdvancedSearchSet` class, a `PersistableObjectSet` class that we wrote to contain the search results. It has one additional feature in that we override the `FinalizeData` method to filter out results that do not belong to the list of selected departments.

```
using System;
using System.Data;
using GW.CMPServices;
using GW.MonitorServices;
using GW.MonitorServices.Logging;
using System.Reflection;
using System.Diagnostics;

namespace GW.Web.ProductCatalog.Data
{
  /// <summary>
  /// Summary description for AdvancedSearchSet.
  /// </summary>
  public class AdvancedSearchSet : PersistableObjectSet
  {
    private string sku;
    private string name;
    private string description;
    private decimal minPrice;
    private decimal maxPrice;
    private string catList;

    public AdvancedSearchSet()
    { }
```

This method has a bit of extra code in it. This is because the SQL query to perform the category filtering would have been a bit too complex, and in testing took far too long due to query nesting. I found that it was actually more effective to get the search results and then use the `FinalizeData` method to filter out those results that don't belong to the selected department list.

```
    public override void FinalizeData()
    {
      GWTrace.EnteringMethod( MethodBase.GetCurrentMethod() );
      // perform finalization of data.
      DataTable rawResults = internalData.Tables[0];
      DataRow[] filteredResults = rawResults.Select(
                           "ParentCategoryID NOT IN (" + catList + ")");

      foreach (DataRow delRow in filteredResults)
      {
        rawResults.Rows.Remove( delRow );
      }
      rawResults.AcceptChanges();
    }

    public string SKU
    {
```

```
      get { return sku; }
      set { sku = value; }
    }

    public string Name
    {
      get { return name; }
      set { name = value; }
    }

    public string Description
    {
      get { return description; }
      set { description = value; }
    }

    public decimal MinPrice
    {
      get {return minPrice; }
      set { minPrice = value; }
    }

    public decimal MaxPrice
    {
      get { return maxPrice; }
      set { maxPrice = value; }
    }

    public string CategoryFilter
    {
      get { return catList; }
      set { catList = value; }
    }
  }
}
```

Advanced Search in Action

When we are all done with our database code and CMP metadata, with our changes to business components and ASP.NET code all set up and ready to go, we get the following search criteria screen:

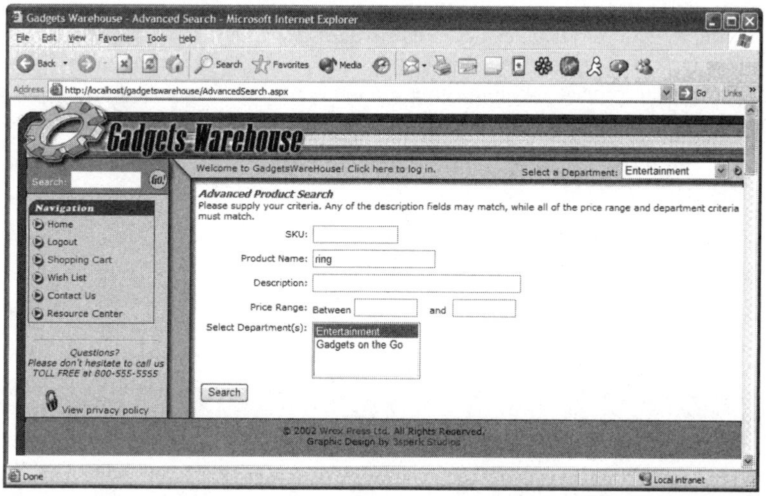

Once the customer fills out that screen and hits the Search button, the next screen containing a list of products appears:

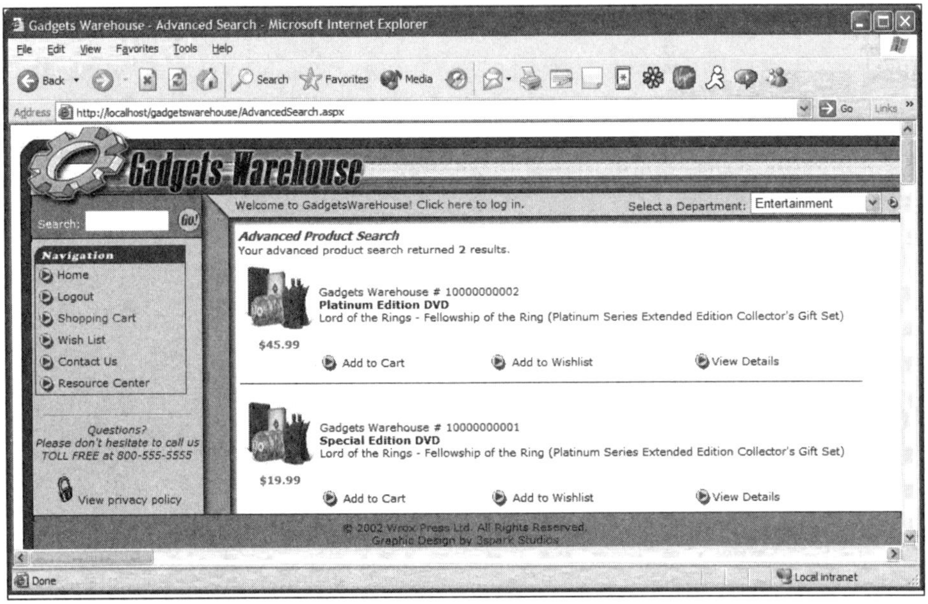

Summary

The previous chapter was all about building the product catalog and making sure that it was reliable, flexible, and friendly enough to provide the customers with a rich and easy experience. This chapter has been about finding your products. When your product catalog grows (and it will grow, and probably quicker than you expected) you need to ensure that your customers can find what they're looking for without having to read a lot of instructions, without having to think too hard about what they're doing, and without having to wait for their results to come back.

We took you through the process of identifying the concerns involved in building product searches and designing your own search solution, and finally we took you through an example of how we built our product search and showed you the source code we used to accomplish it.

CHAPTER 5

5

Shopping Cart

I'm probably beginning to sound like a broken record, starting off each chapter with "this next section is crucial to the success of your website". It's the truth, though. We started by looking at the product catalog, and then moved to the product searching capabilities. Now that customers can find your products, can browse for them and search for them, we need to let them put them into the shopping cart.

This chapter will take you through a discussion of the issues that surround building shopping carts in general. After that we'll take a look at a design that we came up with for our own Gadgets Warehouse shopping cart implementation. Finally, we'll go through an in-depth analysis of the source code that we produced in implementing our design.

By the time you're done with this chapter, you should be familiar with what it takes to build shopping carts, what their purpose is, why they're important, and how to code one from scratch without using third-party tools such as Commerce Server. We will take you through the process creating carts, of adding items to the cart, all the way up to checking out. We'll cover the actual checkout process in the order fulfillment chapter coming up later.

The Problem

Creating a shopping cart used to be a fairly big problem. Back in the early days of e-commerce websites, every single website had its own style and implementation of shopping carts. They all worked differently and they all provided different features. After some evolution, e-commerce consumers have begun to reach a consensus on how they want a shopping cart to work and what they want it to do for them.

The problem of a shopping cart isn't just the technical problem of putting products into some "bin" somewhere. Technologically, shopping carts are not that difficult to create. The hard part of the shopping cart is in the design and in the choice of how much of your solution is going to be "shrink-wrapped" and how much you're going to develop yourself. The biggest decision about a shopping cart (and fulfillment, to a similar extent), is whether you're going to create your own solution or whether you're going to use third-party tools such as Commerce Server. Assuming you do decide to create your own, you'll be faced with decisions such as: When do you require that a user using the shopping cart be authenticated? What information do you want people to have available to them in the shopping cart? Do you want anonymous users to be able to add items to carts? All of those questions and more need to be answered while you're designing your shopping cart in order to provide a simple, reliable, easy-to-use interface to the customer.

The Design

As we just mentioned, there are plenty of things we need to worry about when we're working on the design for our shopping cart implementation. When working on our shopping cart implementation, we came up with the following list of requirements for our cart:

- Flexible
- Guest-friendly
- Durable

Flexible

We want customers to be able to do whatever it is they need to do with regards to their shopping cart from a single point of access. In other words, we want them to be able to modify quantities and remove items from their cart on the same screen with only a single button click.

Guest-friendly

A vast amount of customers for e-commerce websites fall into the category of "impulse" buyers. They are shoppers who, for whatever reason, go to a website with no particular goal in mind and then end up in the checkout screen with a product that caught their eye while they were shopping. Because of the sheer numbers of this type of buyer, we don't want to exclude them. So, our shopping cart will be fully functional while someone is not logged into the site. They will be able to browse the site and still work happily with their cart. When they click the checkout button they will be asked to log in, but by that point they are ready to buy and probably won't mind the inconvenience of a quick sign-up form.

Durable

One thing we don't ever want to happen is a customer to lose what was in their shopping cart. For example, if the cart were session- or cookie-based, the customer would lose the contents of their cart if they closed the browser, or even logged onto the site from another machine. Durable shopping carts do not lose items. After all, the shopping cart is the last step just before the customer checks out and pays us money. If they lose items from the cart and think twice about putting the items back into the cart, we'll lose money. Therefore, it is extremely important that our shopping cart implementation makes sure that there is as little opportunity as possible to have items leave the shopping cart without the customer explicitly pushing a button to make that happen.

The Cart

Before we can come up with a sample UI for our shopping cart, or even with a list of functions we want the cart to perform, we want to be able to narrow down what information we want to display in our shopping cart and how we want it to be displayed. We also need to figure out how we're going to store the shopping cart in the database.

Let's take a look at a diagram of the database table that we want to use to represent our shopping cart:

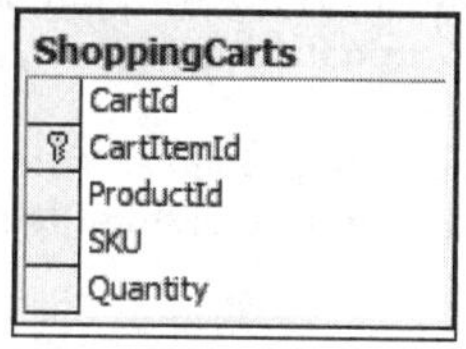

It looks fairly simple, doesn't it?

CartId

This is the ID of the cart itself. It is a `varchar` of size `50`. It needs to be large enough to accommodate the GUID that is generated for anonymously created carts as well as the significantly smaller number used when the `CustomerId` is used for authenticated user-created carts.

The `CartId` is a string that represents a single shopping cart and is what ties all of the items in a particular shopping cart together. Since we want unregistered users to be able to maintain shopping carts just as easily as registered users, we couldn't rely solely on a user ID for the shopping cart identifier.

The way we're going to handle unregistered users is to create an artificial identifier for an anonymous user's shopping cart. When an anonymous user adds something to the shopping cart for the first time, they will be assigned a GUID for their cart identifier, which is written to their client as a cookie. From then on, that customer's access to the shopping cart will be handled using that generated GUID. Authenticated users will simply use their numeric user identifier for their shopping cart.

The one other thing we need to make sure of in the implementation of the shopping cart is that when an anonymous user signs up and registers with the site, their shopping cart contents are not lost, so we will have to modify their cart when they sign up so that their anonymous `CartId` becomes their authenticated user ID.

CartItemId

An identity column indicating the cart item ID. This is the primary key of the table. It is used to uniquely identify a single cart item for use in updating and deleting items in a cart.

ProductId

This is an integer indicating the numeric ID of the product that has been added to the cart.

SKU

This is the SKU of the item added to the cart. The SKU is the lowest level of a product in the cart. Whenever items are added to the cart or removed from the cart, it is done at the SKU level, not the product level. As usual, the SKU is an 11-character `varchar`.

Quantity

This is an integer indicating the quantity of the item in the cart.

The Solution

The solution for our shopping cart involves quite a few different pieces. The first thing that we're going to do is create some stored procedures for working with our shopping cart. These will include functionality like querying cart contents, updating quantities, and removing items from individual carts.

Once the database is prepared for the new shopping cart functionality, we will set up the metadata in our `web.config` file and then we'll move on to creating the shopping cart project and the pages that utilize it.

Stored Procedures

The following is a list of the stored procedures that we're going to need in order to support all of the functionality that we want from our cart. The basic requirements are for querying the contents of the cart, updating and deleting individual items, and finally the ability to migrate a cart from an anonymous guest user to a registered user.

Gw_Select_CartItems

This stored procedure retrieves a list of all of the items that belong to a particular customer, anonymous or otherwise. As usual, we have prefixed the name of the stored procedure with an abbreviation for our application (GadgetsWarehouse.COM): Gw.

```
CREATE PROCEDURE Gw_Select_CartItems
@CartId varchar(50)
AS
  SELECT c.ProductId, c.Sku, c.Quantity, c.CartItemId,
     s.Description as SkuDescription, s.RetailPrice, s.ActualPrice,
     p.Name as ProductName, p.ShortDescription, p.CategoryId,
     ExtAmount = (c.Quantity * s.ActualPrice)
  FROM ShoppingCarts c
     INNER JOIN ProductSkus s ON
        c.Sku = s.Sku
     INNER JOIN Products p on
        c.ProductId = p.ProductID
  WHERE c.CartId = @CartId
GO
```

Gw_Insert_CartItem

This stored procedure will add an item to a customer's shopping cart. If the item (identified uniquely by its Stock Keeping Unit (SKU)) already exists in the cart then its quantity will be increased by one rather than simply adding two of the same item to the cart.

```
CREATE PROCEDURE Gw_Insert_CartItem
  @CartId varchar(50),
```

```
  @SKU varchar(11)
AS
  DECLARE @ProductId int
  DECLARE @CartItemId int
  DECLARE @Quantity int

  SELECT @ProductId = ProductId FROM ProductSkus WHERE Sku = @Sku

  SELECT @CartItemId = CartItemId, @Quantity = Quantity
    FROM ShoppingCarts
    WHERE CartId = @CartId AND Sku = @Sku

  IF @CartItemID IS NULL
    INSERT INTO ShoppingCarts(CartId, SKU, ProductId, Quantity)
                      VALUES ( @CartId, @SKU, @ProductId, 1)
  ELSE
    UPDATE ShoppingCarts SET Quantity = (@Quantity + 1)
    WHERE CartItemId = @CartItemId
GO
```

If a cart has been created for an anonymous user, and that user never comes back, we will be using extra database storage that we don't need. For further expansion, it would be wise to create a job in SQL that will periodically go through and purge anonymous (GUID-based) carts.

Gw_Update_CartItem

This stored procedure will modify the quantity of a particular shopping cart item. This stored procedure will be called once for each modified shopping cart item when the customer clicks a button to update the quantities in the shopping cart.

```
CREATE PROCEDURE Gw_Update_CartItem
  @CartId varchar(50),
  @Sku varchar(11),
  @Quantity int
AS
  UPDATE ShoppingCarts SET Quantity = @Quantity
  WHERE CartId = @CartId AND Sku = @Sku
GO
```

Gw_Delete_CartItem

This stored procedure will remove a product SKU from a customer's shopping cart. This happens when the customer modifies a quantity of an item down to zero or clicks the Delete checkbox from the shopping cart user interface.

```
CREATE PROCEDURE Gw_Delete_CartItem
  @CartId varchar(50),
  @Sku varchar(11)
AS
  DELETE ShoppingCarts WHERE CartId = @CartId AND Sku = @Sku
GO
```

Gw_Convert_ShoppingCart

This stored procedure migrates an anonymous customer's cart items to their newly assigned authenticated user identifier. This is accomplished easily by simply modifying the user ID for each of the anonymous user's cart items.

```
CREATE PROCEDURE Gw_Convert_ShoppingCart
  @OldCartId varchar(50),
  @NewCartId varchar(50)
AS

  UPDATE ShoppingCarts SET CartId = @NewCartId
  WHERE CartId = @OldCartId
GO
```

CMP Metadata

The following is the list of CMP metadata that we need to put in our `web.config` file in order to configure our data services to work with the stored procedures we just wrote. We're only including a few stored procedure metadata definitions in this chapter to make things easier to read. As we saw back in Chapter 2 on our core services, this metadata is essential to creating the object-relational mapping that allows class members to be transferred to/from the database:

```
<ContainerMapping>
  <ContainerMappingId>CartContents</ContainerMappingId>
  <ContainedClass>CartContents</ContainedClass>
  <Select>
    <CommandName>Gw_Select_CartItems</CommandName>
    <Parameter>
      <ClassMember>CartId</ClassMember>
      <ParameterName>@CartId</ParameterName>
      <DbTypeHint>Varchar</DbTypeHint>
      <ParamDirection>Input</ParamDirection>
      <Size>50</Size>
    </Parameter>
  </Select>
</ContainerMapping>
<ContainerMapping>
  <ContainerMappingId>CartMigration</ContainerMappingId>
  <ContainedClass>CartMigration</ContainedClass>
  <Update>
    <CommandName>Gw_Convert_ShoppingCart</CommandName>
    <Parameter>
      <ClassMember>OldCartId</ClassMember>
      <ParameterName>@OldCartId</ParameterName>
      <DbTypeHint>Varchar</DbTypeHint>
      <ParamDirection>Input</ParamDirection>
      <Size>50</Size>
    </Parameter>
    <Parameter>
      <ClassMember>NewCartId</ClassMember>
      <ParameterName>@NewCartId</ParameterName>
```

```
      <DbTypeHint>Varchar</DbTypeHint>
      <ParamDirection>Input</ParamDirection>
      <Size>50</Size>
    </Parameter>
  </Update>
</ContainerMapping>
<ContainerMapping>
```

Shopping Cart Business Classes

With the stored procedures and metadata in place, we can work on creating our business classes. The first thing we'll do is create a new project called `ShoppingCart`. We'll set the default namespace and output filename to `GW.Web.ShoppingCart`. As usual this will be a C# Class Library project.

CartManager

The `CartManager` class serves as the focal point for all of the method calls relating to the shopping cart and shopping cart contents. It contains methods for determining the current shopping cart ID based on whether the user is anonymous or not, as well as methods for adding and removing items, changing quantities, selecting items from the cart, and migrating an anonymous cart to an authenticated user's cart.

```
using System;
using System.Data;
using System.Web;

using GW.CMPServices;
using GW.MonitorServices;
using GW.MonitorServices.Logging;

namespace GW.Web.ShoppingCart
{
  /// <summary>
  /// Summary description for CartManager.
  /// </summary>
  public class CartManager
  {
    private string cartId;

    public CartManager()
    {
      cartId = CartManager.DetermineCurrentCartId();
    }
```

This method will determine the current shopping cart ID. If the user is not authenticated, it will check for an existing shopping cart cookie. If there is no cookie, a new one will be created and the new cart ID (a freshly generated GUID) will be returned. By default, all cookies default to session-expiration, so the cart ID cookie is session-length.

```
    public static string DetermineCurrentCartId()
    {
      HttpContext ctx = HttpContext.Current;
```

```
    if (ctx.User.Identity.Name != "")
      return ctx.User.Identity.Name;
    if (ctx.Request.Cookies["GW_CartId"] != null)
      return ctx.Request.Cookies["GW_CartId"].Value;
    else
    {
      Guid newCartId = Guid.NewGuid();
      string newCartStringId = newCartId.ToString();
      ctx.Response.Cookies["GW_CartId"].Value = newCartStringId;
      return newCartStringId;
    }
  }
```

This next method will retrieve the list of items in the current user's shopping cart. The current cart is retrieved by obtaining the current cart ID using the method listed above.

```
public DataTable GetCartItems()
{

  CartContents cartContents = new CartContents();
  cartContents.CartId = cartId;

  SqlPersistenceContainer spc = new SqlPersistenceContainer(
            CMPConfigurationHandler.ContainerMaps["CartContents"] );
  spc.Select( cartContents );
  return cartContents.ResultSet.Tables[0];
}
```

This next method removes an item from the shopping cart.

```
public void RemoveItem( string SKU )
{
  CartItem ci = new CartItem();
  ci.CartId = cartId;
  ci.SKU = SKU;
  SqlPersistenceContainer spc = new SqlPersistenceContainer(
                CMPConfigurationHandler.ContainerMaps["CartItem"] );
  spc.Delete( ci );
}
```

This method will update the quantity of an item in the current user's cart. The current cart ID is determined automatically by the constructor of the `CartItem` class. We'll see the code listing for that below.

```
public void UpdateItem( string SKU, int newQuantity )
{
  CartItem ci = new CartItem();
  ci.CartId = cartId;
  ci.SKU = SKU;
  ci.Quantity = newQuantity;
  SqlPersistenceContainer spc = new SqlPersistenceContainer(
                CMPConfigurationHandler.ContainerMaps["CartItem"] );
  spc.Update( ci );
}
```

The following method will add a single unit of a SKU to the current user's shopping cart.

```
    public void AddItem( string SKU )
    {
      CartItem ci = new CartItem();
      ci.CartId = cartId;
      ci.SKU = SKU;
      SqlPersistenceContainer spc = new SqlPersistenceContainer(
                      CMPConfigurationHandler.ContainerMaps["CartItem"] );
      spc.Insert( ci );
    }
```

The following method will migrate an anonymous user's cart to the new cart ID belonging to an authenticated user. The cookie created for the anonymous cart will naturally expire when the user's browser is closed.

```
    public void MigrateCart ( string oldCartId, string newCartId )
    {
      CartMigration cm = new CartMigration();
      cm.OldCartId = oldCartId;
      cm.NewCartId = newCartId;
      SqlPersistenceContainer spc = new SqlPersistenceContainer(
                 CMPConfigurationHandler.ContainerMaps["CartMigration"] );
      spc.Update( cm );
    }

    public string CartId
    {
      get { return cartId; }
      set { cartId = value; }
    }
  }
}
```

CartContents

`CartContents` is a `PersistableObjectSet` class that is used to retrieve the list of cart items belonging to a particular shopping cart. `CartContents` contains data members necessary to supply parameter values to the stored procedure for retrieving shopping cart items.

```
using System;

using GW.CMPServices;

namespace GW.Web.ShoppingCart
{
  /// <summary>
  /// Used to retrieve shopping cart contents
  /// </summary>
  public class CartContents : PersistableObjectSet
  {
    private string cartId;
```

```
      public string CartId
      {
        get { return cartId; }
        set { cartId = value; }
      }

      public override void FinalizeData()
      {
        CartContents.FinalizeData( internalData );
      }
    }
  }
```

CartItem

CartItem is a PersistableObject used to represent a single item within a cart. This class is used to pass information to the update, insert, and delete operations on a particular shopping cart item.

```
using System;

using GW.CMPServices;
using GW.MonitorServices;
using GW.MonitorServices.Logging;

namespace GW.Web.ShoppingCart
{
  /// <summary>
  /// Represents a single shopping cart item.
  /// </summary>
  [Serializable()]
  public class CartItem : PersistableObject
  {
    private string cartId;
    private int productId;
    private string sku;
    private int quantity;
    private int cartItemId;

    public CartItem ()
    {
    }

    public string CartId
    {
      get { return cartId; }
      set { cartId = value; }
    }

    public int ProductId
    {
      get { return productId; }
      set { productId = value; }
```

```
    }

    public string SKU
    {
      get { return sku; }
      set { sku = value; }
    }

    public int Quantity
    {
      get { return quantity; }
      set { quantity = value; }
    }

    public int CartItemId
    {
      get { return cartItemId; }
      set { cartItemId = value; }
    }
  }
}
```

CartMigration

`CartMigration` is a `PersistableObject` class used to maintain the information required to migrate a shopping cart from one user to another.

```
using System;
using GW.CMPServices;

namespace GW.Web.ShoppingCart
{
  /// <summary>
  /// Summary description for CartMigration.
  /// </summary>
  public class CartMigration : PersistableObject
  {
    private string oldCartId;
    private string newCartId;
    public CartMigration()
    {

    }

    public string OldCartId
    {
      get { return oldCartId; }
      set { oldCartId = value; }
    }

    public string NewCartId
    {
      get { return newCartId; }
```

```
            set { newCartId = value; }
        }
    }
}
```

Cart Pages

With the stored procedures, data structures, metadata, and business class all complete, the only thing remaining to do in order to complete our shopping cart implementation is actually code the page.

ShoppingCart.aspx

The `ShoppingCart.aspx` page is the main shopping cart interface page. It is called when displaying the shopping cart contents and when an item is going to be added to the shopping cart. Here is a look at in the design view:

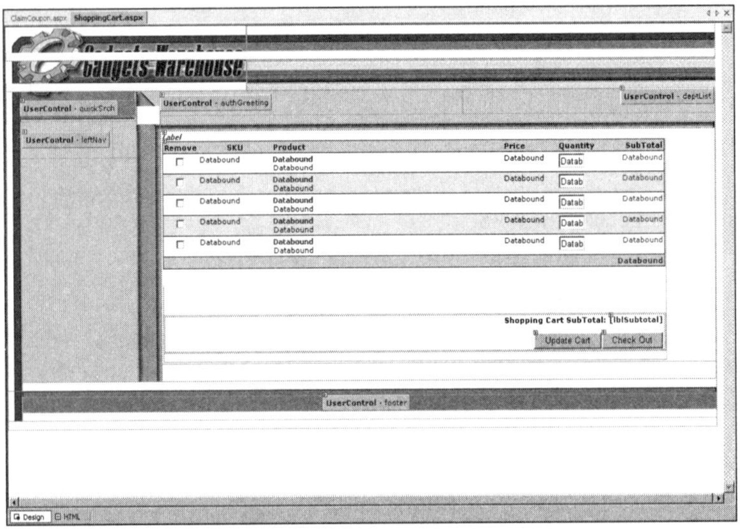

We've seen the code that generates the header, the footer, the left navigation bar, etc., in the previous chapters, so here we're only going to see the top and the important pieces of `ShoppingCart.aspx`, the remainder of the code can be found in the download code of course.

```
<%@ Page language="c#" Codebehind="ShoppingCart.aspx.cs"
    AutoEventWireup="false" Inherits="GW.Web.ShoppingCartPage"%>
<%@ Register TagPrefix="GWU" TagName="TopCategoryDropDown"
   Src="UserControls/TopCategoryDropDown.ascx" %>
<%@ Register TagPrefix="GWU" TagName="Footer"
    Src="UserControls/Footer.ascx" %>
<%@ Register Tagprefix="GWU" TagName="AuthGreeting"
    Src="UserControls/AuthGreeting.ascx" %>
<%@ Register TagPrefix="GWU" TagName="LeftNavigator"
    Src="UserControls/LeftNavigator.ascx" %>
<%@ Register TagPrefix="GWU" TagName="QuickSearch"
```

```
    Src="UserControls/QuickSearch.ascx" %>
<!DOCTYPE HTML PUBLIC "-//W3C//DTD HTML 4.0 Transitional//EN" >
<HTML>
  <HEAD>
    <title>Gadgets Warehouse : Shopping Cart</title>
    <meta name="GENERATOR" Content="Microsoft Visual Studio 7.0">
    <meta name="CODE_LANGUAGE" Content="C#">
    <meta name="vs_defaultClientScript" content="JavaScript">
    <meta name="vs_targetSchema"
          content="http://schemas.microsoft.com/intellisense/ie5">
    <LINK href="Styles/main.css" type="text/css" rel="stylesheet">
  </HEAD>
  <BODY text="#000000" vLink="#000000" aLink="#000000" link="#000000"
        leftMargin="0" topMargin="0">
    <form id="default" method="post" runat="server">
```

I've skipped a considerable amount of less interesting code to get to this point:

```
<TABLE cellSpacing="0" cellPadding="3" width="100%">
  <TBODY>
    <TR>
      <TD vAlign="top">
        <P>
          <asp:Label id="lblMessage" runat="server" EnableViewState="False"
                     Visible="False">Label</asp:Label><BR>
          <asp:Panel ID="pnlCartContents" runat="server">
            <asp:DataGrid id="dgCart" runat="server"
                          AutoGenerateColumns="False" CellPadding="2"
                          GridLines="horizontal" BorderColor="DarkBlue"
                          DataKeyField="Quantity" ShowFooter="True"
                          BorderWidth="1px"
                          BackColor="LightGoldenrodYellow"
                          ForeColor="Black">
              <ItemStyle BackColor="White"></ItemStyle>
              <SelectedItemStyle ForeColor="GhostWhite"
                                 BackColor="DarkSlateBlue">
              </SelectedItemStyle>
              <AlternatingItemStyle BackColor="#eeeeee">
              </AlternatingItemStyle>
              <HeaderStyle Font-Bold="True" BackColor="#e6dfbb">
              </HeaderStyle>
              <FooterStyle BackColor="#e6dfbb"></FooterStyle>
              <Columns>
                <asp:TemplateColumn HeaderText="SKU"
                                    ItemStyle-VerticalAlign="Top"
                                    HeaderStyle-HorizontalAlign="Center"
                                    HeaderStyle-Font-Bold="True"
                                    ItemStyle-Width="110px">
                  <ItemTemplate>
                    <asp:Label ID="lblSKU" Runat="server"
               Text='<%# DataBinder.Eval(Container.DataItem, "Sku")%>'>
                    </asp:Label>
                  </ItemTemplate>
```

```
                </asp:TemplateColumn>
                <asp:TemplateColumn HeaderText="Product"
                                    ItemStyle-Width="400px"
                                    ItemStyle-VerticalAlign="Top">
                  <ItemTemplate>
                    <asp:Label font-bold="True" Font-Name="tahoma"
                               ForeColor="Maroon"
                               ID="prodName" Runat="server"
        Text='<%# DataBinder.Eval(Container.DataItem, "ProductName")%>'>
                    </asp:Label><br>
                    <asp:Label ID="skuDesc" runat="server"
      Text='<%# DataBinder.Eval(Container.DataItem, "SkuDescription")%>'>
                    </asp:Label>
                  </ItemTemplate>
                </asp:TemplateColumn>
                <asp:TemplateColumn HeaderText="Price"
                                    ItemStyle-width="80"
                                    ItemStyle-verticalalign="Top">
                  <ItemTemplate>
                    <asp:Label ID="price" Runat="server"
Text='<%# DataBinder.Eval(Container.DataItem, "ActualPrice", "{0:c}") %>'>
                    </asp:Label>
                  </ItemTemplate>
                </asp:TemplateColumn>
                <asp:TemplateColumn HeaderText="Quantity"
                                    ItemStyle-VerticalAlign="Top">
                  <ItemTemplate>
                   <asp:TextBox ID="txtQuantity" Runat="server"
                                Columns="4" MaxLength="3" Width="40px"
       Value='<%# DataBinder.Eval(Container.DataItem, "Quantity") %>'>
                    </asp:TextBox>
                  </ItemTemplate>
                </asp:TemplateColumn>
                <asp:TemplateColumn HeaderText="SubTotal"
                                    Headerstyle-HorizontalAlign="right"
                                    ItemStyle-Forecolor="Maroon"
                                    ItemStyle-HorizontalAlign="Right"
                                    ItemStyle-width="100px"
                                    ItemStyle-verticalalign="Top">
                  <ItemTemplate>
                    <asp:Label ID="extPrice" Runat="server"
  Text='<%# DataBinder.Eval(Container.DataItem, "ExtAmount", "{0:c}") %>'>
                    </asp:Label>
                  </ItemTemplate>
                </asp:TemplateColumn>
                <asp:TemplateColumn HeaderText="Remove"
                                    ItemStyle-VerticalAlign="Top"
                                    ItemStyle-HorizontalAlign="Center">
                  <ItemTemplate>
                    <asp:CheckBox ID="chkRemove" Runat="server">
                    </asp:CheckBox>
                  </ItemTemplate>
                </asp:TemplateColumn>
              </Columns>
```

```
            </asp:DataGrid>
            <BR>
            <asp:Button id="btnUpdate" runat="server"
                        Text="Update Cart"></asp:Button>
            <asp:Button id="btnCheckOut" runat="server"
                        Text="Check Out"></asp:Button>
          </asp:Panel>
        <P> </P>
      </TD>
    </TR>
  </TBODY>
</TABLE>
```

ShoppingCart.aspx.cs

This is the code-behind class for the shopping cart. It serves three main purposes: to display shopping cart contents, update cart quantities, and add items to the shopping cart. It provides methods for updating the contents of the cart, and event handling routines for dealing with changes to the shopping cart data grid.

Let's begin with `using` directives, private fields and the `Page_Load` method:

```
using System;
using System.Collections;
using System.ComponentModel;
using System.Data;
using System.Drawing;
using System.Web;
using System.Web.SessionState;
using System.Web.UI;
using System.Web.UI.WebControls;
using System.Web.UI.HtmlControls;

using GW.Web.ShoppingCart;

namespace GW.Web
{
  /// <summary>
  /// Summary description for ShoppingCart.
  /// </summary>
  public class ShoppingCartPage : System.Web.UI.Page
  {
    protected System.Web.UI.WebControls.Button btnUpdate;
    protected System.Web.UI.WebControls.Button btnCheckOut;
    protected System.Web.UI.WebControls.Label lblMessage;
    protected System.Web.UI.WebControls.Panel pnlCartContents;
    protected System.Web.UI.WebControls.DataGrid dgCart;

    private void Page_Load(object sender, System.EventArgs e)
    {
      lblMessage.Visible = false;
      // Put user code to initialize the page here
      if (!Page.IsPostBack)
      {
```

```
            LoadData();
        }
    }
```

When one a customer clicks on the Add To Cart button anywhere in the site, the `ShoppingCart.aspx` page is invoked with a `QueryString` parameter called `AddToCart`. This parameter contains the SKU of the product to be added to the user's cart. In our `LoadData` method, we check to see if this parameter is present. If it is, then we will add the item to the cart and then re-direct to the page without the parameter. The reason we do this is that `QueryString` arguments are *retained* on `PostBack`, so we needed a way to avoid adding an item to the cart every time the page is posted back.

```
    private void LoadData()
    {
      CartManager shoppingCart = new CartManager();
      if (Request["AddToCart"] != null)
      {
        shoppingCart.AddItem( Request["AddToCart"] );
        Response.Redirect("ShoppingCart.aspx");
      }
      DataTable cartItems = shoppingCart.GetCartItems();
      if (cartItems.Rows.Count == 0)
      {
        pnlCartContents.Visible = false;
        lblMessage.Text = "<br>There are no items in your shopping cart.";
        lblMessage.Visible = true;
      }
      else
      {
        pnlCartContents.Visible = true;
        dgCart.DataSource = cartItems;
        dgCart.DataBind();
      }
    }
```

The following method will update the cart to reflect changes to quantities and items that have been set to quantity 0 or checked for deletion.

```
    private void UpdateCartItems()
    {
      CartManager shoppingCart = new CartManager();
      for (int i=0; i < dgCart.Items.Count ; i++)
      {
        TextBox txtQuantity = (TextBox)
                          dgCart.Items[i].FindControl("txtQuantity");
        CheckBox chkRemove = (CheckBox)
                            dgCart.Items[i].FindControl("chkRemove");
        int curQuantity;
        try
        {
          curQuantity = Int32.Parse(txtQuantity.Text);

          if ( (curQuantity != (int)dgCart.DataKeys[i]) ||
```

```
                ( chkRemove.Checked ) )
            {
              // quantity has changed or the item has been removed.
              Label lblSku = (Label) dgCart.Items[i].FindControl("lblSKU");
              if ( (curQuantity <= 0) || chkRemove.Checked)
              {
                shoppingCart.RemoveItem( lblSku.Text );
              }
              else
              {
                shoppingCart.UpdateItem( lblSku.Text, curQuantity );
              }
            }
          }
          catch (Exception ex)
          {
            // do something about the errors on the input to the grid.
            lblMessage.Text = "An error occurred in posting (" +
                                                    ex.ToString() + ")";
            lblMessage.Visible = true;
          }
        }
      }
```

Skipping over the designer-generated code, we finally have the event handlers for the Update Cart and Check Out buttons:

```
      private void btnUpdate_Click(object sender, System.EventArgs e)
      {
        UpdateCartItems();
        // Need this to remove deleted cart items.
        LoadData();
      }

      private void btnCheckOut_Click(object sender, System.EventArgs e)
      {
        UpdateCartItems();
        Response.Redirect("Checkout.aspx");
      }
    }
  }
```

Shopping Cart in Action

Here's a look at our shopping cart now that we've gone through the code all the way from the database to the .aspx page. Don't worry about not seeing a sub-total, we're going to add that functionality in the Chapter 7, where we look at coupons and discounts.

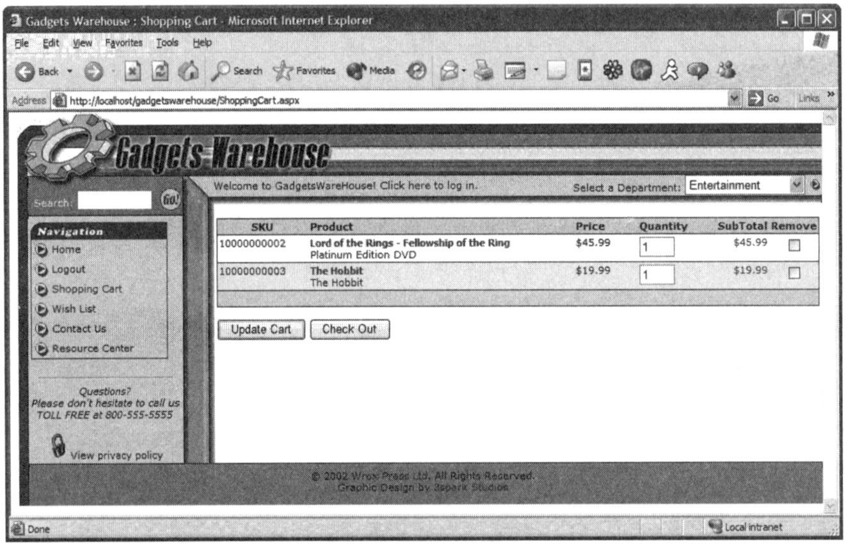

Some highlights on our tour through this page are the quantity textboxes, the Remove checkboxes, and the Update Cart button. We won't be going into the Check Out button in any more detail this chapter. I think there is a very firm difference between the shopping cart and the order fulfillment backend of a website. We are going to devote an entire chapter to the order fulfillment and tracking backend, which will get us into the functionality behind the Check Out button.

Summary

This chapter was all about building a better shopping cart. We talked about what it is we think should be the basic minimum requirements of a good shopping cart, and the need for flexible, reliable, and durable shopping cart items. Then we looked at the design for our shopping cart, which included support for anonymous users shopping as well as authenticated users, and support for anonymous users creating new accounts and migrating their shopping carts. We then discussed all of the code we used to build our shopping cart. At this point you should be very familiar with the concepts behind building a shopping cart and storing products in shopping carts on behalf of your customers. Later on in the book we'll take a look at how to turn the shopping cart into an order and then how to let the customer get access to their order history and status.

CHAPTER 6

6

The Wish List

There are two main types of purchases on e-commerce websites that site planners, architects, marketers, and owners all have to plan for: the impulse purchase and the planned purchase. We looked at how we could design for the impulse purchase in the section covering our shopping cart. We wanted to make sure that the user had a very quick and painless journey from the product page all the way to order completion.

In this chapter we're going to talk about one of the main tools that allows websites to provide for, and encourage, the planned purchase: the wish list. We're going to take a look at the problems that wish lists solve, as well as the kinds of problems that wish lists create. Beyond that, we'll take a look at the design for the wish list implemented by Gadgets Warehouse and then finally we'll walk you through the implementation and source code of the wish list.

The Problem

The problem that we want to solve with the wish list is to be able to support and encourage the informed or cautious buyer and those buyers that plan out their purchases long before they actually buy anything.

As we've mentioned before, there are really two main kinds of browsers on e-commerce websites: people just there looking around and people that are looking for something in particular. We spent an entire chapter discussing product searching, so we already know that if we have a good search engine, then the people who already know what they're looking for will be able to find it on our site.

Once the browser has found what they're looking for, what do they do then? The impulsive buyers or people who want to make a purchase right away will simply add the item to the shopping cart and move right along. However, cautious buyers or people who might not have the money for the purchase right away are almost always considered potential "lost customers". If they leave your site without adding the product they want to their favorites or some database somewhere, they might easily forget they wanted it in the first place and never make the purchase on your website. Hopefully, the community surrounding your website is strong enough to encourage the user to come back to your site. Once they're back, they'll be able to see items they'd previously been interested in by viewing their wish list.

Your goal, as the creator of a wish list system, is to make sure that *everywhere* the customer can look at a product and add it to a shopping cart, they can just as easily add that product to their wish list. By giving the customer the ability to come back to your site and look at a list of things they've found that they like, you're not only saving them the time they might have spent searching for those products a second or third time, but you're making it easier for them to purchase the items they found. Also, never forget that wish lists can easily be turned into a shopping list for a friend, relative, or spouse.

Part of the problem of dealing with a wish list is in dealing with storing the wish list items. We need to decide what information we want to store, and we need to decide what users are allowed to store it. Should guest users be able to have a wish list or is that restricted only to registered users? Those questions and more will be answered by our design.

The Design

The design of our wish list is going to be pretty simple. At the high level, all we really want to do is provide a method that allows customers to add products to a list that belongs to them. From the product browse list control, and from the product pricing box displayed on product detail pages, we want to be able to add products to the wish list just as we can currently add them to our shopping cart.

Once they add the item to their wish list, the customer will be taken to the wish list page. This page allows them to view the contents of their wish list. The design for our wish list actually has a little bit extra that you don't find in too many wish list implementations on the web: room for comments. It's probably enough to allow the customer to add items to their wish list, but we felt that they should be able to add comments to the items. This could be to record information like *why* they added the item to their cart, or *when* they think they'll be able to buy it, or even *who* it might be a gift for. Regardless of how we think the customer will use the comments field, we think that they will find it extremely useful and so we're making sure it is in the design for our wish list.

Wireframes

We're going to try a technique that has quite a bit of benefit when designing user interfaces. Our wish list might not be all that complex, but it all takes place on the same page and we want to make sure that we know what all of the different states of the page are going to look like before we even write a single line of code.

This is where the wireframe comes in. A wireframe is a simple block-and-line diagram that illustrates sample page layouts without bogging you down in the details of creating all of the graphics ahead of time. It lets the programmer see what they're going to need to allow for and it lets the graphic design people see what kind of assets they're going to need to create. We've used the copy of Visio that comes with Microsoft Visual Studio .NET Enterprise Edition to create the wireframe.

Let's take a look at the wireframe for the "default" view of our wish list:

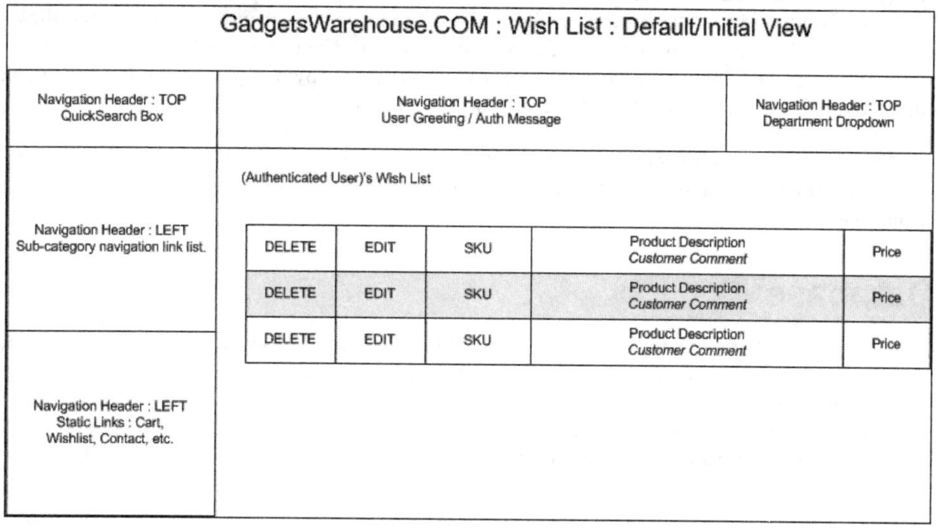

It is pretty simple, just a bunch of rectangles and some text. However, it gives us all the information we need in order to figure out what information we are going to need from the database in order to display a wish list, it tells us what buttons are going to be visible in the default state of the `DataGrid`, and gives the programmer a place to start working on laying things out.

In general, wireframes are an excellent design tool and should be used whenever you have even the slightest thought that your user interface has any complexity to it at all. Many project teams working in ASP and ASP.NET make the production of wireframes a requirement before any development can begin, especially in large team scenarios where some people may not have a clear idea of what the output of the page should look like.

Let's take a look at the wireframe for the same wish list, only this time illustrating the view of the wish list while a customer is editing their comment field:

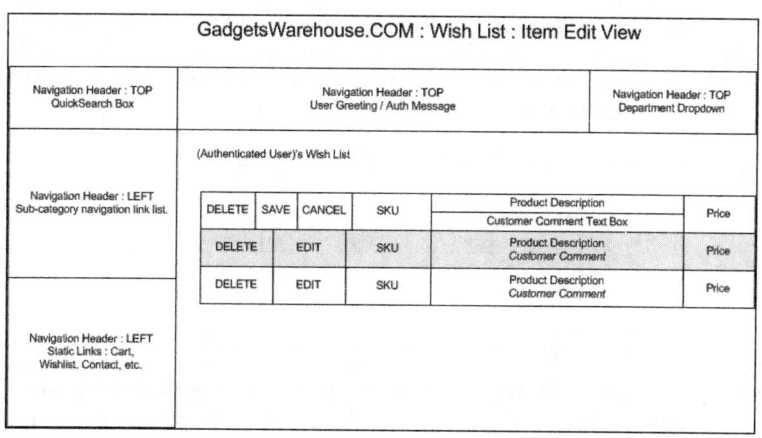

What we can glean from this wireframe is that the customer is going to be able to click the Edit button on any single row in their wish list and it will bring them to a screen that looks like the above. They will have Delete, Save, and Cancel buttons while they edit their comment in a textbox. Once they click Save or Cancel, they will be returned to the default state with the comment having been modified or left alone as necessary. Clicking Delete will remove the current row from the wish list and display the default state of the wish list with the selected item missing.

Even with just these two wireframes to use as a reference, we are in a really good position to start thinking about the database design as well as the design of the code that we're going to need to produce an output like this.

The Database

Now that we know what we want our output to look like, we should have a good idea of what kind of information we're going to need to store in the wish list. In general, a wish list is a simple list of products that are associated with a specific authenticated customer. The database table to store our wish list information will be called `WishlistItems`. In our case, there are two columns of note that will add two additional pieces of information to the product/customer association: `Comment` and `Purchased`.

Comment

We examined the reason for a `Comment` field earlier. We want to make sure that the customer's experience while shopping at the site never prevents them from doing what they want to do. If they are putting items in their wish list, then they should be able to jot down notes about that particular item that might remind them about why they put the item in the wish list, or who they want to buy the item for. Regardless of why the customer uses this field, they should be able to edit it with ease.

Purchased

Many implementations of wish lists automatically remove items from your wish list when you buy them. I personally find that fact frustrating. If I am using a wish list system to purchase Christmas presents for friends, I don't want the item to be removed from my list if I buy it once as I might want to buy it again for someone else or even for myself. I think that removing the item from the wish list when the customer purchases the item infringes on the customer's right to use the site the way they want to. They should be the only ones who decide whether or not the item is removed from the wish list. However, they should be notified in some fashion that they have purchased at least one of the items in their wish list. For that, the `Purchased` column will be a flag for wish list items indicating whether or not they've been purchased. We'll have to make sure that when we get to our order-fulfillment chapter we add code to set this flag to `true` when the customer completes a checkout.

Here's the diagram of our wish list table, with the data types shown:

WishlistItems

	Column Name	Data Type	Length	Allow Nulls
🔑	CustomerId	int	4	
🔑	SKU	varchar	11	
	Comment	varchar	255	
	Purchased	bit	1	

It looks pretty simple, and it is. Keep in mind that we will be pulling all of the product information from the `ProductSKUs` and `Products` tables, so we can keep our wish-list table short and sweet.

Another thing you might have noticed is that we're using `CustomerId` instead of the generated ID as we used with the shopping cart. This is because we are going to require that users be authenticated in order to use the wish list feature. The wish list is really a value-added feature that is designed for registered users of the site. The shopping cart allowing anonymous use is to facilitate impulse buyers and allow them to only register when they check out. Our wish list is for long-term buyers and users of the site, people who are planning on making future purchases with our store, so we want them to be registered on the site to get all of the benefits of registration. As with all of the portions of our website that require authentication, we use Forms Authentication to protect the page. When the user clicks a link leading to the page, they are presented with the login page, which can either log the user in or create a new user. This encourages users to create accounts with us by keeping links to authenticated portions of the site visible.

The Solution

Now that we've come up with what we think is a workable design, its time to take a look at the code that we're going to use to produce our wish list. The first thing we'll do is take a look at the stored procedures that will drive the data-access tier, then we'll take a look at the code we produced that provides the middle-tier support for our wish list.

Stored Procedures

The following is a list of all of the stored procedures that are used to provide data access for the wish list implementation we developed.

Gw_Insert_WishlistItem

This insert procedure will create a new wish list item from a given customer ID and the SKU belonging to the product the customer wants to put in their wish list. There is a little bit of extra coding going on in this procedure that prevents the customer from inserting the same product twice into their wish list. If they do attempt to insert the same product twice into their wish list, the procedure simply does nothing.

```
CREATE PROCEDURE Gw_Insert_WishlistItem
  @CustomerID int,
  @SKU varchar(11)
AS
  DECLARE @FoundSKU varchar(11)

  SELECT @FoundSKU = SKU FROM WishlistItems
  WHERE WishlistItems.SKU = @SKU AND WishlistItems.CustomerID = @CustomerID

  IF @FoundSKU != @SKU
    INSERT INTO WishlistItems(CustomerId, SKU, Purchased)
    VALUES(@CustomerId, @SKU, 0)
GO
```

Gw_Update_WishlistItem

This procedure modifies the user comment for a particular wish list item as indicated by the customer ID and the SKU of the item:

```
CREATE PROCEDURE Gw_Update_WishlistItem
  @CustomerId int,
  @SKU varchar(11),
  @Comment varchar(255)
AS
  UPDATE WishlistItems SET Comment = @Comment
  WHERE CustomerId = @CustomerId AND SKU = @SKU
GO
```

Gw_Remove_WishlistItem

This stored procedure removes a product from a given customer's wish list. Keep in mind that a given customer's wish list item is always represented by the combination of the customer's ID and the SKU of the item.

```
CREATE PROCEDURE Gw_Remove_WishlistItem
  @CustomerId int,
  @SKU varchar(11)
AS
  DELETE FROM WishlistItems WHERE CustomerId= @CustomerId AND SKU = @SKU
GO
```

Gw_Select_WishlistItems

This procedure drives the grid layout display of the customer's entire wish-list contents. It retrieves the list of items in the wish list by joining the `WishListItems` table with the `ProductSkus` table, the results of which are joined with the `Products` table. All of this results in a list of items that is fully described and contains pricing data and enough information to provide links to the detail of that item.

```
CREATE PROCEDURE Gw_Select_WishlistItems
  @CustomerId int
AS

 SELECT wi.SKU, p.Name, p.ShortDescription, ps.ActualPrice, ps.RetailPrice,
        wi.Comment, wi.Purchased

  FROM WishListItems wi INNER JOIN ProductSkus ps ON
  wi.SKU = ps.SKU INNER JOIN
  Products p ON ps.ProductId = p.ProductId
  WHERE wi.CustomerId = @CustomerId
  ORDER BY p.Name
GO
```

CMP Metadata

Now that we know the definitions for the stored procedures we're going to use in order to work with the wish list, we can create the CMP metadata in the `web.config` file. As you've seen before, this metadata is what allows our Container-Managed Persistence tier to function as an object-relational mapping tool. As usual, we're only going to show a portion of the CMP metadata that goes into the `web.config` file to make things easier to read. Here we show the CMP metadata that corresponds to the `Gw_Select_WishlistItems` stored procedure. The other stored procedure metadata is similar, and can be easily pieced together.

```
<ContainerMapping>
  <ContainerMappingId>WishListContents</ContainerMappingId>
  <ContainedClass>WishlistContents</ContainedClass>
  <Select>
    <CommandName>Gw_Select_WishlistItems</CommandName>
    <Parameter>
      <ClassMember>CustomerId</ClassMember>
      <ParameterName>@CustomerId</ParameterName>
      <DbTypeHint>Int</DbTypeHint>
      <ParamDirection>Input</ParamDirection>
      <Size>4</Size>
    </Parameter>
  </Select>
</ContainerMapping>
```

The Wishlist Project

If you are following along with the book and creating your website while reading, then you'll want to stop and add a new C# Class Library to your project. Call it `Wishlist` and set the default namespace and output name to `GW.Web.Wishlist`.

WishlistManager

The `WishlistManager` class is the main workhorse for all of our wish-list code. It contains all of the methods that will perform all wish list operations against the database. You'll notice that this is a trend in that each of our modules has one or more main workhorse classes that serve as the intermediary between the presentation tier and the database.

```
using System;
using System.Reflection;
using System.Diagnostics;

using GW.CMPServices;
using GW.MonitorServices;
using GW.MonitorServices.Logging;

using System.Data;
using GW.Web.Wishlist.Data;

namespace GW.Web.Wishlist
{
  /// <summary>
  /// Summary description for WishlistManager.
  /// </summary>
  public class WishlistManager
  {
    public WishlistManager()
    {
    }
```

The following method will retrieve the entire contents of an authenticated customer's wish list by calling the `Gw_Select_WishlistItems` stored procedure we saw earlier.

```
public DataSet GetWishlistContents( int customerId )
{
  WishListContents wlc = new WishListContents();
  wlc.CustomerId = customerId;

  SqlPersistenceContainer spc = new SqlPersistenceContainer(
        CMPConfigurationHandler.ContainerMaps["WishListContents"] );
  spc.Select( wlc );
  return wlc.ResultSet;
}
```

The RemoveWishlistItem method will take a customer's ID and the SKU of an item, and remove it from the customer's wish list.

```
public void RemoveWishlistItem( int customerId , string SKU )
{
  GWTrace.EnteringMethod( MethodBase.GetCurrentMethod() );
  WishlistItem wli = new WishlistItem();
  wli.CustomerId = customerId;
  wli.SKU = SKU;

  SqlPersistenceContainer spc = new SqlPersistenceContainer(
           CMPConfigurationHandler.ContainerMaps["WishlistItem"] );
  spc.Delete( wli );
}
```

The next method will add the item to the customer's wish list. If the item is already in their wish list, the method (and corresponding stored procedure) will return without displaying any error, since the end result is the same – the item is in the user's wish list.

```
public void AddWishlistItem( int customerId, string SKU )
{
  GWTrace.EnteringMethod( MethodBase.GetCurrentMethod() );
  WishlistItem wli = new WishlistItem();
  wli.CustomerId = customerId;
  wli.SKU = SKU;

  SqlPersistenceContainer spc = new SqlPersistenceContainer(
           CMPConfigurationHandler.ContainerMaps["WishlistItem"] );
  spc.Insert( wli );
}
```

The UpdateWishlistItem method provides the user with a way of changing the comment that is associated with the wish list item. The UI provides this ability through an editable textbox in the bound data grid.

```
public void UpdateWishlistItem( int customerId, string SKU,
                                string comment)
{
  GWTrace.EnteringMethod( MethodBase.GetCurrentMethod() );
  WishlistItem wli = new WishlistItem();
  wli.CustomerId = customerId;
  wli.SKU = SKU;
  wli.Comment = comment;
```

```
        SqlPersistenceContainer spc = new SqlPersistenceContainer(
                   CMPConfigurationHandler.ContainerMaps["WishlistItem"] );
        spc.Update( wli );
      }
    }
  }
```

WishlistContents

WishlistContents is a PersistableObjectSet that is used to hold multiple rows of wish list items.

```
using System;
using System.Data;

using GW.CMPServices;
using GW.MonitorServices;

namespace GW.Web.Wishlist.Data
{
  /// <summary>
  /// Class to hold results of querying wish list items for customer.
  /// </summary>
  public class WishListContents : PersistableObjectSet
  {
    private int customerId;

    public WishListContents()
    { }

    public int CustomerId
    {
      get { return customerId; }
      set { customerId = value; }
    }
  }
}
```

WishlistItem

WishlistItem is a PersistableObject that holds a single wish list item that is used for INSERT, UPDATE, and DELETE operations.

```
using System;
using System.Data;

using GW.CMPServices;
using GW.MonitorServices;

namespace GW.Web.Wishlist.Data
{
  /// <summary>
  /// Class to maintain parameters for wish list item operations.
```

```
    /// </summary>
    public class WishlistItem : PersistableObject
    {
      private int customerId;
      private string sku;
      private string comment;

      public WishlistItem()
      {
      }

      public int CustomerId
      {
        get { return customerId; }
        set { customerId = value; }
      }

      public string SKU
      {
        get { return sku; }
        set { sku = value; }
      }
      public string Comment
      {
        get { return comment; }
        set { comment = value; }
      }
    }
  }
```

Wishlist.aspx

So far in this book and in this application, we haven't used a DataGrid that takes advantage of all of the built-in features that allow you to edit data in place as well as save the changes or cancel changes made while editing. Because the DataGrid on our wish list page allows for all of these things, we're going to go into a bit more detail in the discussion of the ASPX code than we normally do. The DataGrid allows us to create column templates so that we can have tighter control over how the columns are rendered. It also contains ready-made support for Save, Delete, and Edit buttons. We can take advantage of this to create two states for our DataGrid: edit mode and view mode. Each of our columns can render itself differently, depending on whether the grid is in edit mode or view mode. As you'll see, this provides us with an incredibly easy and quick way of creating a fully-featured edit screen.

In the following code, I've cut out the redundant HTML that is used to generate the top and left navigation user interface so that we can skip right to the important portion of the page.

What we're looking at is a DataGrid that is configured to allow items to be edited in place. This is probably one of the most powerful features of the DataGrid for one simple reason: we don't have to write extra code to allow for it. Anytime anyone hands me a stockpile of hundreds of lines of code and tells me I don't have to re-write it, I get happy.

```
<asp:Label ID="lblWishlistHeader" Runat="server" Font-Bold="True" Font-
Names="Tahoma" Font-Size="Larger" ForeColor="#C00000" Font-
Italic="True">Header</asp:Label>
<asp:Label ID="lblMissing" Runat="server"></asp:Label>
<br>
<asp:DataGrid id="dgWishlist" runat="server"
   AutoGenerateColumns="False" CellPadding="2" GridLines="horizontal"
   BorderColor="DarkBlue" DataKeyField="SKU" ShowFooter="True"
   BorderWidth="1px" BackColor="LightGoldenrodYellow" ForeColor="Black">
   <ItemStyle BackColor="White"></ItemStyle>
   <SelectedItemStyle ForeColor="GhostWhite"
      ackColor="DarkSlateBlue"></SelectedItemStyle>
   <AlternatingItemStyle BackColor="#eeeeee"></AlternatingItemStyle>
   <HeaderStyle Font-Bold="True" BackColor="#e6dfbb"></HeaderStyle>
   <FooterStyle BackColor="#e6dfbb"></FooterStyle>
   <Columns>
    <asp:ButtonColumn ButtonType="PushButton"
      CommandName="Delete" Text="Delete"
      ItemStyle-VerticalAlign="Top"
      ItemStyle-Width="8%"></asp:ButtonColumn>
```

Here's our first treat. The `DataGrid` automatically handles being in edit mode, we just have to supply templates for what each of our columns looks like in edit mode, and then (as we'll see later) we just respond to the Save, Edit, and Cancel buttons and it works.We really have very little work to do in order to get this functionality.

```
    <asp:EditCommandColumn ButtonType="PushButton"
      EditText="Edit" CancelText="Cancel"
      UpdateText="Save" ItemStyle-VerticalAlign="Top"
      ItemStyle-Width="8%"></asp:EditCommandColumn>

    <asp:TemplateColumn ItemStyle-Font-Bold="True" HeaderText="SKU"
      ItemStyle-VerticalAlign="Top" ItemStyle-Width="8%">
      <ItemTemplate>
        <asp:Label ID="lblSKU" Runat="server"
          Text='<%#DataBinder.Eval(Container.DataItem, "SKU")%>'>
        </asp:Label>
      </ItemTemplate>
    </asp:TemplateColumn>

    <asp:TemplateColumn HeaderText="Product" ItemStyle-Width="50%">
      <ItemTemplate>
        <%# DataBinder.Eval(Container.DataItem, "ShortDescription")%>
        <br>
        <br>
        <font color="Maroon"><i>
        <%# DataBinder.Eval(Container.DataItem, "Comment")%>
        </i></font>
      </ItemTemplate>
```

Here we can see that for our product description, when we're in regular mode only the product description is displayed. However, when we're in edit mode, the textbox will be displayed allowing the customer to modify their personal comment on the wish list item:

```
        <EditItemTemplate>
          <%# DataBinder.Eval(Container.DataItem, "ShortDescription")%>
          <br>
          <br>
          <asp:TextBox ID="txtComment" Runat="server" MaxLength="254"
            Width="90%"
            Text='<%# DataBinder.Eval(Container.DataItem, "Comment")%>'>
        </asp:TextBox>
    </EditItemTemplate>
</asp:TemplateColumn>

<asp:TemplateColumn HeaderText="Price" ItemStyle-Width="10%"
   ItemStyle-VerticalAlign="Top" ItemStyle-ForeColor="Maroon"
   ItemStyle-Font-Bold="True" ItemStyle-HorizontalAlign="Center"
   HeaderStyle-HorizontalAlign="Center">
  <ItemTemplate>
    <%# DataBinder.Eval(Container.DataItem, "ActualPrice", "{0:c}") %>
  </ItemTemplate>
</asp:TemplateColumn>
```

In this next section of code, you can see that for the read-only version of the template column `Purchased`, we're invoking a method called `DisplayPurchased`. The `DisplayPurchased` is a *public* method in the code-behind class for this page that takes a Boolean value as input, and returns a string to be displayed in-place that contains an indicator to the user that the item in their cart has been purchased.

```
<asp:TemplateColumn HeaderText="Purchased" ItemStyle-Width="10%"
                    ItemStyle-VerticalAlign="Top"
                    ItemStyle-HorizontalAlign="Center">
   <ItemTemplate>
     <%# DisplayPurchased ( System.Convert.ToBoolean(
                   DataBinder.Eval(Container.DataItem, "Purchased"))) %>
   </ItemTemplate>
</asp:TemplateColumn>

<asp:ButtonColumn ButtonType="PushButton" CommandName="AddToCart"
  Text="Buy" ItemStyle-Width="6%"></asp:ButtonColumn>
</Columns>
</asp:DataGrid>
```

The rest of the code on the page is just the closing tags and cleanup/footer code for the UI and navigation interface and isn't worth spending any time discussing here.

Wishlist.aspx.cs

Now we'll take a look at the code-behind class for our `Wishlist` page. This code-behind class is a little bit different from some others that we've seen so far in that it contains a public method used by the `DataBinder` object on the page to render a string. It also contains code to add an item to the wish list, as well as event handlers for the Save, Edit, and Delete buttons.

One thing you won't find in this page is a check for authenticated users. Because of the Forms Authentication setup we're using, we don't need to do that check. By adding `<location>` tags to the `web.config` file like so:

```
<location path="Wishlist.aspx">
  <system.web>
    <authorization>
      <deny users="?"/>
    </authorization>
  </system.web>
</location>
```

We can restrict access to specific pages. When an anonymous user hits a restricted page, they will be taken to the login screen. From there, they can either log in or register as a new user. When they're done, they will be given access to the restricted page.

```
using System;
using System.Collections;
using System.ComponentModel;
using System.Data;
using System.Drawing;
using System.Web;
using System.Web.SessionState;
using System.Web.UI;
using System.Web.UI.WebControls;
using System.Web.UI.HtmlControls;

using GW.Web.Wishlist;
using GW.Web.Wishlist.Data;
using GW.MonitorServices;
using GW.MonitorServices.Logging;
using System.Reflection;
using System.Diagnostics;
namespace GW.Web
{
  /// <summary>
  /// Class that provides code-behind functionality for wish list page.
  /// </summary>
  public class WishlistPage : System.Web.UI.Page
  {
    protected System.Web.UI.WebControls.DataGrid dgWishlist;
    protected System.Web.UI.WebControls.Label lblMissing;
    protected System.Web.UI.WebControls.Label lblWishlistHeader;

    private int customerId;

    private void Page_Load(object sender, System.EventArgs e)
    {
```

As we've seen earlier in this book on our Forms Authentication scheme, when we authenticate users, we set their "name" to their customer ID. This gives us easy, quick access to the database key for a particular user without having to do additional lookups. The user's full name is stored as a session-scope cookie that also allows us to avoid unnecessary database hits. If the `AddToList` query string parameter is correct, the value of that parameter is used as the SKU to add to the user's wish list. We have to re-direct back to this page to remove that parameter from `ViewState` since postbacks will leave that parameter in the query string.

```
    customerId = System.Convert.ToInt32(User.Identity.Name);
    if (Request["AddToList"]!= null)
    {
      WishlistManager wm = new WishlistManager();
      wm.AddWishlistItem( customerId, Request["AddToList"] );
      Response.Redirect("Wishlist.aspx");
    }
    // Put user code to initialize the page here
    lblWishlistHeader.Text = Request.Cookies["GW_FullName"].Value +
                                                          "'s Wishlist";

    if (!Page.IsPostBack)
    {
      LoadData();
    }
  }

  private void LoadData()
  {
    int customerId = System.Convert.ToInt32(User.Identity.Name);
    WishlistManager wm = new WishlistManager();
    DataSet wishList = wm.GetWishlistContents( customerId );
    if (wishList.Tables[0].Rows.Count == 0)
    {
      lblMissing.Visible = true;
      lblMissing.Text = "<br>Your Wish List does not contain any items.";
      dgWishlist.Visible = false;
    }
    else
    {
      lblMissing.Visible = false;
      dgWishlist.Visible = true;
      dgWishlist.DataSource = wishList.Tables[0];
      dgWishlist.DataBind();
    }
  }
```

The `DisplayPurchased` method is called by the `DataBinder` when the binding on the main page takes place. If the Boolean value `purchased` is `true`, then an `IMG` tag will be rendered on the page indicating that the customer has purchased the item.

```
  public string DisplayPurchased( bool purchased )
  {
    if (purchased)
      return "<img src=\"images/checkmark.gif\" alt=\"Yes\">";
    else
      return "";
  }
```

The rest of the code is web-forms designer auto-generated code that we can safely leave out of the chapter.

This next event handler for the DataGrid ItemCommand event is invoked when the user clicks the Buy button from the wish list. It will send the user to the ShoppingCart page and add the item from their wish list to the cart. The SKU to add to the customer's shopping cart is passed in the query string so that it can be read by the ShoppingCart.aspx page from the AddToCart parameter.

```
private void dgWishlist_ItemCommand(object source,
                 System.Web.UI.WebControls.DataGridCommandEventArgs e)
{
  GWTrace.EnteringMethod( MethodBase.GetCurrentMethod() );
  DataGridItem dgItem = e.Item;
  string sku = ((Label)dgItem.FindControl("lblSKU")).Text;

  if (e.CommandName == "AddToCart")
  {
    Response.Redirect("ShoppingCart.aspx?AddToCart=" + sku);
  }
}
```

This event handler is called when the user clicks the Edit button on a given row. It will convert the DataGrid into edit mode by setting the EditItemIndex. Because the change to edit mode can't take place until the grid is re-bound in the new mode, we have to call LoadData again.

```
private void dgWishlist_EditCommand(object source,
                 System.Web.UI.WebControls.DataGridCommandEventArgs e)
{
  DataGridItem dgItem = e.Item;
  dgWishlist.EditItemIndex = dgItem.ItemIndex;

  // Changing the EditItemIndex of a DataGrid doesn't actually
  // show anything until DataBind() is
  // called on it, so we need to re-bind after putting it in Edit mode.
  LoadData();
}
```

This event handler is called when the user clicks the Cancel button while in edit mode. It simply turns off edit mode and does not persist the changes made to the database.

```
private void dgWishlist_CancelCommand(object source,
                 System.Web.UI.WebControls.DataGridCommandEventArgs e)
{
  dgWishlist.EditItemIndex = -1;

  // Need to re-bind after taking it out of edit mode for
  // the changes to be visible to the user.
  LoadData();
}
```

This method sends the changes made to the database and then turns off edit mode. The visible effect is that the text in the comment text box becomes read-only label text after you click the update button.

```
private void dgWishlist_UpdateCommand(object source,
                System.Web.UI.WebControls.DataGridCommandEventArgs e)
{
  DataGridItem dgItem = e.Item;
  int customerId = System.Convert.ToInt32(User.Identity.Name);
  string sku = ((Label)dgItem.FindControl("lblSKU")).Text;
  string comment = ((TextBox)dgItem.FindControl("txtComment")).Text;

  WishlistManager wm = new WishlistManager();
  wm.UpdateWishlistItem( customerId, sku, comment );

  dgWishlist.EditItemIndex = -1;
  LoadData();
}
```

The Delete button is available in all modes, and will remove the selected item from the wish list.

```
    private void dgWishlist_DeleteCommand(object source,
                    System.Web.UI.WebControls.DataGridCommandEventArgs e)
    {
      DataGridItem dgItem = e.Item;
      int customerId = System.Convert.ToInt32(User.Identity.Name);
      string sku = ((Label)dgItem.FindControl("lblSKU")).Text;

      WishlistManager wm = new WishlistManager();
      wm.RemoveWishlistItem( customerId, sku );

      LoadData();
    }
  }
}
```

Modifying Templates

Because we want to be able to make sure that the product displays in all locations throughout the website are updated to allow customers to add products to their wish lists, we'll have to modify the various item templates we created in the product catalog chapter.

SkuItemTemplate

This is the modified `BindData` method from the `SkuItem` template in the `ProductCatalog` project, which is displayed whenever the product pricing box control is rendered:

```
public void BindData( object sender, EventArgs e)
{
  Literal l = (Literal)sender;
  DataListItem container = (DataListItem)l.NamingContainer;
  DataRowView currentRowView = (DataRowView) container.DataItem;

  StringBuilder sb = new StringBuilder();
  sb.Append ("<table width=\"100%\" border=\"0\" cellspacing=0 "+
```

```
                                                        "cellpadding=0>");
    sb.Append("<tr><td valign=\"top\" width=\"65%\">");
    sb.AppendFormat("<B>{0}</B>",
      currentRowView["Description"]);
    sb.Append("<br>");
    sb.AppendFormat("<a href=\"ShoppingCart.aspx?AddToCart={0}\">" +
      "<img border=\"0\" src=\"images/gad_arrow.gif\" " +
      "align=\"absmiddle\"></a> Add to Cart ",
      currentRowView["SKU"]);
    sb.AppendFormat("<a href=\"Wishlist.aspx?AddToList={0}\">" +
      "<img src=\"images/gad_arrow.gif\" align=\"absmiddle\" "+
      " border=\"0\"></a> Add to Wishlist",
      currentRowView["SKU"]);
    sb.Append("</td>");
    sb.Append("<td width=\"35%\" align=\"right\" valign=\"top\">");
    sb.AppendFormat("<b>Our Price: <font color=\"red\">${0}</font></b>",
                    currentRowView["ActualPrice"]);
    sb.AppendFormat("<br>Retail: <s>${0}</s>",
                    currentRowView["RetailPrice"]);
    sb.Append("</td></tr></table><br>");
    l.Text = sb.ToString();
  }
```

ProductItemTemplate

The following is the modified `BindData` method from the `ProductItemTemplate` in the `ProductCatalog` project that now includes a link that allows the customer to add the product to their wish list:

```
public void BindData( object sender, EventArgs e)
{
  Literal l = (Literal)sender;
  DataListItem container = (DataListItem)l.NamingContainer;
  DataRowView currentRowView = (DataRowView) container.DataItem;

  StringBuilder sb = new StringBuilder();

  if ((categoryId == null) || (categoryId == ""))
    categoryId = currentRowView["ParentCategoryId"].ToString();
  sb.Append("<table width=\"650\" border=\"0\" cellspacing=2 " +
                                                  "cellpadding=0>");
  sb.Append("<tr>");
  sb.Append("<td vAlign=\"center\" width=\"80\" align=\"center\">\n");
  sb.AppendFormat("<img src=\"products/images/tn/{0}.jpg\" " +
    "alt=\"{1}\" width=\"80\" height=\"80\" border=\"0\"><br>",
    currentRowView["ProductId"], currentRowView["Name"]);
  sb.AppendFormat("<font color=\"red\"><b>${0}</b></font>",
    currentRowView["ActualPrice"]);
  sb.Append("</td>");
  sb.Append("<td colspan=\"3\" vAlign=\"center\" width=\"550\">");
  sb.AppendFormat("Gadgets Warehouse # {0}\n<br>",
    currentRowView["SKU"]);
  sb.AppendFormat("<b>{0}</b><br>\n", currentRowView["SkuDesc"]);
```

```
        sb.Append(currentRowView["ShortDescription"]);
        sb.Append("<br>");
        sb.Append("</td>");
        sb.Append("</tr><tr>");
        sb.Append("<td><Br></td>");
        sb.AppendFormat("<td><a href=\"ShoppingCart.aspx?AddToCart={0}\">" +
           "<img align=\"absmiddle\" src=\"images/gad_arrow.gif\" " +
           "border=\"0\"></a> Add to Cart</td>",
          currentRowView["SKU"]);
        sb.AppendFormat("<td><a href=\"Wishlist.aspx?AddToList={0}\">" +
          "<img align=\"absmiddle\" src=\"images/gad_arrow.gif\" " +
          "border=\"0\"></a>",
          currentRowView["SKU"]);
        sb.Append(" Add to Wishlist</td>");

        sb.Append("<td>");
        sb.AppendFormat("<a href=\"ProductDetail.aspx?productId={0}" +
          "&categoryId={1}&SubcategoryId={2}\">",
          currentRowView["ProductId"], categoryId,
          currentRowView["CategoryId"]);
        sb.Append("<img align=\"absmiddle\" src=\"images/gad_arrow.gif\" "+
                                  "border=\"0\"></a>View Details</td>");


        sb.Append("</tr>");
        sb.Append("</table>\n");
        l.Text = sb.ToString();
      }
```

Summary

This chapter has been all about the purpose, problems, designs, and solutions involved in creating a wish list. We emphasized that if your customers don't have the ability to use your site for comparison shopping and to mark items they might want to buy later, you could potentially lose their business. As a result, it is essential that the website provide a simple, and easy-to-use wish list solution that not only helps the customer maintain a list of items they want, but helps you retain your customers and encourage future purchases.

CHAPTER 7

7

Discounting, Coupons, and Sales

If you remember the last time you walked through a shopping center or mall, you probably remember seeing that no matter what time of year, or what occasion, most stores had some kind of promotion, or sale going on. Department stores have furniture sales, toy stores have promotions for video games, board games, and everything else that you can imagine.

Those of us who remember the days before online shopping was as popular as it is now remember how important it was to find a sale. If a customer was in the vicinity of a sale, the idea was that they would be more likely to take advantage of it, because they just didn't know where or when the next sale might come from.

The age of the Internet Shopper has made customers far more discerning. You need to accept and prepare for the fact that any customer can probably compare your prices against all of your competitors without ever having to get up out of their chair. Gone are the days of salespeople and marketers counting on the customer not *knowing* that there are better deals out there. Today, you must assume that the customer knows *exactly* who has the best price on the product they're looking for. This means that to get their business, your website either needs to have the best price, or needs to do something else better than all of your competitors. When we talk about community building, we'll talk about building additional services that might set you apart from your competitors.

For now, this chapter is all about the price. We'll talk about the problems involved with discounts and coupons and then we'll tackle the unexpectedly complex problem of designing a good, reliable, efficient way of managing sales. After the design, we'll take you through the source code for handling discounts and coupons, which may be some of the most complex code we've looked at in the book so far.

The Problem

The problem we are faced with in this chapter is dealing with sales. In our own opinions, no matter how good our site is, and no matter how robust our product catalog is, people will think it sorely lacking if they don't see sales, discounts, coupons, or other promotional content. Changing, promotional content is one thing that encourages your customers to come back to your site. If they know you are frequently putting items on sale, they are more likely to come back and check your site. If you are e-mailing your customers notification of sales and coupons, they are also more likely to come back for a purchase they might have otherwise made at a competitor's site.

So, what is our problem? We need to be able to set our site up so that it can support dynamic promotional materials that we can change programmatically without having to spend hours manually editing HTML or modifying the contents of our product catalog. We can't have people manually adjusting 300 prices to put all products within a particular category on sale.

This means that our problem is that we need to be able to handle standard discounts (or sales) as well as code-activated coupons that we can include in targeted mailings or advertisements.

The Design

As with all of our other modules, once we've identified the problem we're trying to solve, we can get right into the work of actually designing our solution. For our sales and promotional code, we are going to implement the solution in two pieces: Discounts and Coupons.

Discounts

There is a fine line of difference between a discount and a coupon. We need to make sure that we have the concept of a *discount* clearly defined before we can continue and definitely before we write a single line of code. For our purposes, and for the development of GadgetsWarehouse.com, we're going to define a discount as *any reduction in price brought about when the contents of a customer's shopping cart meet all rules outlined by any active discounts in our database.*

What that really means is that discounts are sales. If we want to put all DVDs up for sale at 15% off of our regular price, that is a discount. If we are selling a brand-new product that we want lots of people to buy, and we want to give customers $10 off that product, that is a discount.

Our discounts will work this way: We will define a discount value and a value type (either a percentage or a raw value, such as $5 off). That value will be applied to the actual price of the product on which the discount is based. Discounts can also apply to an entire category, in which case everything in the customer's shopping cart that is in the affected category will receive the appropriate price reduction.

Coupons

To provide the simplest definition we can, a coupon is a *code-triggered discount.* In other words, there is a specific type of discount that does not automatically show up in a customer's shopping cart when they meet the rules of the discount. To satisfy the rules of the coupon-based discount, the customer needs to *claim* the coupon.

Our coupon implementation will basically work by providing the customer with claim codes. A claim code will be distributed to customers either through demographically-filtered direct mailings, or through advertisings or other promotions through retail outlets or other affiliates. We're not actually going to implement the claim code delivery system. There are plenty of third-party direct-mail software packages, and Commerce Server also supports delivering correspondence to customers this way.

Once the customer claims the coupon, they will see the applicable coupon in their shopping cart. We will have to spend a little bit of time modifying the shopping cart implementation we came up with earlier to accommodate the display of a claimed coupon. Our implementation of coupons can only apply discount values to the entire contents of the cart. So, when we send out coupons, they will be in the form of "Claim this coupon and get 20% off your entire purchase", etc. The framework is there for you to expand on this for your own site and create far more complex and involved coupon implementations that might allow for such things as claiming multiple coupons at once.

The Database

Let's discuss the data structures that we're going to need in our database to support the new discounting and coupon system. The following is a diagram of the four tables we're going to use in our implementation:

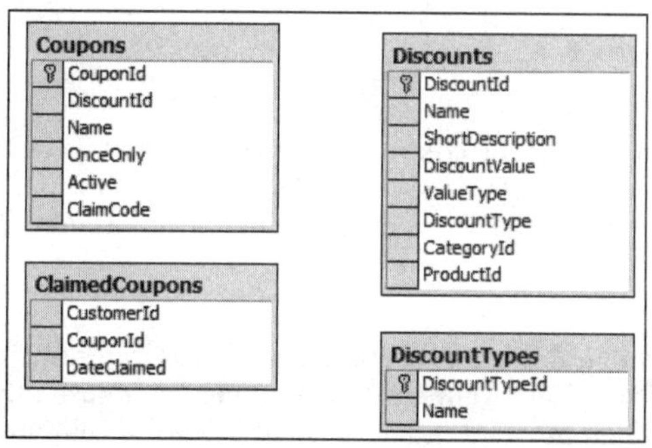

Discounts

This is the table for discounts. It contains the fields necessary to describe discounts, such as the discount's name (the text that the fulfillment people/system will see, more on that in the fulfillment chapter), a short, user-friendly description, and the details about the discount such as the value type, value, discount type, and to what the discount applies. Let's take a more detailed look at some of the less obvious columns:

DiscountValue

This column actually contains the value of the discount. This is *always* a whole number. If the discount is for 10% then this column will contain the number 10. If the discount is for $10 then this column will contain the number 10.

ValueType

This column indicates how the discount is to be applied. If the value of this column is 1, then the discount is a percentage-based discount. Otherwise, it is a raw discount and the value is subtracted directly from the product price.

DiscountType

This column indicates the type of discount. If this value is one, then the discount applies to all products within the supplied category. If the value is two, then the discount applies to a single product. If the discount type is any other value, then by default it will be a discount that can only be used by a claimed coupon, as only types one and two will be displayed in the non-coupon space of the shopping cart.

ProductId

This column will contain a `-1` on category-wide discounts; otherwise it will contain the product ID on which the discount is based.

CategoryId

This column will contain a `-1` when the discount is a product-specific discount. When the discount is based on a specific category, this column will contain the ID of the category on which the discount is based.

DiscountTypes

This is a simple lookup table that contains the list of discount types. This is used for reference and for administration and isn't actually used for any user-facing features. Our table for our own testing purposes contains the following discount types: Category-wide Discount, Single Product Discount, and Coupon-Activated Discount.

Coupons

This is the main table that contains the coupons applicable to our site. This table contains information about the coupon itself and also a reference to the discount that the coupon will activate if a customer claims it. The following is a discussion of some of the more important fields in this table.

OnceOnly

This is a Boolean (bit) field that indicates whether this coupon can only be claimed once. Some discounts are so good that you don't want customers to be able to use them over and over again, otherwise your site will lose money and the purpose of using the coupon to attract new customers will be pretty much voided.

Active

This column indicates whether or not the coupon is active. Inactive coupons cannot be claimed, even if the customer has the claim code correct and has never claimed it before.

ClaimCode

This is the character string that the customer must type *exactly*, including proper case, in order to be able to claim the coupon.

ClaimedCoupons

This table keeps track of which customers have claimed which coupons, and when. This allows the system to reject multiple attempts to claim *once-only* coupons as well as giving site administrators and marketers the ability to track demographics and other figures on how well different campaigns are working.

The Code Design

Before we get into discussing the actual code, let's take a look at the design for the classes we're going to need for our coupon and discount management systems:

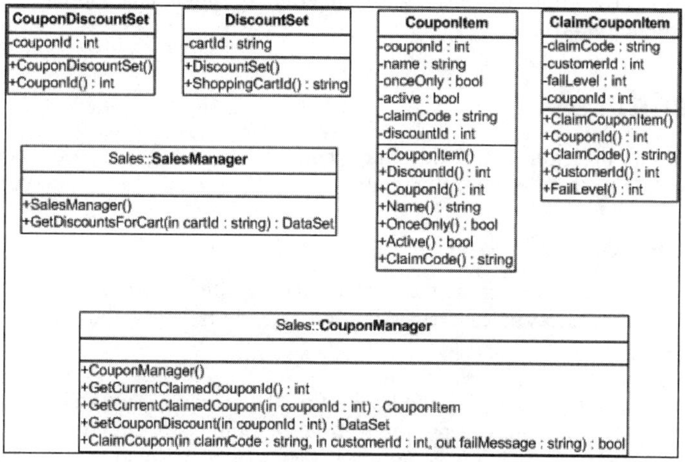

CouponManager

The `CouponManager` class is responsible for handling the tasks we need accomplished with regards to our coupons. It provides methods for obtaining the discount that belongs to a specific coupon, as well as getting information on the currently claimed coupon. The currently claimed coupon will be stored in the form of a session-length cookie.

SalesManager

The `SalesManager` class is responsible for pulling the list of discounts that apply to the contents of the customer's shopping cart.

CouponDiscountSet

This is the `PersistableObjectSet` responsible for containing the results of a query that returns a coupon discount.

DiscountSet

The `PersistableObjectSet` responsible for containing the results of a query that returns a list of discounts.

CouponItem

A single `PersistableObject` that represents a coupon.

ClaimCouponItem

A `PersistableObject` that represents a single row in the `ClaimedCoupons` table.

The Solution

So far we've talked about the problem we need to solve and presented a design that I think will produce a very nice sales and discounting solution. We're going to take a look at the stored procedures (some of which are fairly complex) for accomplishing this, the data-tier metadata and classes, and the code that goes into the presentation layer.

Stored Procedures

This next section is an in-depth look at the source code for the stored procedures that form the core of our data functionality for the discounts and coupons.

Gw_Insert_ClaimCoupon

This stored procedure is used to log the fact that a customer attempted to claim a coupon. There is an output variable called `FailLevel` that is used to indicate the type of failure (if any) that occurred while trying to claim a coupon.

If the `FailLevel` is equal to `0`, the website knows that the customer successfully claimed the coupon. If `FailLevel` is equal to `1`, that indicates to the website that the claim code being submitted by the customer does not belong to any known coupon. If `FailLevel` is equal to `2`, that indicates that the customer has already claimed that coupon *and* that the coupon is a once-only coupon. Finally, if `FailLevel` is equal to `3`, then the claim code was accurate, and the customer has not already claimed that coupon, but the coupon is now inactive and cannot be claimed. This output variable is key to providing a rich interactive experience with useful feedback to the customer on the coupon-claiming page.

```
CREATE PROCEDURE Gw_Insert_ClaimCoupon
  @ClaimCode varchar(50),
  @CustomerId int,
  @FailLevel int output,
  @CouponId int output
AS
  DECLARE @CoupActive bit
  DECLARE @OnceOnly bit

  -- figure out the coupon Id based on the claim code
  SELECT @CouponId = CouponId, @CoupActive = Active, @OnceOnly = OnceOnly
  FROM Coupons
  WHERE ClaimCode = @ClaimCode

  IF @CouponId IS NULL
  BEGIN
    SET @CouponId = -1
    SET @FailLevel = 1
    RETURN
  END

  -- check if the customer has claimed this coupon already
  SELECT DateClaimed FROM ClaimedCoupons
```

```
    WHERE CustomerId = @CustomerId AND CouponId = @CouponId

     IF (@@ROWCOUNT > 0) AND @OnceOnly = 1
      SET @FailLevel = 2
    ELSE IF (@CoupActive = 0)
      SET @FailLevel = 3
    ELSE
      BEGIN
        -- coupon is active, and has not been claimed or has been claimed
      -- but is not once-only
        INSERT INTO ClaimedCoupons(CouponId, CustomerId)
                            VALUES(@CouponId, @CustomerId)
        SET @FailLevel = 0
      END
  GO
```

Gw_Select_Coupon

This is a fairly straightforward procedure that loads all relevant data on a single coupon into output variables. Stored procedures that return individual items are generally used to view or edit a single item. In our case, this procedure is used to retrieve all of the properties of an individual coupon.

```
CREATE PROCEDURE Gw_Select_Coupon
  @CouponId int,
  @Active  bit out,
  @ClaimCode varchar(50) out,
  @DiscountId  int out,
  @Name varchar(50) out,
  @OnceOnly bit out
AS
  SELECT @Active = Active,
         @ClaimCode = ClaimCode,
         @DiscountId = DiscountId,
         @Name = Name,
         @OnceOnly = OnceOnly
  FROM Coupons
  WHERE CouponId = @CouponId
GO
```

Gw_Select_Coupon_Discount

This stored procedure loads all of the discount information that belongs to the discount that is linked with the specified coupon. In our situation, we don't need ever to retrieve a list of coupons and a list of discounts at the same time; the nature of our UI/presentation means that all of that information is not required for a single page.

```
CREATE PROCEDURE Gw_Select_Coupon_Discount
  @CouponId int
AS

  SELECT disc.DiscountId, disc.Name, disc.ShortDescription,
       disc.DiscountValue, disc.ValueType, coup.Name AS CouponName,
```

```
        Coup.CouponId
    FROM Discounts disc
    INNER JOIN Coupons coup ON disc.DiscountId = coup.DiscountId
    WHERE coup.CouponId = @CouponId
GO
```

Gw_Select_Discounts_From_Cart

This stored procedure takes advantage of the `UNION` operator and retrieves both type one and type two discounts (category-wide and product-specific). It does this by grabbing all type one discounts that apply to any of the categories represented in the specified shopping cart. This result is then combined with the list of discounts represented by all of the products in the cart. The resulting list is used to build the discount display that we'll look at later.

```
CREATE PROCEDURE Gw_Select_Discounts_From_Cart
    @CartId varchar(50)
AS
    SELECT disc.DiscountId, disc.Name, disc.ShortDescription,
           disc.DiscountValue, disc.ValueType, disc.ProductId,
           disc.CategoryId, disc.DiscountType
    FROM Discounts disc
    WHERE disc.DiscountId IN
    (
    -- Select all category-wide discounts
    SELECT DISTINCT dc.DiscountId
    FROM ShoppingCarts cart
    INNER JOIN Products p ON cart.ProductId = p.ProductId
    INNER JOIN Discounts dc ON p.CategoryId = dc.CategoryId
    WHERE cart.CartId = @CartId AND dc.DiscountType = 1

    UNION
    -- Select all product-specific discounts
    SELECT DISTINCT dc.DiscountId
    FROM ShoppingCarts cart
    INNER JOIN Products p ON cart.ProductId = p.ProductId
    INNER JOIN Discounts dc ON p.ProductId = dc.ProductId
    WHERE Cart.Cartid = @CartId AND dc.DiscountType = 2
    )
GO
```

One behavior you might want to add into this stored procedure is to work with a temporary table, and remove discounts that have already been applied. For example, you might want to make a change so that if you have a discount on one movie, and a discount on all movies in the Horror category, you don't discount the same movie twice. This could be done by removing any duplicate `ProductID` and `CategoryId` from the resulting set.

In our case, we decided not to do this filtering. The (fictitious) administrators of the site decided that they might occasionally want to double-discount an item, so they've decided to leave it up to them and the data entry operators to avoid any unwanted double-discounting.

CMP Metadata

Now that we've seen the stored procedure definitions, as usual, we need to add the Container-Managed Persistence XML metadata to our `web.config` file. By now you should have a pretty firm grasp of how to map the stored procedure information to the XML metadata. I'll include just one of the stored procedure mappings we created to keep things brief and easy to read:

```
<ContainerMapping>
  <ContainerMappingId>DiscountList</ContainerMappingId>
  <ContainedClass>DiscountSet</ContainedClass>
  <Select>
    <CommandName>Gw_Select_Discounts_From_Cart</CommandName>
    <Parameter>
      <ClassMember>ShoppingCartId</ClassMember>
      <ParameterName>@CartId</ParameterName>
      <DbTypeHint>Varchar</DbTypeHint>
      <ParamDirection>Input</ParamDirection>
      <Size>50</Size>
    </Parameter>
  </Select>
</ContainerMapping>
```

The Sales Project

As usual, if you're following along and typing the solution into your website as you read rather than downloading the entire thing at once, you need to stop and create a new project here. Call the project `Sales` and set the default namespace and output filename to `GW.Web.Sales`. The following is a list of the classes that belong to the `Sales` project:

CouponManager

The `CouponManager` class is responsible for retrieving information about coupons from the database. It provides methods for claiming coupons and loading data on a single coupon, as well as a method for retrieving the discount information that belongs to a given coupon. As with most of our simple business objects, it is just an object-oriented front-end for interfacing with the SQL Server Container for Container Managed Persistence.

```
using System;
using System.Reflection;
using System.Diagnostics;
using System.Data;
using System.Web;

using GW.Web.Sales.Data;

using GW.CMPServices;
using GW.MonitorServices;
using GW.MonitorServices.Logging;

namespace GW.Web.Sales
{
```

```
/// <summary>
/// Summary description for CouponManager.
/// </summary>
public class CouponManager
{
  public CouponManager()
  {
    //
    // TODO: Add constructor logic here
    //
  }
```

In the next method, we retrieve the currently claimed coupon ID. We decided to make this a session-based cookie because in our design, the customer can only maintain a single coupon per session. In a typical scenario, the customer comes to the page as a result of some marketing campaign and claims a coupon. Once they claim the coupon, the record of that claim is put in the database and the ID of the currently claimed coupon is placed in a cookie to be used by most stages of the shopping cart and checkout process.

```
  public int GetCurrentClaimedCouponId()
  {
    int currentId = -1;

    HttpCookie claimedCoupon =
                  HttpContext.Current.Request.Cookies["GW_ClaimedCoupon"];
    if (claimedCoupon != null)
    {
      currentId = System.Convert.ToInt32(claimedCoupon.Values["CouponId"]);
    }

    return currentId;
  }
```

The next method is a front-end for the above method. It will invoke the `Gw_Select_Coupon` stored procedure to retrieve all the relevant data on the currently claimed coupon.

```
  public CouponItem GetCurrentClaimedCoupon( int couponId )
  {
    CouponItem ci = new CouponItem();
    ci.CouponId = couponId;

    SqlPersistenceContainer spc = new SqlPersistenceContainer(
                      CMPConfigurationHandler.ContainerMaps["Coupon"]);
    spc.Select( ci );

    return ci;
  }
```

This next method will retrieve the discounting information, such as the discount type and value that is associated with the currently claimed coupon.

```
public DataSet GetCouponDiscount( int couponId )
{
  CouponDiscountSet csd = new CouponDiscountSet();
  csd.CouponId = couponId;

  SqlPersistenceContainer spc = new SqlPersistenceContainer(
           CMPConfigurationHandler.ContainerMaps["CouponDiscountSet"]);
  spc.Select( csd );
  csd.FinalizeData();
  return csd.ResultSet;
}
```

Our next method will attempt to claim a coupon. If the customer claims the coupon successfully, then the method returns `true`. If, for any reason, the customer is unable to claim the coupon, the method returns `false` and a user-friendly message indicating *why* the coupon could not be claimed is returned in the `out` parameter, `failMessage`.

```
public bool ClaimCoupon( string claimCode, int customerId,
                         out string failMessage )
{
  // returns true if customer has claimed the coupon,
  // false if coupon is not claimable.
  failMessage = "";

  ClaimCouponItem cci = new ClaimCouponItem();
  cci.CustomerId = customerId;
  cci.ClaimCode = claimCode;

  SqlPersistenceContainer spc = new SqlPersistenceContainer(
           CMPConfigurationHandler.ContainerMaps["ClaimCouponItem"] );
  spc.Insert( cci );

  switch ( cci.FailLevel )
  {
    case 1:
      failMessage = "There was no coupon found with that claim code.";
      break;
    case 2:
      failMessage = "You have already claimed a coupon with that " +
                                                       "claim code.";
      break;
    case 3:
      failMessage = "You attempted to claim a coupon that is no " +
                                                     "longer active.";
      break;
  }

  if (failMessage == "")
  {
    // place the claimed coupon cookie
```

This next section may seem unnecessary, but it is a side-effect of team programming. At this point we may not be sure if anyone else's code has modified the claimed coupon cookie. If it has, and we add the cookie to the Response collection, we could have incorrect values. As a safety precaution, we only add a cookie to the Response collection if it isn't there.

```
        if (HttpContext.Current.Response.Cookies["GW_ClaimedCoupon"] != null)
        {
          HttpCookie oldCookie =
                    HttpContext.Current.Response.Cookies["GW_ClaimedCoupon"];
          oldCookie.Values.Clear();
          oldCookie.Values["CouponId"] = cci.CouponId.ToString();
        }
        else
        {
          HttpCookie newCookie = new HttpCookie("GW_ClaimedCoupon");
          newCookie.Values["CouponId"] = cci.CouponId.ToString();
          HttpContext.Current.Response.Cookies.Add( newCookie );
        }
        return true;
      }
      else
        return false;

    }
  }
}
```

SalesManager

The SalesManager class provides all of the access methods that our presentation layer needs for dealing with discounts and related data. At the moment, this class has only one purpose: retrieving the list of all discounts that are applicable to a particular shopping cart. We've created a fully-fledged class because there is no way to tell what sort of expansion we might need in this area. For now, it only implements one method – GetDiscountsForCart.

```
using System;
using System.Reflection;
using System.Diagnostics;
using System.Data;

using GW.Web.Sales.Data;

using GW.CMPServices;
using GW.MonitorServices;
using GW.MonitorServices.Logging;

namespace GW.Web.Sales
{
  /// <summary>
  /// Summary description for SalesManager.
  /// </summary>
  public class SalesManager
  {
```

```
    public SalesManager()
    {
      //
      // TODO: Add constructor logic here
      //
    }

    public DataSet GetDiscountsForCart( string cartId )
    {
      DiscountSet ds = new DiscountSet();
      ds.ShoppingCartId = cartId;

      SqlPersistenceContainer spc = new SqlPersistenceContainer(
                  CMPConfigurationHandler.ContainerMaps["DiscountList"] );
      spc.Select( ds );
      ds.FinalizeData();
      return ds.ResultSet;
    }
  }
}
```

DiscountSet

This class is a `PersistableObjectSet` that contains rows of discounts returned from a stored procedure. As with all `PersistableObjectSet` classes, it maintains data members that are used as parameters to a stored procedure, and the results are returned in the `ResultSet` property inherited from the base `PersistableObjectSet` class.

```
using System;
using System.Reflection;
using System.Diagnostics;

using GW.CMPServices;
using GW.MonitorServices;
using GW.MonitorServices.Logging;

namespace GW.Web.Sales.Data
{
  /// <summary>
  /// Summary description for DiscountSet.
  /// </summary>
  public class DiscountSet : PersistableObjectSet
  {
    private string cartId;

    public DiscountSet()
    {

    }

    public string ShoppingCartId
    {
      get { return cartId; }
      set { cartId = value; }
    }
  }
}
```

CouponItem

The CouponItem class is a PersistableObject that contains properties that represent a single coupon. As we saw above, we have a stored procedure that is used to retrieve a single coupon item. This class contains property definitions for each of that stored procedure's parameters. Once the stored procedure is executed, all of the output parameter values will be set on the appropriate properties, giving us a class instance that represents a single coupon as stored in the database.

```
using System;
using System.Reflection;
using System.Diagnostics;
using System.Xml;
using System.Xml.Serialization;

using GW.CMPServices;
using GW.MonitorServices;
using GW.MonitorServices.Logging;

namespace GW.Web.Sales.Data
{
  /// <summary>
  /// Summary description for CouponItem.
  /// </summary>
  [Serializable()]
  public class CouponItem : PersistableObject
  {
    private int couponId;
    private string name;
    private bool onceOnly;
    private bool active;
    private string claimCode;
    private int discountId;

    public CouponItem()
    {
      // TODO: Add constructor logic here
    }

    public int DiscountId
    {
      get { return discountId; }
      set { discountId = value; }
    }

    public int CouponId
    {
      get { return couponId; }
      set { couponId = value; }
    }

    public string Name
    {
      get{ return name; }
```

```
      set{ name = value; }
    }

    public bool OnceOnly
    {
      get { return onceOnly; }
      set { onceOnly = value; }
    }

    public bool Active
    {
      get { return active; }
      set { active = value; }
    }

    public string ClaimCode
    {
      get { return claimCode; }
      set { claimCode = value; }
    }
  }
}
```

CouponDiscountSet

This `PersistableObjectSet` is responsible for containing data from a query for the discount related to a coupon. The reason why we have a separate storage for discount data that belongs to a coupon is that our interface does not always need the discount information whenever a coupon is loaded. By making this a separate stored procedure and separate retrieval class, we only retrieve the discounting data for a coupon when it is necessary.

```
using System;
using System.Reflection;
using System.Diagnostics;
using System.Xml;
using System.Xml.Serialization;

using GW.CMPServices;
using GW.MonitorServices;
using GW.MonitorServices.Logging;

namespace GW.Web.Sales.Data
{
  /// <summary>
  /// Summary description for CouponDiscountSet.
  /// </summary>
  public class CouponDiscountSet : PersistableObjectSet
  {
    private int couponId;

    public CouponDiscountSet()
    {
      // TODO: Add constructor logic here
```

```
    }

    public int CouponId
    {
      get { return couponId; }
      set { couponId = value; }
    }
  }
}
```

ClaimCouponItem

The `ClaimCouponItem` class is a `PersistableObject` that represents a row of data in the `ClaimedCoupons` table. It contains properties that map directly to the columns in the `ClaimedCoupons` table that are used to supply parameters to the stored procedure to claim a coupon, such as the claim code the customer entered and the `failLevel` (if any) returned by the stored procedure.

```
using System;
using System.Reflection;
using System.Diagnostics;
using System.Xml;
using System.Xml.Serialization;

using GW.CMPServices;
using GW.MonitorServices;
using GW.MonitorServices.Logging;

namespace GW.Web.Sales.Data

{
  /// <summary>
  /// Summary description for CouponClaimItem.
  /// </summary>
  [Serializable()]
  public class ClaimCouponItem : PersistableObject
  {
    private string claimCode;
    private int customerId;
    private int failLevel;
    private int couponId;

    public ClaimCouponItem()
    {
      // TODO: Add constructor logic here
    }

    public int CouponId
    {
      get { return couponId; }
      set { couponId = value; }
    }
```

```
    public string ClaimCode
    {
      get { return claimCode; }
      set { claimCode = value; }
    }

    public int CustomerId
    {
      get { return customerId; }
      set { customerId = value; }
    }

    public int FailLevel
    {
      get { return failLevel; }
      set { failLevel = value; }
    }
  }
}
```

Claim Coupon Page

In addition to making some additional changes to our shopping cart to display the currently claimed coupon and adjust the final price accordingly, we've also created a new page that we're using as a base for claiming coupons. The shopping cart will link off to this page to allow the customer to claim coupons, and direct mailing and advertising can include this page in links to take the customer directly to a coupon-claiming page.

ClaimCoupon.aspx

Here's a look at `ClaimCoupon.aspx` in the design view:

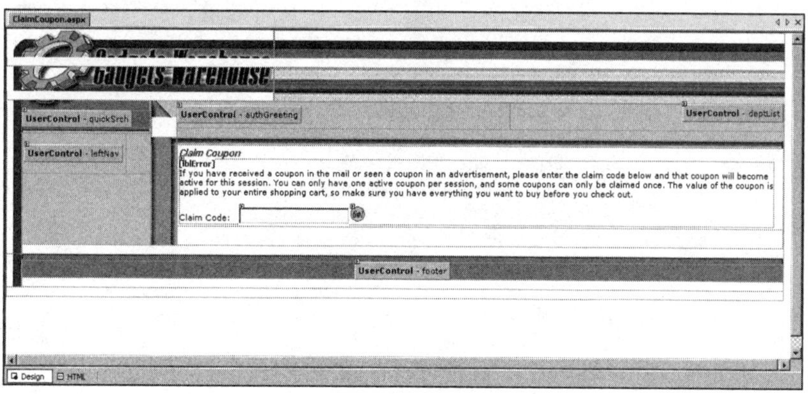

Here's the code for the HTML designer portion of our coupon-claiming page. Unfortunately one side effect of having a fairly complex user interface is that, in general, the code behind the designer is pretty painstaking to type in on your own. In the interest of keeping things simple, I'll only show the portion of the HTML that applies to what we're doing. You've seen the ASPX pages enough times and have access to the code download to reconstruct it on your own if you need to:

```
<%@ Page language="c#" Codebehind="ClaimCoupon.aspx.cs"
    AutoEventWireup="false" Inherits="GW.Web.ClaimCoupon" %>
<%@ Register TagPrefix="GWU" TagName="TopCategoryDropDown"
    Src="UserControls/TopCategoryDropDown.ascx" %>
<%@ Register TagPrefix="GWU" TagName="Footer"
    Src="UserControls/Footer.ascx" %>
<%@ Register Tagprefix="GWU" TagName="AuthGreeting"
    Src="UserControls/AuthGreeting.ascx" %>
<%@ Register TagPrefix="GWU" TagName="LeftNavigator"
    Src="UserControls/LeftNavigator.ascx" %>
<%@ Register TagPrefix="GWU" TagName="QuickSearch"
    Src="UserControls/QuickSearch.ascx" %>
<!DOCTYPE HTML PUBLIC "-//W3C//DTD HTML 4.0 Transitional//EN" >
<HTML>
  <HEAD>
    <title>Claim Coupon</title>
    <meta name="GENERATOR" Content="Microsoft Visual Studio 7.0">
    <meta name="CODE_LANGUAGE" Content="C#">
    <meta name="vs_defaultClientScript" content="JavaScript">
    <meta name="vs_targetSchema"
          content="http://schemas.microsoft.com/intellisense/ie5">
    <LINK href="Styles/main.css" type="text/css" rel="stylesheet">
  </HEAD>
  <BODY text="#000000" vLink="#000000" aLink="#000000" link="#000000"
        leftMargin="0" topMargin="0">
    <form id="default" method="post" runat="server">
```

Let's get straight on to the important HTML here for the panel that provides information to the user about the use of the coupon and asks for the claim code – we'll skip over the standard HTML for the navigation bar and footers, and so on.

```
  <TABLE cellSpacing="0" cellPadding="3" width="100%">
  <TBODY>
      <TR>
        <TD vAlign="top">
          <font color="maroon" size="2" face="Tahoma">
          <b><i>Claim Coupon</i></b></font><br>
          <asp:Panel ID="pnlMain" Runat="server">
          <asp:Label id="lblError" Runat="server"
                     Visible="false" Font-Name="Tahoma" Font-Bold="True"
                     ForeColor="Maroon"></asp:Label>
           <BR>If you have received a coupon in the mail or seen a
           coupon in an advertisement, please enter the claim
           code below and that coupon will become active for
           this session. You can only have one active coupon
           per session, and some coupons can only be claimed
           once. The value of the coupon is applied to your
           entire shopping cart, so make sure you have
           everything you want to buy before you check
           out.<BR><BR>Claim Code:  
           <asp:TextBox id="txtClaimCode" Runat="server"
                        MaxLength="50"></asp:TextBox>
           <asp:ImageButton id="ImageButton1" runat="server"
```

```
                                  ImageUrl="images/gad_gobutton.gif"
                                  Height="20px"></asp:ImageButton>
            </asp:Panel>
         </TD>
      </TR>
    </TBODY>
  </TABLE>
```

ClaimCoupon.aspx.cs

Here's the code-behind class code for our coupon-claiming page. It contains our `Page_Load` event and the event handlers to respond to the button click on the page:

```
using System;
using System.Collections;
using System.ComponentModel;
using System.Data;
using System.Drawing;
using System.Web;
using System.Web.SessionState;
using System.Web.UI;
using System.Web.UI.WebControls;
using System.Web.UI.HtmlControls;

using GW.Web.Sales;

namespace GW.Web
{
  /// <summary>
  /// Summary description for ClaimCoupon.
  /// </summary>
  public class ClaimCoupon : System.Web.UI.Page
  {
    protected System.Web.UI.WebControls.ImageButton ImageButton1;
    protected System.Web.UI.WebControls.Label lblError;
    protected System.Web.UI.WebControls.Panel pnlMain;
    protected System.Web.UI.WebControls.TextBox txtClaimCode;
```

Unlike most of our other pages, there's no data binding that needs to take place before we display the UI to the user for the first time. It is a pure input form, so everything is ready to go without having to query the database.

```
    private void Page_Load(object sender, System.EventArgs e)
    {
      // Put user code to initialize the page here
    }

    #region Web Form Designer generated code
    override protected void OnInit(EventArgs e)
    {
      //
      // CODEGEN: This call is required by the ASP.NET Web Form Designer.
```

```
    //
    InitializeComponent();
    base.OnInit(e);
  }

  /// <summary>
  /// Required method for Designer support - do not modify
  /// the contents of this method with the code editor.
  /// </summary>
  private void InitializeComponent()
  {
    this.ImageButton1.Click += new
            System.Web.UI.ImageClickEventHandler(this.ImageButton1_Click);
    this.Load += new System.EventHandler(this.Page_Load);

  }
  #endregion
```

Let's look at the event handler that is invoked when the user clicks the button to claim the coupon. Because we're using the customer ID as the user's name in our Forms Authentication solution, we can easily grab the customer ID by checking `User.Identity.Name`. Once we have that, we can create an instance of the `CouponManager` business class and attempt to claim the coupon represented by the claim code the user supplied. If the claim attempt fails, we can activate our error label and display the message returned by the business object:

```
  private void ImageButton1_Click(object sender,
                                System.Web.UI.ImageClickEventArgs e)
  {
    int customerId = System.Convert.ToInt32( User.Identity.Name );
    CouponManager cm = new CouponManager();
    string failMessage;

    if (!cm.ClaimCoupon( txtClaimCode.Text, customerId, out failMessage ))
    {
      lblError.Text = "You were not able to claim the coupon: " +
                                                failMessage + "<br><br>";
      lblError.Visible = true;
    }
    else
    {
      lblError.Text = "You have successfully claimed the coupon. " +
    "You will see it the next time you examine your shopping cart.<br><br>";
      lblError.Visible = true;
    }
  }
 }
}
```

When we're all done with our coupon claim page, we get a screenshot that looks like this:

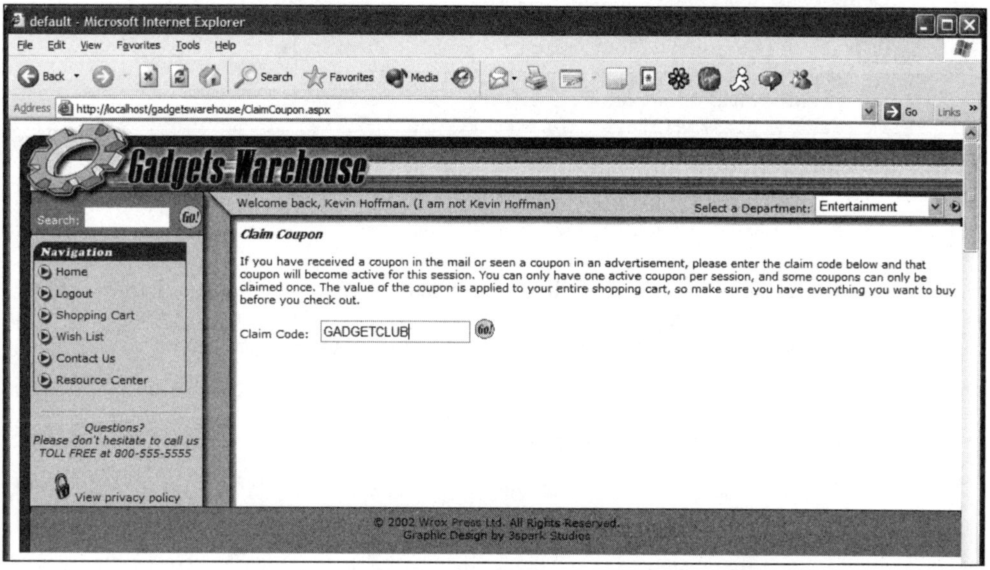

The New Shopping Cart

In order for our shopping cart to work with the new discounts and coupons, we needed to add a considerable amount of code to the existing cart we developed in Chapter 5.

ShoppingCart.aspx

This is the code for the HTML designer portion of the new `ShoppingCart.aspx` page. We'll show the pieces of the code that apply to the modifications we needed to make to accommodate the coupon display. You can compare this code with the code from the shopping cart to see the complete HTML. As it stands, the code from the HTML designer is too large and dense to include here in its entirety:

```
<%@ Page language="c#" Codebehind="ShoppingCart.aspx.cs" AutoEventWireup="false"
Inherits="GW.Web.ShoppingCartPage"%>
<%@ Register TagPrefix="GWU" TagName="TopCategoryDropDown"
Src="UserControls/TopCategoryDropDown.ascx" %>
<%@ Register TagPrefix="GWU" TagName="Footer"
    Src="UserControls/Footer.ascx" %>
<%@ Register Tagprefix="GWU" TagName="AuthGreeting"
Src="UserControls/AuthGreeting.ascx" %>
<%@ Register TagPrefix="GWU" TagName="LeftNavigator"
Src="UserControls/LeftNavigator.ascx" %>
<%@ Register TagPrefix="GWU" TagName="QuickSearch"
Src="UserControls/QuickSearch.ascx" %>
<!DOCTYPE HTML PUBLIC "-//W3C//DTD HTML 4.0 Transitional//EN" >
<HTML>
  <HEAD>
```

```
    <title>Gadgets Warehouse : Shopping Cart</title>
    <meta name="GENERATOR" Content="Microsoft Visual Studio 7.0">
    <meta name="CODE_LANGUAGE" Content="C#">
    <meta name="vs_defaultClientScript" content="JavaScript">
    <meta name="vs_targetSchema"
         content="http://schemas.microsoft.com/intellisense/ie5">
    <LINK href="Styles/main.css" type="text/css" rel="stylesheet">
  </HEAD>
  <BODY text="#000000" vLink="#000000" aLink="#000000" link="#000000"
        leftMargin="0" topMargin="0">
    <form id="default" method="post" runat="server">
```

Here I've cut out the usual code to generate the top navigation strip, the quick search button, the navigation bar on top, and the category navigator on the left. This code is the same for nearly all of the pages on the website, so you should be able to piece it together from virtually any other page you may have typed in or downloaded.

```
<TABLE cellSpacing="0" cellPadding="3" width="100%">
 <TBODY>
  <TR>
   <TD vAlign="top">
    <P><asp:Label id="lblMessage" runat="server"
                  EnableViewState="False" Visible="False"
                  ForeColor="#C00000" Font-Bold="True"
                  Font-Names="Tahoma" Font-Italic="True">Label</asp:Label><BR>
       <asp:Panel ID="pnlCartContents" runat="server">
```

In this section I took out the code to generate the DataGrid that contains the standard shopping cart contents. The following code displays the discount details and the coupon DataGrid controls:

```
         <BR>
         < asp:Label id="lblDiscountHeader" ForeColor="#C00000"
                     Font-Bold="True" Runat="server"
                     Font-Names="Tahoma" Font-Italic="True"></asp:Label>
          <BR>
          <asp:DataGrid id="dgDiscounts" runat="server"
                        AutoGenerateColumns="False" CellPadding="2"
                        GridLines="horizontal" BorderColor="DarkBlue"
                        DataKeyField="DiscountId" ShowFooter="True"
                        BorderWidth="1px" BackColor="LightGoldenrodYellow"
                        ForeColor="Black" width="775px">
          <SelectedItemStyle ForeColor="GhostWhite"
                             BackColor="DarkSlateBlue"></SelectedItemStyle>
          <AlternatingItemStyle BackColor="#EEEEEE"></AlternatingItemStyle>
          <ItemStyle BackColor="White"></ItemStyle>
          <HeaderStyle Font-Bold="True" BackColor="#E6DFBB"></HeaderStyle>
          <FooterStyle BackColor="#E6DFBB"></FooterStyle>
          <Columns>
            <asp:BoundColumn HeaderText="Discount"
                             HeaderStyle-HorizontalAlign="Left"
                             ItemStyle-VerticalAlign="Top"
                             DataField="Name" ItemStyle-Width="140px"
```

```
                    HeaderStyle-Width="140px"></asp:BoundColumn>
      <asp:TemplateColumn HeaderText="Product(s)"
                          ItemStyle-ForeColor="Maroon"
                          ItemStyle-Width="350px"
                          ItemStyle-VerticalAlign="Top"
                          HeaderStyle-Width="350px">
          <ItemTemplate>
            <%# IterateAssociatedProducts(
         System.Convert.ToInt32( DataBinder.Eval(Container.DataItem,
                                                  "DiscountType") ),
         System.Convert.ToInt32( DataBinder.Eval(Container.DataItem,
                                                    "ProductId") ),
         System.Convert.ToInt32( DataBinder.Eval(Container.DataItem,
                                                  "CategoryId") ) )%>
          </ItemTemplate>
        </asp:TemplateColumn>
        <asp:TemplateColumn HeaderText="Savings"
                            ItemStyle-ForeColor="Maroon"
                            ItemStyle-HorizontalAlign="Right"
                            HeaderStyle-HorizontalAlign="Right"
                            FooterStyle-HorizontalAlign="Right"
                            ItemStyle-VerticalAlign="Top"
                            ItemStyle-Width="285px"
                            HeaderStyle-Width="285px"
                            FooterStyle-ForeColor="Maroon"
                            FooterStyle-Font-Bold="True">
          <ItemTemplate>
            <%# IterateAssociatedProductValues( System.Convert.ToInt32(
               DataBinder.Eval( Container.DataItem, "DiscountId" )) )%>
          </ItemTemplate>
          <FooterTemplate>
            <%# CheckCurrentRunningSavingsTotal() %>
          </FooterTemplate>
        </asp:TemplateColumn>
      </Columns>
    </asp:DataGrid>
    <BR>
    <TABLE cellSpacing="2" cellPadding="0" width="400" border="0">
      <TR>
        <TD vAlign="center">
          <asp:Label id="lblCouponDisplay" runat="server"
                     ForeColor="#C00000" Font-Bold="True"
                     Font-Names="Tahoma"
                     Font-Italic="True"></asp:Label></TD>
        <TD vAlign="center">
          <asp:Button id="btnClaimOrClear" runat="server"
                      Text="Button"></asp:Button></TD>
      </TR>
    </TABLE>
    <asp:DataGrid id="dgCoupon" runat="server"
                  AutoGenerateColumns="False" CellPadding="2"
                  GridLines="horizontal" BorderColor="DarkBlue"
                  DataKeyField="DiscountId" ShowFooter="True"
                  BorderWidth="1px" BackColor="LightGoldenrodYellow"
```

```
                    ForeColor="Black" width="775px">
            <SelectedItemStyle ForeColor="GhostWhite"
                               BackColor="DarkSlateBlue"></SelectedItemStyle>
            <AlternatingItemStyle BackColor="#EEEEEE"></AlternatingItemStyle>
            <ItemStyle BackColor="White"></ItemStyle>
            <HeaderStyle Font-Bold="True" BackColor="#E6DFBB"></HeaderStyle>
            <FooterStyle BackColor="#E6DFBB"></FooterStyle>
            <Columns>
              <asp:BoundColumn DataField="ShortDescription"
                               HeaderText="Sale Description">
              </asp:BoundColumn>
              <asp:TemplateColumn ItemStyle-HorizontalAlign="Right"
                                  HeaderText="Total Savings"
                                  HeaderStyle-HorizontalAlign="Right"
                                  ItemStyle-ForeColor="Maroon"
                                  ItemStyle-Font-Bold="True">
                <ItemTemplate>
                  <%# FigureCouponDiscount(
                          (System.Data.DataRowView)Container.DataItem ) %>
                </ItemTemplate>
              </asp:TemplateColumn>
            </Columns>
          </asp:DataGrid>
        </asp:Panel>
```

After this point, the rest of the `ShoppingCart.aspx` code remains unchanged.

ShoppingCart.aspx.cs

`ShoppingCart.aspx.cs` is the source listing for the code-behind class that drives our shopping cart. To make things easy, we'll include the entire listing, but I've highlighted the pieces of the shopping cart code-behind class that we've modified in order to include discounts and coupon displays.

```
using System;
using System.Collections;
using System.ComponentModel;
using System.Data;
using System.Drawing;
using System.Web;
using System.Web.SessionState;
using System.Web.UI;
using System.Web.UI.WebControls;
using System.Web.UI.HtmlControls;

using GW.Web.ShoppingCart;
using GW.Web.Sales;
using GW.Web.Sales.Data;
using GW.Web.OrdersClient;

using GW.MonitorServices;
using GW.MonitorServices.Logging;

using System.Reflection;
using System.Diagnostics;
```

```
namespace GW.Web
{
  /// <summary>
  /// Summary description for ShoppingCart.
  /// </summary>
  public class ShoppingCartPage : System.Web.UI.Page
  {
    protected System.Web.UI.WebControls.Button btnUpdate;
    protected System.Web.UI.WebControls.Button btnCheckOut;
    protected System.Web.UI.WebControls.Label lblMessage;
    protected System.Web.UI.WebControls.Panel pnlCartContents;
    protected System.Web.UI.WebControls.DataGrid dgDiscounts;
    protected System.Web.UI.WebControls.DataGrid dgCart;

    private DataTable cartItems;
    private DataSet discountItems;
    private CouponItem currentCoupon;

    private decimal currentRunningTotal = 0;
    protected System.Web.UI.WebControls.DataGrid dgCoupon;
    protected System.Web.UI.WebControls.Label lblCouponDisplay;
    protected System.Web.UI.WebControls.Button btnClaimOrClear;
    private decimal currentRunningSavingsTotal = 0;
    protected System.Web.UI.WebControls.Label lblSubtotal;
    protected System.Web.UI.WebControls.Label lblDiscountHeader;
    private decimal currentCouponSavings = 0;

    private void Page_Load(object sender, System.EventArgs e)
    {
      lblMessage.Visible = false;
      lblDiscountHeader.Visible = false;

      // Put user code to initialize the page here
      //if (!Page.IsPostBack)
      //{
        LoadData();
      //}
```

Now the text of the btnClaimOrClear button is modified depending on whether there is a coupon to be claimed or not:

```
      // Now deal with the coupons
      CouponManager cm = new CouponManager();
      int couponId = cm.GetCurrentClaimedCouponId();
      if (couponId != -1)
      {
        currentCoupon = cm.GetCurrentClaimedCoupon( couponId );
        lblCouponDisplay.Text = "Current Coupon - <font color=\"black\">" +
                                      currentCoupon.Name + "</font>";
        btnClaimOrClear.Text = "Clear Coupon";
        DataSet couponDiscount = cm.GetCouponDiscount( couponId );
        dgCoupon.DataSource = couponDiscount.Tables[0];
        dgCoupon.DataBind();
```

```
    }
    else
    {
      lblCouponDisplay.Text = "Current Coupon - None";
      btnClaimOrClear.Text = "Claim Coupon";
      dgCoupon.Visible = false;
    }
  }
```

The LoadData method is modified to bind the discount information to the dgDiscounts DataGrid:

```
  private void LoadData()
  {
    CartManager shoppingCart = new CartManager();
    if ( (Request["AddToCart"] != null) && (Request["AddToCart"] != ""))
    {
      shoppingCart.AddItem( Request["AddToCart"] );
      Response.Redirect("ShoppingCart.aspx");
    }
    cartItems = shoppingCart.GetCartItems();
    if ( (cartItems == null) || (cartItems.Rows.Count == 0))
    {
      pnlCartContents.Visible = false;
      lblMessage.Text = "<br>There are no items in your shopping cart.";
      lblMessage.Visible = true;
    }
    else
    {
      lblMessage.Text = "Current Cart Contents:";
      lblMessage.Visible = true;
      SalesManager sm = new SalesManager();
      discountItems = sm.GetDiscountsForCart( User.Identity.Name );
      pnlCartContents.Visible = true;
      dgCart.DataSource = cartItems;
      dgCart.DataBind();
      if (discountItems.Tables[0].Rows.Count > 0)
      {
        lblDiscountHeader.Text = "Applicable Sale Items:";
        lblDiscountHeader.Visible = true;
        dgDiscounts.DataSource = discountItems.Tables[0];
        dgDiscounts.DataBind();
      }
    }
  }
```

The IterateAssociatedProducts method produces a list of products that are covered by the discount represented by the currently bound row. We will either list the single product the discount applies to, or we'll list all the products in the cart belonging to the category to which the discount applies.

```
  public string IterateAssociatedProducts( int discountType, int productId,
                                           int categoryId )
  {
```

```
    string outString = "";
    DataRow[] assocRows;
    if (discountType == 1)
    {
      // category-wide
      assocRows = cartItems.Select("CategoryId = " + categoryId.ToString());
    }
    else
    {
      // product-specific
      assocRows = cartItems.Select("ProductId = " + productId.ToString() );
    }

    foreach (DataRow assocRow in assocRows)
    {
      outString += assocRow["ProductName"] + "<BR>";
    }
    return outString;
  }
```

The `IterateAssociatedProductValues` method produces the list of discounted product values that corresponds to the list of products affected by the discount. It shows the value of the discount. Thus, if a product costs $50, and the discount applies to that product is for 10%, then the string produced by this method will display $5. This method and the others like it that we'll see next are used in the discount `DataGrid`.

```
  public string IterateAssociatedProductValues( int discountId  )
  {
    string outString = "";
    decimal adjDiscount;
    DataRow discRow = discountItems.Tables[0].Select("DiscountId = " +
                                            discountId.ToString() )[0];
    int productId;
    int categoryId;
    int discountType;
    int valueType;
    decimal productPrice;


    productId = (int) discRow["ProductId"];
    categoryId = (int) discRow["CategoryId"];
    discountType = (int) discRow["DiscountType"];
    valueType = (int) discRow["ValueType"];

    DataRow[] assocRows;
    if (discountType == 1)
      assocRows = cartItems.Select("CategoryId = " + categoryId.ToString());
    else
      assocRows = cartItems.Select("ProductID = " + productId.ToString());

    if (valueType == 1)
    {
      foreach (DataRow assocRow in assocRows)
      {
        // percentage off of source product
        productPrice = (decimal)assocRow["ActualPrice"];
```

We now enter into a rather elaborate little piece of mathematical tomfoolery to ensure that calculated discount is correct, so that 10% of 14.99 does indeed produce 1.49 rather than 1.50. It's the appropriate way to calculate the discount as any store owner will tell you – unfortunately, the .NET Framework doesn't currently include a class with a "financial/sale round" method!

```
          adjDiscount = (productPrice *
                        ((decimal)discRow["DiscountValue"]/100)) *
                        (int)assocRow["Quantity"];
          adjDiscount = (decimal)(Math.Floor(
                                        (double)(adjDiscount * 100) ) / 100);
          adjDiscount = -1 * adjDiscount;
          currentRunningSavingsTotal += adjDiscount;
          outString += string.Format("{0:c}", adjDiscount) + "<BR>";
        }
      }
      else
      {
        for (int i=0; i< assocRows.Length; i++)
        {
          // raw value off of entire cart purchase
          adjDiscount = -1 * (int)discRow["DiscountValue"];
          currentRunningSavingsTotal += adjDiscount;
          outString += string.Format("{0:c}", adjDiscount) + "<BR>";

        }
      }
      return outString;
    }
```

These next methods are used to print out the current running total as it stands at the time of binding. It is included in the discounting and coupon displays as well as the regular shopping cart contents grid.

```
    public string CheckCurrentRunningTotal()
    {
      lblSubtotal.Text = string.Format("{0:c}", currentRunningTotal);
      return lblSubtotal.Text;
    }

    public string CheckCurrentRunningSavingsTotal()
    {
      lblSubtotal.Text = string.Format("{0:c}", currentRunningTotal +
                                                currentRunningSavingsTotal);
      return string.Format("{0:c}", currentRunningSavingsTotal);
    }

    public string RenderAndSum( DataRowView currentRow )
    {
      GWTrace.EnteringMethod( MethodBase.GetCurrentMethod() );
      if (currentRow == null)
        return "---";

      decimal extPrice=System.Convert.ToDecimal(currentRow.Row["ExtAmount"]);
```

```
    currentRunningTotal += extPrice;
    return string.Format("{0:c}", extPrice );
  }

  public string FigureCouponDiscount( DataRowView currentRow )
  {
    decimal discountValue = System.Convert.ToDecimal(
                                        currentRow["DiscountValue"] );
    decimal valueType = System.Convert.ToDecimal( currentRow["ValueType"] );
    decimal adjDiscount;
    if (valueType == 1)
    {
      // take a percentage off of the entire cart contents
      adjDiscount = (currentRunningTotal + currentRunningSavingsTotal) *
                                        ((decimal)discountValue/100);
      adjDiscount = (decimal)(Math.Floor((double)adjDiscount * 100) / 100);
      adjDiscount = -1 * adjDiscount;
    }
    else
    {
      adjDiscount = -1 * discountValue;
    }
    currentCouponSavings = adjDiscount;


    lblSubtotal.Text = string.Format( "{0:c}", currentRunningTotal +
                   currentRunningSavingsTotal + currentCouponSavings );
    return string.Format("{0:c}", adjDiscount);
  }
```

We also have to add the event-handler for the `btnClaimOrClear` button:

```
        private void InitializeComponent()
        {
          this.btnClaimOrClear.Click += new
                            System.EventHandler(this.btnClaimOrClear_Click);
          this.btnUpdate.Click += new System.EventHandler(this.btnUpdate_Click);
          this.btnCheckOut.Click += new
                                System.EventHandler(this.btnCheckOut_Click);
          this.Load += new System.EventHandler(this.Page_Load);

        }
```

Finally, we have the event handler itself, which redirects the user to the page that allows them to claim a coupon if they haven't yet claimed one. If they have claimed a coupon, this event handler will remove the claimed coupon cookie.

```
        private void btnClaimOrClear_Click(object sender, System.EventArgs e)
        {
          GWTrace.EnteringMethod( MethodBase.GetCurrentMethod() );
          CouponManager cm = new CouponManager();
          int couponId = cm.GetCurrentClaimedCouponId();
```

```
        if (couponId == -1)
          Response.Redirect("ClaimCoupon.aspx");
        else
        {
          HttpContext.Current.Response.Cookies[
                                         "GW_ClaimedCoupon"].Values.Clear();
          HttpContext.Current.Response.Cookies["GW_ClaimedCoupon"].Expires =
                                                   DateTime.Now.AddMinutes(-1);
          // the cookie isn't actually expired until the page is loaded again.
          Response.Redirect("ShoppingCart.aspx");
        }
      }

    }
  }
```

All of this code combines and we get the following set of images of our new shopping cart. The first picture below is of the standard shopping cart with a single item in it. There are no coupons or discounts applicable and the subtotal is displaying accordingly.

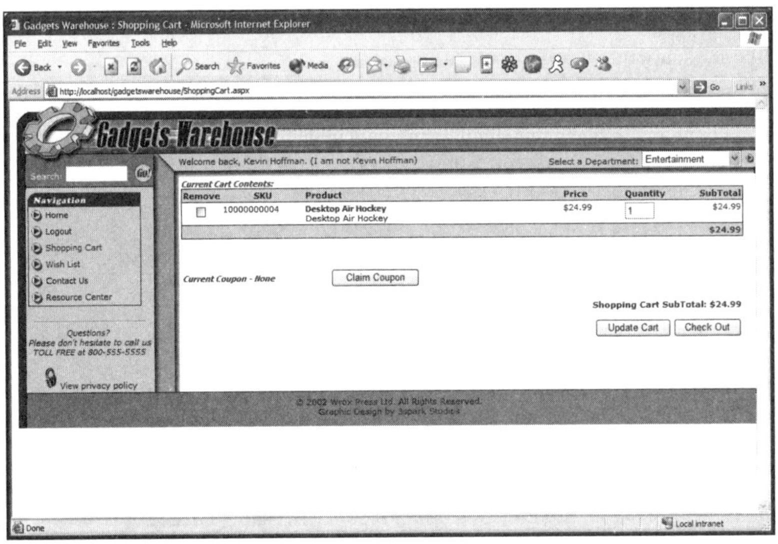

This next screenshot illustrates the discount display. We can see from the contents of the shopping cart here that there are two discounts active, combining to provide three price reductions since two discounts happen to apply to the same product (because of a product-specific discount as well as a category-wide discount).

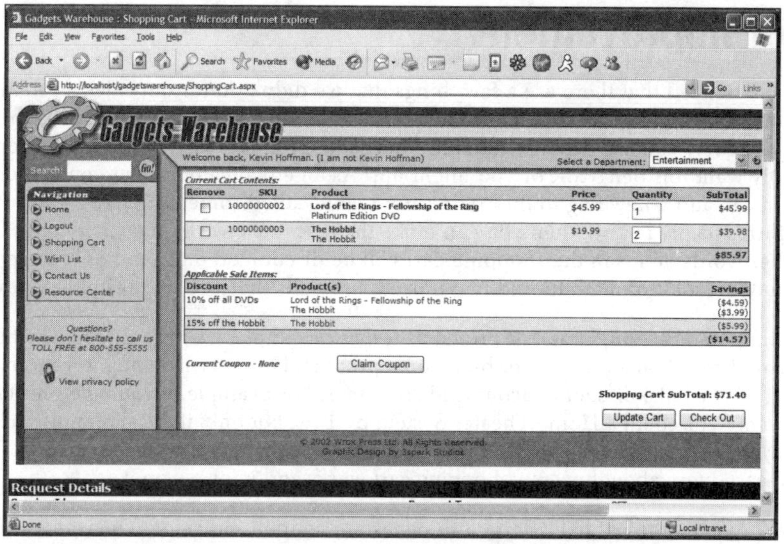

Finally, the following image is of the shopping cart with discounts *and* coupons displayed. You can see that the customer has claimed the Gadget Club Promotion coupon and also has the other discounts still active all for a respectable reduction in price. You can see that all of the discount prices are displaying in parentheses, which is the default way of displaying negative currency/money values.

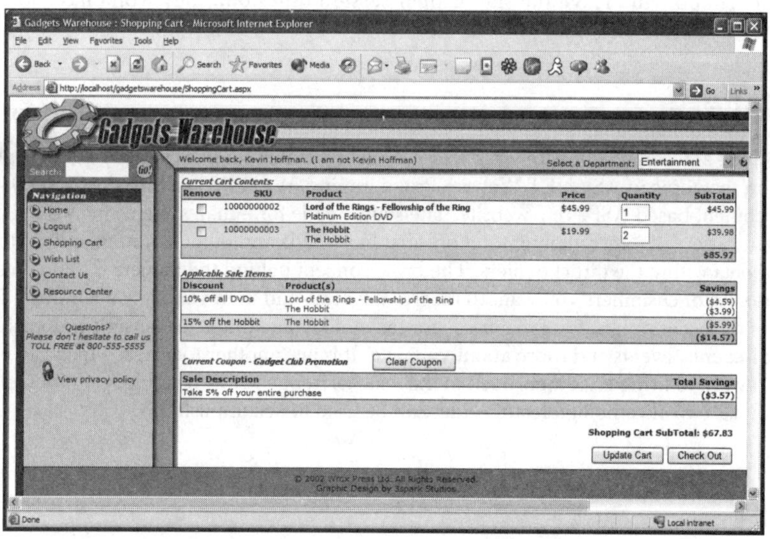

Room for Improvement

You may have noticed that there are a few things that we didn't do for our sales implementation. For example, you probably noticed that if you have a discount on a category, and a discount on a product within that category, you can actually discount that same product twice in the same shopping cart. You might actually want this behavior, or you might not. As an enhancement that you can do yourself as an exercise, you can add a new flag to the `Discounts` table called something like `Repeatable` or `Overlap`. If this flag is `false`, then you can make the discounts work on a "first-come first-served" basis. In other words, items in the shopping cart will be discounted once and only once. This prevents people from doing a bit of math to find maximized discounts that you might not have expected.

The other thing we didn't implement is prerequisites. For example, we have discounts where you can apply a discount based on a category or based on a product. However, you might want to add additional requirements that act like discount-encouraged cross-sells. For example, if your site sells home electronics, you might want to discount a Home Theater System by 10%, but only if the shopping cart also contains something from the Speakers category. This is also another enhancement that you can add as an exercise to help you learn more about how our shopping cart works and improve on it.

Another thing you might feel like adding is a persistent-coupon indicator. The way our coupon claiming system works, once you claim the coupon it resides in a cookie until your session ends. You might want to make some graphical change to the navigation bars on the site so that the customer has an ever-present reminder that they have recently claimed a coupon. Something like this might keep customers from forgetting their coupons and thereby cut down on possible lost sales. Another bit of reliability might be added to delay the recording of a claimed coupon until the customer checks out. This way, if they claim the coupon and leave the site or their session times out, they won't have lost their opportunity to claim the coupon.

Direct Mailers

We didn't include any code on how to write a direct mailing system in this chapter. There is plenty of excellent information on that topic in ASP.NET Website Programming, Wrox Press (ISBN 1-86100-693-4), where we developed a content-based ASP.NET website. The source code for e-mail systems in .NET is freely available, and there are a variety of direct mailing solutions that have APIs and other scripting options that allow you to use your own data within the direct mailers. The basic concept behind the mailers is that you start with a query, which returns a list of customers you want to receive the mail, and then you have a template (form letter) that is sent to each of those customers. One major use for technology like this is to transmit coupons and information about sales, discounts, events and more about your site. It is just another tool with which site managers and marketers can work to bring customers back to their site as frequently as possible. Commerce Server from Microsoft also has e-mail campaign features that can be used to accomplish this.

Summary

This chapter started off with a discussion of sales, marketing departments, advertising, and coupons. We discussed discounts and sales, and then we discussed coupons. Using our coupon system, you can easily plug into a direct mailing system and send demographically targeted coupons to large numbers of your customers. A flexible, scalable, powerful discounting and coupon system can provide a website with that added edge that might be the one difference between it and its competitors. In the next chapter we're going to go to the next page after the shopping cart, and cover checking out, product tracking, and fulfillment.

CHAPTER 8

8

Order Tracking and Fulfillment

This chapter will take us through the complex problem of taking orders, processing them, and providing customers with feedback on the status of individual orders and their order histories with the site. After we've had a walk-through of the common problems associated with order tracking and fulfillment, we'll talk about the design of GadgetsWarehouse.com's order tracking and fulfillment solution. Finally, we'll go through all of our source code for order tracking and displaying order status.

The Problem

There are many different kinds of problems that we need to take into consideration when dealing with order submissions, tracking, and status display. First and foremost, we need to be aware of the legal ramifications of how we deal with orders. There are rules that apply to when customers can be charged for their orders and how long you must retain records of customer purchases. Someone with the appropriate legal experience should determine all of this before you begin working on your order handling solution. For example, there are legalities involved in making sure that your shipping prices are publicly available, and that you'll never charge a customer for their product until it is shipped to them. Many business rules built into third-party commerce engines are done so in order to comply with various legal requirements.

Fortunately, other people typically deal with these problems. This leaves us more time to spend worrying about the problems we can solve by programming. We need to figure out how we're going to accomplish the following:

- Record new orders
- Update existing orders
- Display order history and details for the customer
- Communicate orders between website and fulfillment system (such as the warehouse)

Our design will have to provide answers for all of the above requirements.

The Design

There are a few of things that our design needs to allow for. We listed those above. What we want is to be able to submit orders from the website, and we need to be able to update the customers with their order history and the status of each of their orders. In addition to all of that, we also want to make sure that our fulfillment system is not tightly coupled with our website. This will allow us to mimic the majority of real-life commercial websites that have Unix mainframes or other disparate systems running their shipping/receiving/fulfillment systems that are not part of the main web application. Loosely coupling our site with our order fulfillment allows us to the flexibility to react quickly to change. The fulfillment system might change several times over the course of a few months, but our website might not. While our product catalog remains fixed, the way in which we send those products might change. For example, if we're continually expanding, we might be adding warehouses across the country to decrease shipping time and costs, and we might also be upgrading our fulfillment software. In order for our website to remain reliable and stable while all this change is taking place, we don't want this software to be directly tied to our web application.

The Order Pipeline

If you have used Commerce Server or have been a part of e-commerce development you are probably familiar with the concept of an order pipeline. The order pipeline is the flow of customer experience through the order capturing process. Think of it like an assembly line in a factory. Think of a piece of candy (our shopping cart). It starts off at the beginning of the pipeline and as it travels along the pipeline, more decoration is added. Finally, the wrapping is added and it is packaged and put in a box to be sent to stores.

Our order pipeline follows the same principal. The first step in the pipeline is the shopping cart. A new, almost empty order begins its life there. Then, as the customer continues through the order pipeline, more and more data is added. This is where the shipping address is added to the order, and where sales tax and shipping calculations would be performed and placed on the order. When the pipeline is complete, the end result should be a fully populated order that stands on its own as a single unit. This order can then be stored in the database and transmitted in its entirety to fulfillment systems or any other location.

The following diagram should help illustrate the process of building an order and the communication of orders between our application and other applications responsible for updating orders and modifying order status.

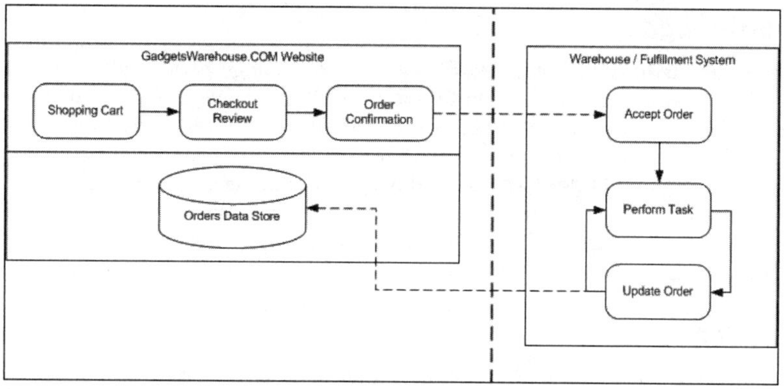

The Database

The following is a diagram of the tables we're going to use in our order tracking system:

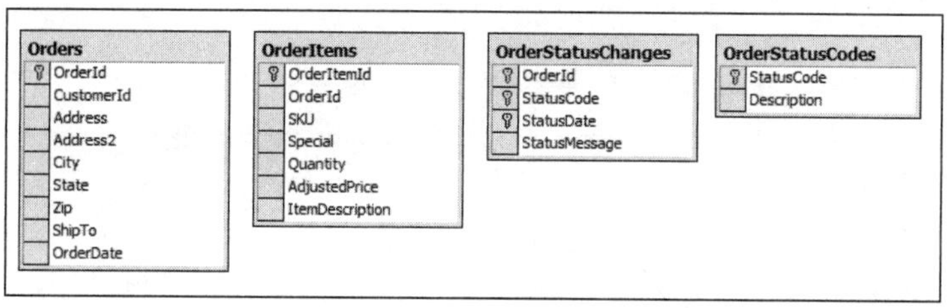

Orders

This table contains the orders. It is important to remember that, in our design, the website will create the order and order items, but will never make modifications after that. All subsequent modifications are the responsibility of whatever back-end fulfillment solution is in use.

OrderItems

This is a typical order item table. It contains the `SKU`, `Quantity`, `AdjustedPrice` (adjusted for quantity as well), and an `ItemDescription`. The `ItemDescription` is there so that our fulfillment system can display to warehouse operators a description of the product *without* having to refer back to our database. Remember that our system is loosely coupled, and the fulfillment system should not have to depend on any particular field in our database to accomplish its task. In addition to that, there is a `Special` flag. This is a Boolean (bit) field, which indicates whether the item is to be considered "special". By "special", we mean that the item is not a tangible product, but is some other form of line item that cannot be shipped. Coupons and Discounts applied to an order are stored as special order items with the `AdjustedPrice` being the amount of the discount in dollars. The `AdjustedPrice` is the final amount the customer will be charged.

OrderStatusChanges

Many websites simply have a field called Status that will change periodically based on the status of the order. Therefore, if your order goes from Ordered to Shipped, everything is good and no one has any reason to complain. However, what if your order goes from Ordered to Backordered? If there is no historical log of status changes, there will be no record that your order ever had a status of Ordered. By considering the Order and Order Item as 'read only' and making all changes to the status of an order in a separate table, we not only provide a historical account of all status changes, but we provide a greater degree of accountability. Customers will feel very comfortable with our system because not only will they know what their order status is, they will know *exactly when* that order status changed.

OrderStatusCodes

This table contains a look-up list of descriptions for numeric status codes. This table currently only contains status descriptions, but it can be upgraded at some later date to support a workflow that describes a chain of sequential status codes. In other words, it could be coded in the database that an order can only change from Accepted to Shipped, and cannot change from Accepted to Pending, for example.

The Code

The following is a class diagram of the classes we're going to be putting in our `OrdersClient` project:

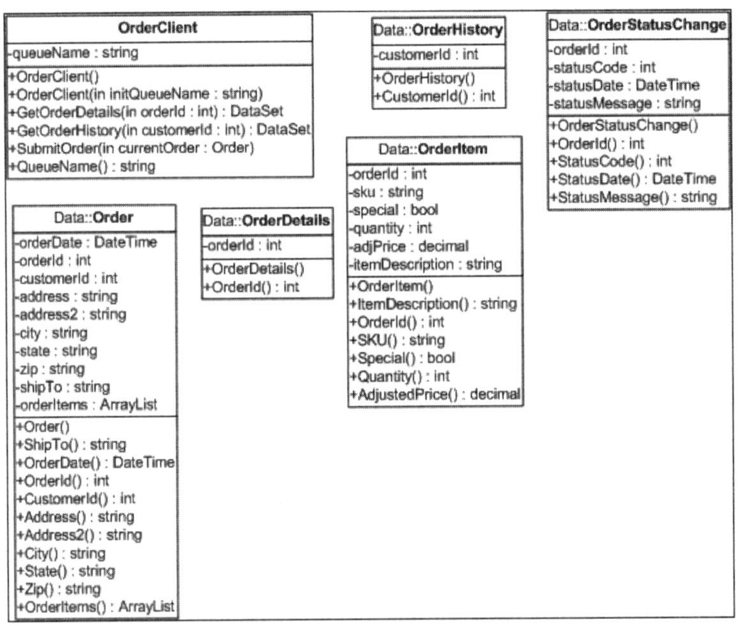

The `OrderClient` class is the most interesting class here and we'll talk about that in more detail in a moment, the other classes are wrappers for the relevant database object.

The Solution

Now that we've taken a look at the design we can look at the source code for our solution. Keep in mind that the solution we're developing is the website's client to the order fulfillment system. We haven't coded anything that actually performs any fulfillment, so all of the orders on our site as it stands now will remain at the first stage of status and not be fulfilled. We'll talk more about what you can do to implement a "stub" fulfiller later. Our purpose here is to show you how to integrate a fulfillment system into your web application, not how to write a fulfillment system. That would probably take up another book on its own. In most cases, you'll probably be integrating with a commercial or previously-written fulfillment solution.

Stored Procedures

The following is the list of stored procedures that we created for our `OrdersClient` project:

Gw_Insert_Order

This stored procedure creates a new order in the database and returns the new order ID as an output parameter. It is called by the final stage of the checkout pipeline from the `OrdersClient` project we'll be developing later:

```
CREATE PROCEDURE Gw_Insert_Order
  @CustomerId int,
  @Address varchar(100),
  @Address2 varchar(100),
  @City varchar(50),
  @State varchar(2),
  @Zip varchar(14),
  @ShipTo varchar(50),
  @OrderId int out
AS
  INSERT INTO Orders(CustomerId, Address, Address2, City, State,
                     Zip, ShipTo)
              VALUES(@CustomerId, @Address, @Address2, @City, @State,
                     @Zip, @ShipTo)

  SET @OrderId = @@IDENTITY
GO
```

Gw_Insert_OrderItem

This stored procedure creates a new order item that will be associated with a pre-existing order. If the item being purchased is a product (as opposed to a discount or a coupon) and that product is in the customer's wish list, the *purchased* flag on that product within the wish list will be set, giving the customer a visual indication that they purchased that product. Remember that the fulfillment system will need to be able to see the discounts and coupons applied to the cart as line items. This allows the receipt packaged with the customer's product to include that information. It is absolutely imperative that at each stage of fulfillment, it is known what the product originally cost, and how much the customer paid for it, and why they paid less than the original price, if applicable.

```
CREATE PROCEDURE Gw_Insert_OrderItem
  @OrderId int,
  @SKU varchar(11),
  @Special bit,
  @Quantity int,
  @AdjustedPrice money,
  @ItemDescription varchar(255)
AS
  DECLARE @CustomerId int

  SELECT @CustomerId = CustomerId FROM Orders WHERE OrderId = @OrderId

  INSERT INTO OrderItems(OrderId, SKU, Special, Quantity,
                         AdjustedPrice, ItemDescription)
                  VALUES(@OrderId, @SKU, @Special, @Quantity,
                         @AdjustedPrice, @ItemDescription)
```

In this next section of the stored procedure, we will modify the user's wish list to set the `Purchased` flag. Because discounts and coupons are "special" line items, we only do this for regular products.

```
  IF @Special = 0
    UPDATE WishListItems SET Purchased = 1
    WHERE CustomerId = @CustomerId  AND SKU = @SKU
GO
```

Gw_Insert_OrderStatusChange

Because our system is designed so that our website does not have the ability to modify individual records belonging to an order or an order item, we need to insert rows into the `OrderStatusChanges` table in order to indicate an order's change in status by the fulfillment backend. Each time a record is inserted in this table, the `StatusDate` field is automatically populated with the current date and time when the record was inserted, giving us a timestamp for the status change:

```
CREATE PROCEDURE Gw_Insert_OrderStatusChange
  @OrderId int,
  @StatusCode int,
  @StatusMessage varchar(100)
AS
  INSERT INTO OrderStatusChanges(OrderId, StatusCode, StatusMessage)
  VALUES(@OrderId, @StatusCode, @StatusMessage)
GO
```

Gw_Select_OrderStatusChanges

This procedure returns a list of all of the status changes that have occurred with regard to a particular order. This will show the customer the status change history for an order when viewing order details:

```
CREATE PROCEDURE Gw_Select_OrderStatusChanges
  @OrderId int
AS
  SELECT os.OrderId, os.StatusCode, os.StatusDate, os.StatusMessage,
         osc.Description CodeDescription
```

```
  FROM OrderStatusChanges os
  INNER JOIN OrderStatusCodes osc ON os.StatusCode = osc.StatusCode
  WHERE os.OrderId = @OrderId
  ORDER BY os.StatusDate DESC
GO
```

Gw_Select_OrderItems

This procedure will return a list of items belonging to a particular order:

```
CREATE PROCEDURE Gw_Select_OrderItems
  @OrderId int
AS
  SELECT oi.OrderItemId, oi.OrderId, oi.SKU, oi.Special, oi.Quantity,
         oi.AdjustedPrice, oi.ItemDescription FROM OrderItems oi
  WHERE OrderId = @OrderId
  ORDER BY OrderItemId
GO
```

Gw_Select_OrderHistory

This stored procedure returns a list of all orders for a particular customer in reverse chronological order:

```
CREATE PROCEDURE Gw_Select_OrderHistory
  @CustomerId int
AS
  SELECT o.OrderId, o.CustomerId, o.Address, o.Address2, o.City,
       o.State, o.Zip, o.ShipTo, o.OrderDate,
       Total = ( SELECT SUM(AdjustedPrice)
              FROM OrderItems
              WHERE OrderItems.OrderId = o.OrderId )
  FROM Orders o
  WHERE o.CustomerId = @CustomerID
  ORDER BY o.OrderDate DESC
GO
```

CMP Metadata

Here is the list of CMP metadata markup that we put into the `web.config` file to complete the object-relational mapping to drive our data tier for the order fulfillment section. To keep things clear and easy to read, we'll just show a little bit of the XML required. The rest of it should be easy to figure out or you can find it in the final `web.config` in the code download.

```
<ContainerMapping>
<ContainerMappingId>OrderItem</ContainerMappingId>
<ContainedClass>OrderItem</ContainedClass>
<Insert>
  <CommandName>Gw_Insert_OrderItem</CommandName>
  <Parameter>
    <ClassMember>OrderId</ClassMember>
    <ParameterName>@OrderId</ParameterName>
```

```
      <DbTypeHint>Int</DbTypeHint>
      <ParamDirection>Input</ParamDirection>
      <Size>4</Size>
    </Parameter>
    <Parameter>
      <ClassMember>SKU</ClassMember>
      <ParameterName>@SKU</ParameterName>
      <DbTypeHint>Varchar</DbTypeHint>
      <ParamDirection>Input</ParamDirection>
      <Size>11</Size>
    </Parameter>
    <Parameter>
      <ClassMember>Special</ClassMember>
      <ParameterName>@Special</ParameterName>
      <DbTypeHint>Bit</DbTypeHint>
      <ParamDirection>Input</ParamDirection>
      <Size>1</Size>
    </Parameter>
    <Parameter>
      <ClassMember>Quantity</ClassMember>
      <ParameterName>@Quantity</ParameterName>
      <DbTypeHint>Int</DbTypeHint>
      <ParamDirection>Input</ParamDirection>
      <Size>4</Size>
    </Parameter>
    <Parameter>
      <ClassMember>AdjustedPrice</ClassMember>
      <ParameterName>@AdjustedPrice</ParameterName>
      <DbTypeHint>Money</DbTypeHint>
      <ParamDirection>Input</ParamDirection>
      <Size>8</Size>
    </Parameter>
    <Parameter>
      <ClassMember>ItemDescription</ClassMember>
      <ParameterName>@ItemDescription</ParameterName>
      <DbTypeHint>Varchar</DbTypeHint>
      <ParamDirection>Input</ParamDirection>
      <Size>255</Size>
    </Parameter>
  </Insert>
  </ContainerMapping>
```

The OrdersClient Project

If you're following along instead of using the code download, you should add a new C# Class Library project to the main solution. Call it `OrdersClient` and perform the usual operation of setting up the linked `SharedAssemblyInfo.cs` file and reducing the `AssemblyInfo.cs` file that VS .NET created. Set the default namespace and project output name to `GW.Web.OrdersClient`.

OrderClient

The `OrderClient` class is the main worker class for dealing with order management from the website. It contains methods for retrieving details on a particular order, retrieving the order history for a particular customer, and submitting an order, which writes an order to our database and submits it to the loosely coupled fulfillment backend.

```
using System;
using System.Data;
using System.Diagnostics;
using System.Reflection;

using GW.CMPServices;
using GW.MonitorServices;
using GW.MonitorServices.Logging;

using System.Messaging;

namespace GW.Web.OrdersClient
{
  /// <summary>
  /// Summary description for OrderClient.
  /// </summary>
  public class OrderClient
  {
    private string queueName;

    public OrderClient()
    {
    }
```

This is the constructor we will be using. It creates an instance of this class and sets the name of the MSMQ Queue to which we will be submitting orders. We don't actually instantiate the queue here since it is not required for all methods on this class.

```
    public OrderClient( string initQueueName)
    {
      queueName = initQueueName;
    }
```

The `GetOrderDetails` method will retrieve several types of information for a particular order. It will retrieve all of the items that belong to the order, as well as all of the order status history changes. In order to get both of those result sets to appear in the same `DataSet`, we create a new `DataSet`, into which we merge the results of two different stored procedure operations.

```
    public DataSet GetOrderDetails( int orderId )
    {
      GWTrace.EnteringMethod( MethodBase.GetCurrentMethod() );
      DataSet finalData = new DataSet();
      OrderDetails od = new OrderDetails();
      od.OrderId = orderId;

      SqlPersistenceContainer spc = new SqlPersistenceContainer(
                   CMPConfigurationHandler.ContainerMaps["OrderItems"] );
      spc.Select( od );
      od.ResultSet.Tables[0].TableName = "OrderItems";
      finalData.Merge( od.ResultSet.Tables[0] );
      spc.ContainerMapping =
              CMPConfigurationHandler.ContainerMaps["OrderStatusHistory"];
```

```
        OrderDetails od2 = new OrderDetails();
        od2.OrderId = orderId;
        spc.Select( od2 );
        od2.ResultSet.Tables[0].TableName = "OrderStatusItems";
        finalData.Merge( od2.ResultSet.Tables[0], true,
                         MissingSchemaAction.Add  );
        return finalData;
    }
```

This method will retrieve an order history for a particular customer by invoking the appropriate stored procedure.

```
    public DataSet GetOrderHistory( int customerId )
    {
        GWTrace.EnteringMethod( MethodBase.GetCurrentMethod() );
        OrderHistory oh = new OrderHistory();
        oh.CustomerId = customerId;

        SqlPersistenceContainer spc = new SqlPersistenceContainer(
                    CMPConfigurationHandler.ContainerMaps["OrderHistory"]);
        spc.Select( oh );
        oh.FinalizeData();
        return oh.ResultSet;
    }
```

The `SubmitOrder` method will take a fully populated `Order` object and submit it to the back-end fulfillment system. This is done by creating the order entry in the database and then submitting that order to a private Microsoft Message Queue.

```
    public void SubmitOrder( Order currentOrder )
    {
        GWTrace.EnteringMethod( MethodBase.GetCurrentMethod() );
        GWTrace.Trace(TraceLevel.Info, "Queue Name: {0}", queueName );

        SqlPersistenceContainer spc = new SqlPersistenceContainer(
                         CMPConfigurationHandler.ContainerMaps["Order"] );
        spc.Insert( currentOrder );
        spc.ContainerMapping =
                        CMPConfigurationHandler.ContainerMaps["OrderItem"];
        for (int i=0; i< currentOrder.OrderItems.Count; i++)
        {
          OrderItem oi = (OrderItem)currentOrder.OrderItems[i];
          oi.OrderId = currentOrder.OrderId;
          spc.Insert( oi );
        }
```

This next section of code will submit a copy of the order to a private message queue on the local machine. We won't be going into the details of message queing here – for a deep exploration of this topic see *Data-Centric .NET Programming with C#*, (Wrox Press, ISBN 1-86100-592-X). In a production environment, we would be submitting it to a public queue accessible by the back-end fulfillment system. However, since most of us are writing this on our own machines and don't have our own domains, private queues are the only things to which we have access. The name of the queue is stored in the `web.config` file and passed to the constructor of this class. By sending the order to a queue, we have the advantage of passing off the order asynchronously using a reliable messaging system to the back-end facility. Because MSMQ can be bridged to MQ Series for IBM mainframes, we can theoretically use any back-end fulfillment system that we like for enhanced flexibility and scalability. The purpose here is that each time the fulfillment system changes the status of an order, it will update the main website accordingly by inserting status change records.

```
      MessageQueue mq = new MessageQueue( queueName );

      mq.DefaultPropertiesToSend.Recoverable = true;

      mq.Send( currentOrder );
      mq.Close();

      spc.ContainerMapping =
              CMPConfigurationHandler.ContainerMaps["OrderStatusChange"];
      OrderStatusChange osc = new OrderStatusChange();
      osc.OrderId = currentOrder.OrderId;
      osc.StatusCode = 1;
      osc.StatusMessage = "Order Submitted by Customer";
      spc.Insert( osc );
```

Once the order status change has been submitted, we empty the user's shopping cart. Once they've purchased something, it should always be removed from their cart. The stored procedure will take care of flagging their wish list with purchased items.

```
      spc.ContainerMapping =
                CMPConfigurationHandler.ContainerMaps["CartContents"];
      ShoppingCart.CartContents cc = new ShoppingCart.CartContents();
      cc.CartId = currentOrder.CustomerId.ToString();
      spc.Delete( cc );
    }

    public string QueueName
    {
      get { return queueName; }
      set { queueName = value; }
    }
  }
}
```

ShoppingCart.aspx.cs Changes

The following is a new listing for `ShoppingCart.aspx.cs`. I've highlighted the changes that we made to support the notion of `Order` and `OrderItems`. The basic principal behind what we're doing here is that each page in the order pipeline is going to add more data to the order or further refine the existing data on an order. When the customer is completely done submitting their order, the order will be submitted as we saw in the code above.

```
...
    private decimal currentCouponSavings = 0;
    private Order currentOrder;
```

This next property will make the order object instance available to the next page in the pipeline. We do this by using the `Server.Transfer` method to transfer execution context to the next page. Using that method, we can reference public properties of a page like the one below from another page without having to worry about complex `QueryString` parameters. There is a limitation to this, however, and we'll discuss that when we get to the `Checkout.aspx.cs` code.

```
    public Order CurrentOrder
    {
      get { return currentOrder; }
    }

    private void Page_Load(object sender, System.EventArgs e)
    {
```

In this next block of code, if the user is authenticated, then we will make a new order object for them.

```
      if (User.Identity.IsAuthenticated)
      {
        currentOrder = new Order();
        currentOrder.CustomerId = System.Convert.ToInt32(
                                                    User.Identity.Name );
        currentOrder.OrderDate = System.DateTime.Now;
      }
      lblMessage.Visible = false;
      lblDiscountHeader.Visible = false;

      // Put user code to initialize the page here
      if (!Page. IsPostBack)
      {
        LoadData();
      }
```

We've cut out a lot of code that hasn't been changed. In the `IterateAssociatedProductValues` method, we see the following sections of code where we're creating new order item objects. The SKU for a discount is going to contain the prefix `DISCOUNT` so that the fulfillment system can easily make distinctions.

```
      public string IterateAssociatedProductValues( int discountId  )
      {
        ...
          // add order item
          OrderItem oi = new OrderItem();
          oi.SKU = "DISCOUNT" + discRow["DiscountId"].ToString();
          oi.ItemDescription = discRow["Name"].ToString();
          oi.Special = true;
          oi.Quantity = 1;
          oi.AdjustedPrice = adjDiscount;
          currentOrder.OrderItems.Add( oi );

        }
      }
      else
      {
        for (int i=0; i< assocRows.Length; i++)
        {
          // raw value off entire cart purchase
          adjDiscount = -1 * (int)discRow["DiscountValue"];
          currentRunningSavingsTotal += adjDiscount;
          outString += string.Format("{0:c}", adjDiscount) + "<BR>";
```

```
            OrderItem oi = new OrderItem();
            oi.SKU = "DISCOUNT" + discRow["DiscountId"].ToString();
            oi.ItemDescription = discRow["Name"].ToString();
            oi.Special = true;
            oi.Quantity = 1;
            oi.AdjustedPrice = adjDiscount;
            currentOrder.OrderItems.Add( oi );
          }
        }
        return outString;
      }
```

Next we show changes to the RenderAndSum method where we are adding new order items for the products themselves (as opposed to coupons or discounts):

```
    public string RenderAndSum( DataRowView currentRow )
      {
        GWTrace.EnteringMethod( MethodBase.GetCurrentMethod() );
        if (currentRow == null)
          return "--";

        decimal extPrice = System.Convert.ToDecimal(
                                           currentRow.Row["ExtAmount"] );

        OrderItem oi = new OrderItem();
        oi.AdjustedPrice = extPrice;
        oi.ItemDescription = currentRow["SkuDescription"].ToString();
        oi.Quantity = (int)currentRow["Quantity"];
        oi.SKU = (string)currentRow["SKU"];
        oi.Special = false;
        currentOrder.OrderItems.Add( oi );

        currentRunningTotal += extPrice;
        return string.Format("{0:c}", extPrice );
      }
```

The following are changes to the FigureCouponDiscount method where we create an order item for a coupon. We are using the coupon ID and the coupon name for the current row passed to this method to create a new order item. Each order item we create is added to the currentOrder object. The currentOrder object is made available to the next page in the pipeline via the Server.Transfer method and page referencing.

```
      public string FigureCouponDiscount( DataRowView currentRow )
      {
        decimal discountValue = System.Convert.ToDecimal(
                                            currentRow["DiscountValue"] );
        decimal valueType = System.Convert.ToDecimal(
                                              currentRow["ValueType"] );
        decimal adjDiscount;
        if (valueType == 1)
        {
          // take a percentage off of the entire cart contents
          adjDiscount = (currentRunningTotal + currentRunningSavingsTotal) *
```

```
                                            ((decimal)discountValue/100);
          adjDiscount = (decimal)(Math.Floor( (double)adjDiscount * 100) /
                                                                   100 );

          adjDiscount = -1 * adjDiscount;
        }
        else
        {
          adjDiscount = -1 * discountValue;
        }
        currentCouponSavings = adjDiscount;

        OrderItem oi = new OrderItem();
        oi.Special = true;
        oi.SKU = "COUPON" + currentRow["CouponId"].ToString();
        oi.ItemDescription = currentRow["CouponName"].ToString();
        oi.AdjustedPrice = adjDiscount;
        oi.Quantity = 1;
        currentOrder.OrderItems.Add( oi );

        lblSubtotal.Text = string.Format( "{0:c}", currentRunningTotal +
                        currentRunningSavingsTotal + currentCouponSavings );
        return string.Format("{0:c}", adjDiscount);
      }
```

We've already seen quite a few screenshots of the shopping cart and since our changes to the cart were entirely behind the scenes, we won't show another image here.

Checkout.aspx

The following is the code for the HTML portion of the `Checkout` page. This page presents the user with an input form that asks for their shipping information. Because our solution doesn't actually collect credit information, you won't see that. However, this page or another page inserted into the pipeline after this one would be an ideal location for collecting payment information. As usual, we'll skip through the redundant HTML and cut right to the portion of the HTML that is relevant to the page:

```
<font color="maroon" size="3" face="Tahoma"><i><b>Confirm Your
Order</b></i></font><br>
<asp:Label id="lblOrderSummary" runat="server">Label</asp:Label><br>
<br>
<b>Shipping Details</b>
</P>
<table width="100%" border="0" cellspacing="2" cellpadding="2" ID="Table1">
<tr>
    <td width="200" align="right">
    Ship To:
    </td>
    <td>
    <asp:TextBox ID="txtShipTo" Runat="server" MaxLength="50"
                Width="300px"></asp:TextBox>
    </td>
</tr>
```

```
<tr>
    <td width="200" align="right">
    Address
    </td>
    <td>
    <asp:TextBox ID="txtAddress" Runat="server" maxlength="100"
                 Width="300px"></asp:TextBox>
    </td>
</tr>
<tr>
    <td align="right">
    Address (Add'l)
    </td>
    <td>
    <asp:TextBox ID="txtAddress2" Runat="server" MaxLength="100"
                 Width="300px"></asp:TextBox>
    </td>
</tr>
<tr>
    <td align="right">
    City / State / Zip
    </td>
    <td>
    <asp:TextBox ID="txtCity" MaxLength="50" Width="100px"
                 Runat="server"></asp:TextBox>, 
    <asp:TextBox ID="txtState" MaxLength="2" Width="20px"
                 Runat="server"></asp:TextBox>  
    <asp:TextBox ID="txtZip" MaxLength="14" Width="40px"
                 Runat="server"></asp:TextBox>
    </td>
</tr>
<tr>
    <td><br>
    </td>
    <td>
    <asp:Button ID="btnNext" Runat="server"
                Text="Checkout >>"></asp:Button> 
    <asp:Button ID="btnCancel" Runat="server" Text="Cancel"></asp:Button>
```

Checkout.aspx.cs

The following is the code for the code-behind class that drives the `Checkout` page, the second page in our order pipeline:

```
using System;
using System.Collections;
using System.ComponentModel;
using System.Data;
using System.Drawing;
using System.Web;
using System.Web.SessionState;
using System.Web.UI;
```

```
using System.Web.UI.WebControls;
using System.Web.UI.HtmlControls;
using System.Text;
using System.IO;

using System.Xml.Serialization;
using System.Xml;

using GW.Web.ShoppingCart;
using GW.Web.OrdersClient;

namespace GW.Web
{
  /// <summary>
  /// Summary description for Checkout.
  /// </summary>
  public class Checkout : System.Web.UI.Page
  {
    protected System.Web.UI.WebControls.TextBox txtAddress;
    protected System.Web.UI.WebControls.TextBox txtAddress2;
    protected System.Web.UI.WebControls.TextBox txtCity;
    protected System.Web.UI.WebControls.TextBox txtState;
    protected System.Web.UI.WebControls.TextBox txtZip;
    protected System.Web.UI.WebControls.Label lblOrderSummary;

    protected Order currentOrder;
    protected System.Web.UI.WebControls.Button btnNext;
    protected System.Web.UI.WebControls.Button btnCancel;
    protected System.Web.UI.WebControls.TextBox txtShipTo;
```

This next section of code may look a little unfamiliar. What we're doing is using a page reference. This means that by using `Server.Transfer`, we can retain in memory all the public members of the page from which we came. The next property definition will make the current order object available to the *next* page in the pipeline.

```
    public GW.Web.ShoppingCartPage cartPage;

    public Order CurrentOrder
    {
      get { return currentOrder; }
    }

    private void Page_Load(object sender, System.EventArgs e)
    {
      // Put user code to initialize the page here
      if (!Page.IsPostBack)
      {
        LoadData();
      }
    }
```

The first few lines of this next method are fairly important. The problem we have here is this: we are obtaining a reference to the previous page by utilizing the page reference functionality because we know that when being sent via `Server.Transfer`, the `Context.Handler` property contains a reference to the sending page. We can use that to read property values from the sending page. This is what we do below to get a reference to the previous page's `Order` object. The thing that we must do is serialize that order object to `ViewState` immediately after retrieving it from the previous page. This is because that `Context.Handler` property will actually contain a reference to the current page after a `PostBack`, thereby losing a reference to the previous page and its associated public properties and data. To get around this little issue, we're going to store the previous page's order instance in the view state. When we post back, we'll load it from `ViewState` and make it available in the `CurrentOrder` public property we saw above for the next page in the pipeline to do the same thing.

```
private void LoadData()
{
  cartPage = (GW.Web.ShoppingCartPage)Context.Handler;
  currentOrder = cartPage.CurrentOrder;
  currentOrder.CustomerId = System.Convert.ToInt32(
                                        User.Identity.Name );
```

We need to serialize the object because the `ViewState` collection actually imposes restrictions on reference types being placed in it. It is easier for us just to implement a serialization of our class so we don't have to worry about breaking any of the rules of the `ViewState` collection.

```
  ViewState["CurrentOrder"] = currentOrder.ToXmlString();

  decimal subTotal = 0;

  for (int i=0; i < currentOrder.OrderItems.Count; i ++)
  {
    subTotal += ((OrderItem)currentOrder.OrderItems[i]).AdjustedPrice;
  }
  lblOrderSummary.Text = string.Format(
    "Current Order Sub-Total : {0} item(s) for <b><i><font " +
    "color=\"Maroon\">{1:c}</font></b></i>",
    currentOrder.OrderItems.Count,
    subTotal );

  CartManager shoppingCart = new CartManager();

}
```

In our next method, you can see the order being added to in preparation for being passed to the next page. We are deserializing the previous order instance from `ViewState` (since we no longer have a valid reference to the previous page) and then adding more information to it. Again, keep in mind the analogy of a product going through a manufacturing assembly line, having more parts added to it at each stage in the pipeline until it is finally shrink-wrapped and shipped at the end of the line.

```
    private void btnNext_Click(object sender, System.EventArgs e)
    {
      XmlSerializer xs = new XmlSerializer( typeof(
                                    GW.Web.OrdersClient.Order ));
      StringReader sr = new StringReader(
                              ViewState["CurrentOrder"].ToString() );
      currentOrder = (GW.Web.OrdersClient.Order)xs.Deserialize( sr );

      currentOrder.ShipTo = txtShipTo.Text;
      currentOrder.Address = txtAddress.Text;
      currentOrder.Address2 = txtAddress2.Text;
      currentOrder.City = txtCity.Text;
      currentOrder.State = txtState.Text;
      currentOrder.Zip = txtZip.Text;
      Server.Transfer("FinalCheckout.aspx");
    }

    private void btnCancel_Click(object sender, System.EventArgs e)
    {
      Response.Redirect("ShoppingCart.aspx");
    }
  }
}
```

Let's take a look at the checkout confirmation page (address request) page in action:

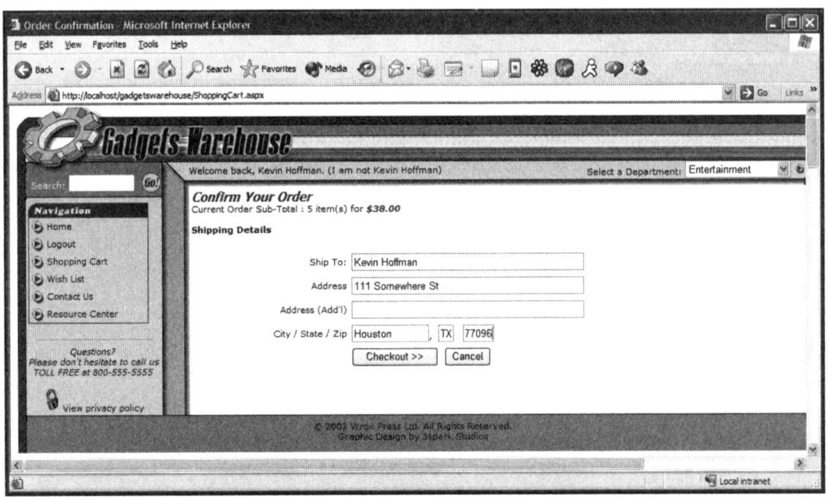

Finalcheckout.aspx

The `FinalCheckout` page is responsible for displaying the final order as it will be sent to the fulfillment system. Here the user will see their order items, discounts, coupons, and the shipping address. This is also their last chance to cancel the order. If they click Complete Order, the order will be recorded and sent to the fulfillment system. Here is the source code to the `FinalCheckout.aspx` page without the redundant UI elements:

```
<tr>
  <td width="100" align="right" valign="top">
  <b>Ship To:</b>
</td>
<td valign="top">
  <asp:Label id="lblShipTo" runat="server">Label</asp:Label><BR>
</td>
</tr>
</table>
<br>
<asp:Panel ID="pnlFinalCheckout" Runat="server">
  <asp:DataGrid id="dgOrderItems" runat="server"
                BorderStyle="Solid" BorderWidth="1px"
                BorderColor="Black" GridLines="None"
                AutoGenerateColumns="False" CellPadding="3"
                width="100%" ShowFooter="True">
    <HeaderStyle Font-Bold="True" BackColor="PaleGoldenrod"></HeaderStyle>
    <FooterStyle BackColor="PaleGoldenrod"></FooterStyle>
    <Columns>
      <asp:BoundColumn DataField="SKU" HeaderText="SKU">
        <HeaderStyle HorizontalAlign="Center" Width="100px"></HeaderStyle>
        <ItemStyle HorizontalAlign="Center" Width="100px"></ItemStyle>
      </asp:BoundColumn>
      <asp:TemplateColumn HeaderText="Item">
        <HeaderStyle width="400px"></HeaderStyle>
        <ItemStyle Width="400px"></ItemStyle>
        <ItemTemplate>
          <%# DisplayItemDescription(
                    (bool)DataBinder.Eval(Container.DataItem, "Special"),
          (string)DataBinder.Eval(Container.DataItem, "ItemDescription"))%>
        </ItemTemplate>
      </asp:TemplateColumn>
      <asp:BoundColumn DataField="Quantity" HeaderText="Quantity">
        <HeaderStyle HorizontalAlign="Center" Width="50px"></HeaderStyle>
        <ItemStyle HorizontalAlign="Center" Width="50px"></ItemStyle>
      </asp:BoundColumn>
      <asp:TemplateColumn HeaderText="Amount">
        <HeaderStyle HorizontalAlign="Center" Width="80px"></HeaderStyle>
        <ItemStyle Font-Bold="True" HorizontalAlign="Center"
                   ForeColor="Maroon" Width="80px"></ItemStyle>
        <ItemTemplate>
         <%# DataBinder.Eval( Container.DataItem,"AdjustedPrice", "{0:c}")%>
        </ItemTemplate>
        <FooterStyle Font-Bold="True" ForeColor="Maroon"
                     BackColor="PaleGoldenrod" HorizontalAlign="Center"
                     Width="80px"></FooterStyle>
        <FooterTemplate>
          <%# DisplayFinalCost() %>
        </FooterTemplate>
      </asp:TemplateColumn>
    </Columns>
  </asp:DataGrid>
  <BR>
  <asp:Button id="btnComplete" Runat="server"
```

```
            Text="Complete Order >>"></asp:Button>
</asp:Panel>
<asp:Label ID="lblFinalSummary" runat="server" Visible="False">
Your order has been submitted to our fulfillment department. You will be able to
see your order status once the fulfillment department has begun your order
processing.</asp:Label>
```

FinalCheckout.aspx.cs

Now here is the code-behind class for `FinalCheckout.aspx.cs`, which is essentially just an intermediate page that is used to display the order itself before it is submitted to the fulfillment backend. Keep in mind that the user cannot get to this page without having been authenticated because it is secured as a location in our `web.config` file.

```
using System;
using System.Collections;
using System.ComponentModel;
using System.Data;
using System.Drawing;
using System.Web;
using System.Web.SessionState;
using System.Web.UI;
using System.Web.UI.WebControls;
using System.Web.UI.HtmlControls;

using System.Xml;
using System.Xml.Serialization;
using System.IO;

using GW.Web.OrdersClient;

namespace GW.Web
{
  public class FinalCheckout : System.Web.UI.Page
  {
    protected GW.Web.Checkout checkoutPage;
    protected System.Web.UI.WebControls.DataGrid dgOrderItems;
    protected System.Web.UI.WebControls.Label lblShipTo;
    protected System.Web.UI.WebControls.Panel pnlFinalCheckout;
    protected System.Web.UI.WebControls.Label lblFinalSummary;
    protected System.Web.UI.WebControls.Button btnComplete;
    protected Order currentOrder;

    private void Page_Load(object sender, System.EventArgs e)
    {
      if (!Page.IsPostBack)
      {
        Load_Data();
      }
    }
```

This next method is used to display to the user the final amount they're going to be billed, including all of their coupons, discounts, and products.

```
public string DisplayFinalCost()
{
  decimal finalTotal = 0;
  for (int i=0; i<currentOrder.OrderItems.Count; i++)
  {
    finalTotal +=
           ((OrderItem)currentOrder.OrderItems[i]).AdjustedPrice;
  }
  return string.Format("{0:c}", finalTotal);
}
```

This method is used so that when regular products are displayed in the order output, they are displayed in bold, while coupons and discounts are displayed in regular typeface.

```
public string DisplayItemDescription( bool special,
                                      string itemDescription )
{
  if (special)
    return itemDescription;
  else
    return "<B>" + itemDescription + "</B>";
}
```

Yet again, take note of the little bit of work we're doing to obtain the current instance of a single order and then serializing that order into `ViewState` so that the `PostBack` events for this page can have access to that data and not require a reference to the previous page.

```
public void Load_Data()
{
  checkoutPage = (GW.Web.Checkout)Context.Handler;
  currentOrder = checkoutPage.CurrentOrder;
  ViewState["CurrentOrder"] = currentOrder.ToXmlString();
  lblShipTo.Text = currentOrder.ShipTo + "<BR>";
  lblShipTo.Text += currentOrder.Address + "<BR>";
  if (currentOrder.Address2.Length > 0)
    lblShipTo.Text += currentOrder.Address2 + "<br>";
  lblShipTo.Text += currentOrder.City + ", " + currentOrder.State
                 + " " + currentOrder.Zip;

  dgOrderItems.DataSource = currentOrder.OrderItems;
  dgOrderItems.DataBind();
}

private void btnComplete_Click(object sender, System.EventArgs e)
{
  pnlFinalCheckout.Visible = false;

  XmlSerializer xs = new XmlSerializer( typeof(
                                GW.Web.OrdersClient.Order ));
  StringReader sr = new StringReader(
                          ViewState["CurrentOrder"].ToString() );
  currentOrder = (GW.Web.OrdersClient.Order)xs.Deserialize( sr );
```

```
        OrderClient oc = new OrderClient(
      System.Configuration.ConfigurationSettings.AppSettings["OrderQueue"] );
        oc.SubmitOrder( currentOrder );

        lblFinalSummary.Visible = true;
      }
    }
  }
```

Let's take a look at the `FinalCheckout.aspx` page output:

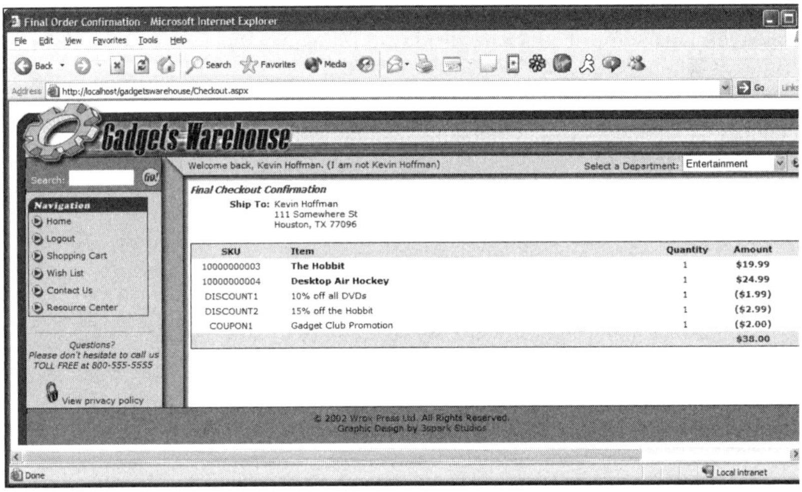

and after we submit this final checkout:

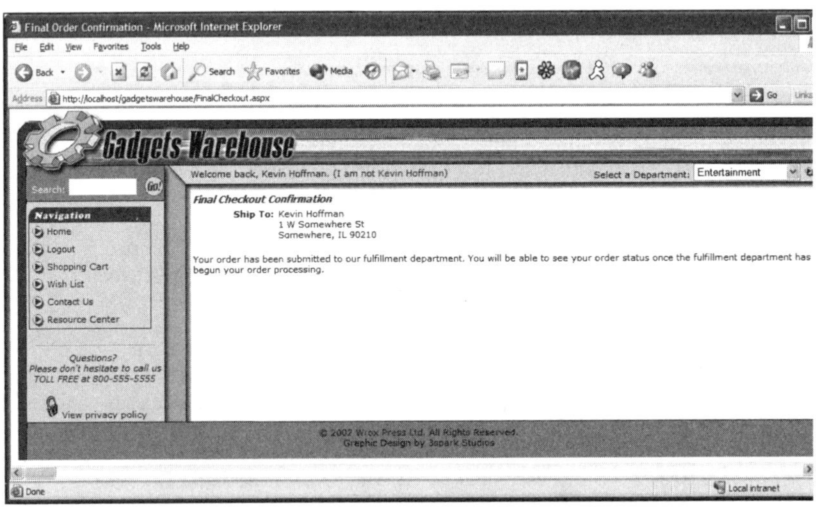

OrderHistory.aspx

In addition to being able to submit orders, customers have to be able to view their history. The OrderHistory.aspx page is secured in web.config via the <location> element, so only authenticated users are allowed to view it. The following page allows customers to view their history as well as click on a particular order and view a detailed list of all items on that order as well as a history of all status changes for that order. The display of order history will be contained in a DataGrid that is in a <div> tag with an overflow style attribute of auto. What this does is create the DataGrid within a scrollable IFRAME if the DataGrid output is bigger than the size of the <div> tag. This makes it so that we can see the *parent* rows all of the time while the detail information is also visible on the screen. We'll see an example of how this looks after looking at the code. Again, we've removed the redundant UI elements to make things easier to read:

```
<div style="BORDER-RIGHT:#000000 1px solid;
            BORDER-TOP:#000000 1px solid;
            OVERFLOW:auto;
            BORDER-LEFT:#000000 1px solid;
            WIDTH:752px; BORDER-BOTTOM:#000000 1px solid;
            HEIGHT:90px;BACKGROUND-COLOR:#e6dfbb">
<asp:DataGrid id="dgOrderHistory" runat="server"
              AutoGenerateColumns="False" Width="733px"
              CellSpacing="0" CellPadding="2"
              GridLines="horizontal" BorderColor="DarkBlue"
              BorderWidth="1">
  <SelectedItemStyle ForeColor="Black"   BackColor="#C0C0FF">
  </SelectedItemStyle>
  <AlternatingItemStyle BackColor="#EEEEEE"></AlternatingItemStyle>
  <ItemStyle BackColor="White"></ItemStyle>
  <HeaderStyle Font-Bold="True" BackColor="#E6DFBB"></HeaderStyle>
  <FooterStyle BackColor="#E6DFBB"></FooterStyle>
  <Columns>
  <asp:BoundColumn Visible="False" DataField="OrderId"></asp:BoundColumn>
    <asp:ButtonColumn Text="View" ButtonType="PushButton"
                      HeaderText="Details"
                      CommandName="Detail"></asp:ButtonColumn>
    <asp:TemplateColumn HeaderText="Shipped To">
      <HeaderStyle Width="450px"></HeaderStyle>
      <ItemStyle Width="450px" VerticalAlign="Top"></ItemStyle>
      <ItemTemplate>
        <%# DataBinder.Eval( Container.DataItem, "ShipTo") %>
        <br>
        <%# DisplayAddress( (System.Data.DataRowView) Container.DataItem)%>
     </ItemTemplate>
    </asp:TemplateColumn>
    <asp:BoundColumn DataField="OrderDate" HeaderText="Order Date">
      <ItemStyle VerticalAlign="Top"></ItemStyle>
    </asp:BoundColumn>
    <asp:TemplateColumn HeaderText="Total">
      <HeaderStyle HorizontalAlign="Right"></HeaderStyle>
      <ItemStyle Font-Bold="True" HorizontalAlign="Right"
                 ForeColor="Maroon" VerticalAlign="Top"></ItemStyle>
      <ItemTemplate>
```

```
        <%# DataBinder.Eval( Container.DataItem, "Total", "{0:c}" ) %>
      </ItemTemplate>
    </asp:TemplateColumn>
  </Columns>
</asp:DataGrid>
</div>
<asp:Panel ID="pnlDetail" Runat="server">
<HR width="100%" color="maroon" SIZE="1">
<FONT face="Tahoma" color="maroon" size="2">
<B><I>Order Status</I></B></FONT><BR>
<BR>
<asp:DataGrid id="dgStatusChanges" runat="server"
     AutoGenerateColumns="False" Width="750px"
     BorderColor="darkblue" BorderWidth="1"
     GridLines="Horizontal" Cellpadding="2">
  <Columns>
    <asp:BoundColumn DataField="StatusDate" HeaderText="Date"
                     HeaderStyle-HorizontalAlign="Center"
                     ItemStyle-HorizontalAlign="Center"
                     ItemStyle-Width="150px"
                     HeaderStyle-Width="150px"
                     HeaderStyle-Font-Bold="True"></asp:BoundColumn>
    <asp:BoundColumn DataField="CodeDescription" HeaderText="Status"
                     HeaderStyle-HorizontalAlign="Center"
                     ItemStyle-HorizontalAlign="Center"
                     Itemstyle-width="150px"
                     HeaderStyle-Width="150px"
                     HeaderStyle-Font-Bold="True"
                     ItemStyle-Font-Bold="True"></asp:BoundColumn>
    <asp:BoundColumn DataField="StatusMessage" HeaderText="Information"
                     HeaderStyle-HorizontalAlign="Left"
                     ItemStyle-Width="450px"
                     HeaderStyle-Width="450px"></asp:BoundColumn>
  </Columns>
</asp:DataGrid>
<BR>
<FONT face="Tahoma" color="maroon" size="2">
<B><I>Order Items</I></B></FONT><BR>
<BR>
<asp:DataGrid id="dgOrderItems" runat="server"
              AutoGenerateColumns="False" BorderWidth="1"
              BorderColor="darkblue" GridLines="Horizontal"
              CellPadding="2" CellSpacing="0" Width="750px">
  <SelectedItemStyle ForeColor="Black" BackColor="#C0C0FF">
  </SelectedItemStyle>
  <AlternatingItemStyle BackColor="#EEEEEE"></AlternatingItemStyle>
  <ItemStyle BackColor="White"></ItemStyle>
  <HeaderStyle Font-Bold="True" BackColor="#E6DFBB"></HeaderStyle>
  <FooterStyle BackColor="#E6DFBB"></FooterStyle>
  <Columns>
    <asp:BoundColumn DataField="SKU" HeaderText="SKU"
                     ItemStyle-Width="80px"
                     HeaderStyle-Width="80px"></asp:BoundColumn>
    <asp:BoundColumn DataField="Quantity" HeaderText="Quantity"
                     ItemStyle-HorizontalAlign="Center"
```

```
                        HeaderStyle-Width="80px"
                        HeaderStyle-HorizontalAlign="Center"></asp:BoundColumn>
    <asp:TemplateColumn HeaderText="Final Price"
                        ItemStyle-ForeColor="Maroon"
                        ItemStyle-font-bold="True"
                        ItemStyle-Font-Name="Tahoma"
                        ItemStyle-Width="150px"
                        HeaderStyle-Width="150px"
                        ItemStyle-HorizontalAlign="Center"
                        HeaderStyle-HorizontalAlign="Center">
      <ItemTemplate>
        <%# DataBinder.Eval(Container.DataItem, "AdjustedPrice", "{0:c}") %>
      </ItemTemplate>
    </asp:TemplateColumn>
    <asp:TemplateColumn HeaderText="Description"
                        ItemStyle-Width="300px"
                        HeaderStyle-Width="440px">
      <ItemTemplate>
        <%# DisplayDescription((System.Data.DataRowView)Container.DataItem )%>
      </ItemTemplate>
    </asp:TemplateColumn>
  </Columns>
</asp:DataGrid>
```

OrderHistory.aspx.cs

Here is the code-behind class for our `OrderHistory` page, which contains the code necessary for allowing the user to select a parent row (`Order`) from the scrollable `DataGrid` and view a set of details (the order history) for that order:

```
using System;
using System.Collections;
using System.ComponentModel;
using System.Data;
using System.Drawing;
using System.Web;
using System.Web.SessionState;
using System.Web.UI;
using System.Web.UI.WebControls;
using System.Web.UI.HtmlControls;

using GW.Web.OrdersClient;

namespace GW.Web
{

  public class OrderHistory : System.Web.UI.Page
  {
    protected System.Web.UI.WebControls.Panel pnlDetail;
    protected System.Web.UI.WebControls.DataGrid dgOrderItems;
    protected System.Web.UI.WebControls.DataGrid dgStatusChanges;
    protected System.Web.UI.WebControls.DataGrid dgOrderHistory;
```

```
private void Page_Load(object sender, System.EventArgs e)
{
  pnlDetail.Visible = false;
  // Put user code to initialize the page here
  if (!Page.IsPostBack)
  {
    Load_Data();
  }
}
```

This method retrieves the user's entire order history (remember the two table `DataSet` from the `OrderClient` project?) and binds the parent table to the top grid.

```
private void Load_Data()
{
  OrderClient oc = new OrderClient();
  DataSet dsHistory = oc.GetOrderHistory( System.Convert.ToInt32(
                                            User.Identity.Name ) );
  dgOrderHistory.DataSource = dsHistory.Tables[0];
  dgOrderHistory.DataBind();
}
```

This method is used by the ASPX page to display the address to which an order was shipped as one formatted item rather than as multiple columns.

```
protected string DisplayAddress( DataRowView currentRow )
{
  string outString = (string)currentRow["Address"] + "<BR>";
  if ( (string)currentRow["Address2"] != "")
    outString += (string)currentRow["Address2"] + "<BR>";
  outString += (string)currentRow["City"] + ", " +
        (string)currentRow["State"] + " " + (string)currentRow["Zip"];
  return outString;
}
```

This next event handler method is called whenever the button is clicked on the parent grid to view the details of a particular order. It will invoke the `Load_Order_Details` method to populate the data in the bottom portion of the web page.

```
private void dgOrderHistory_ItemCommand(object source,
              System.Web.UI.WebControls.DataGridCommandEventArgs e)
{
  DataGridItem dgi = e.Item;
  dgOrderHistory.SelectedIndex = dgi.ItemIndex;
  Load_Data();
  Load_Order_Details( System.Convert.ToInt32( e.Item.Cells[0].Text ));
}
```

The `DisplayDescription` method is used to embolden regular products while leaving coupons and discounts in regular typeface.

```
protected string DisplayDescription( DataRowView currentRow )
{
  if ( (bool)currentRow["Special"] )
    return (string)currentRow["ItemDescription"];
  else
    return "<B>"  + (string)currentRow["ItemDescription"] + "</B>";
}
```

The Load_Order_Details method will retrieve the items and status change history for a particular order selected by the customer, and makes sure that the region of the web form that contains the order history detail will be visible and each DataGrid is bound.

```
private void Load_Order_Details( int orderId )
{
  OrderClient oc = new OrderClient();
  DataSet dsDetail = oc.GetOrderDetails( orderId );

  dgOrderItems.DataSource  = dsDetail.Tables["OrderItems"];
  dgStatusChanges.DataSource = dsDetail.Tables["OrderStatusItems"];
  dgOrderItems.DataBind();
  dgStatusChanges.DataBind();
  pnlDetail.Visible = true;
}


    }
  }
```

Now let's take a look at what this code produces for output:

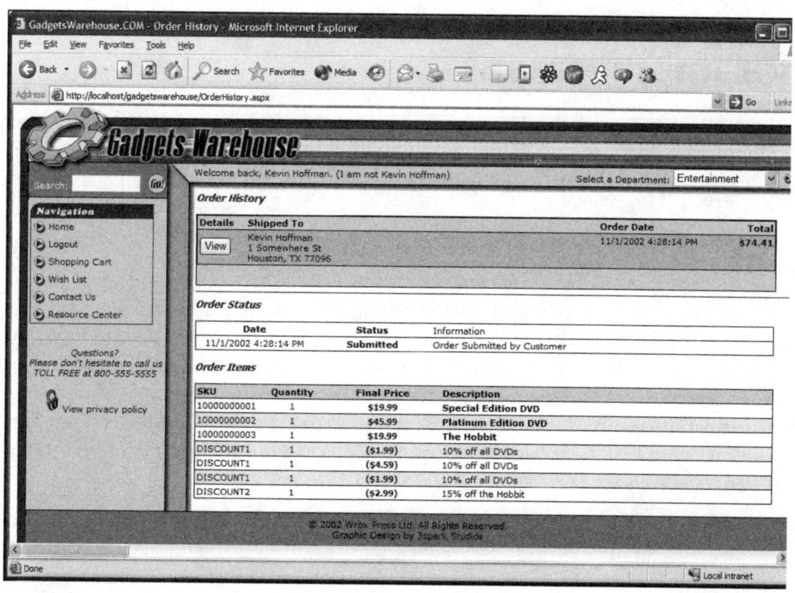

That is what the output looks like when we only have one order in our history, and the details of that order fit within the height attribute of our `<div>` tag. Let's see what it looks like when we have more than one order in our history:

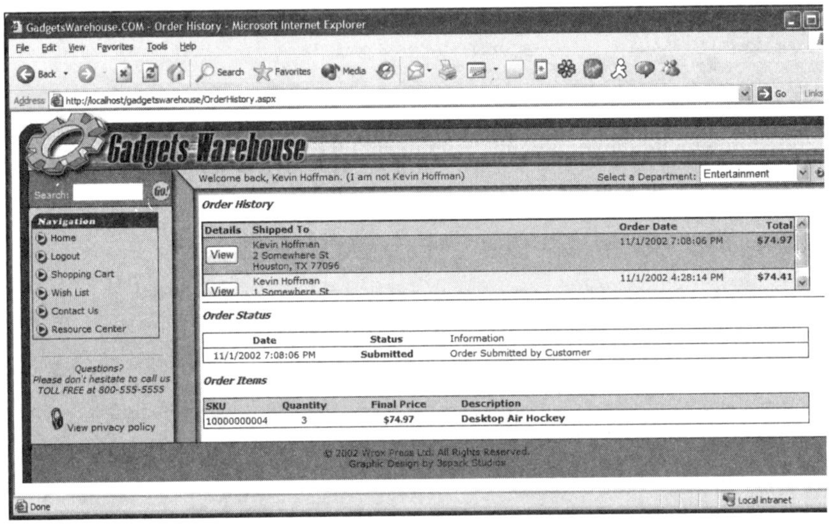

From the above, you can see that the list of orders in our history is embedded in the page in a scrollable `IFRAME` so that we can look at all of the details *and* see the selected item in the `DataGrid` and scroll. Clicking the View button brings up the order details that you see in the bottom half of the screen. If this page were viewed with a browser that doesn't support the `IFRAME` tag, then the top portion would appear in its entirety, making the user perform the scrolling on their own by scrolling the whole page.

Room for Improvement

The solution that we have proposed here in this chapter is sufficient, but it is far from perfect. Our goal with the code in this book is to show you how we implement *our* solutions to various problems associated with e-commerce website programming. Our solution is definitely not the only solution.

Fulfillment

Our fulfillment solution is basically vaporware. What we've done is create a framework that can be used to submit orders to a backend. We're working on the assumption that most people have back-end fulfillment systems in place, or they plan on using third-party tools or tools developed by other projects or teams. To facilitate these scenarios, we've loosely coupled our backend using Microsoft Message Queuing (MSMQ) to provide the most flexibility. Let's take a look at the MSMQ entries that are created by our order handling solution – you can view these by opening Computer Management from Administrative Tools in the Control Panel:

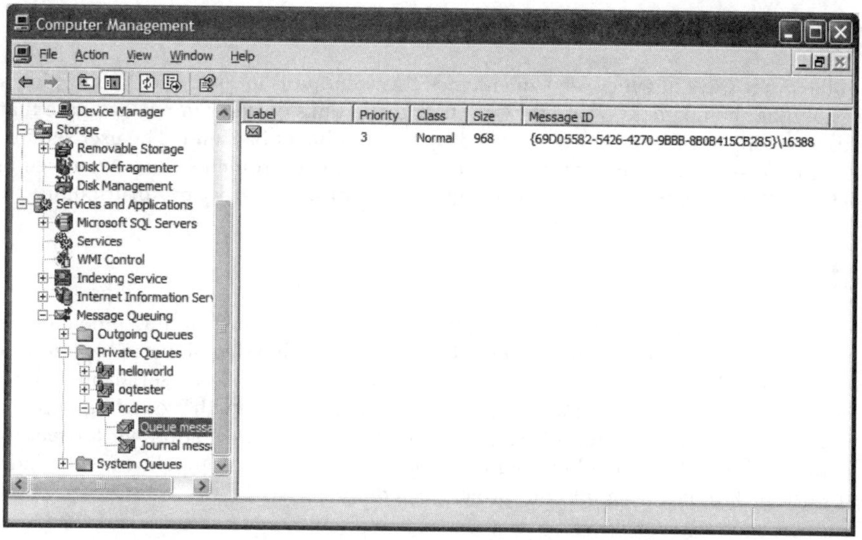

This screenshot shows an MSMQ called **orders** in the **Private Queues** section. You can see that there is an order sitting in the queue that was submitted as a result of the user completing the order pipeline. If we double-click that order, we can see the serialized XML output of the `Order` object sitting in the body of that message:

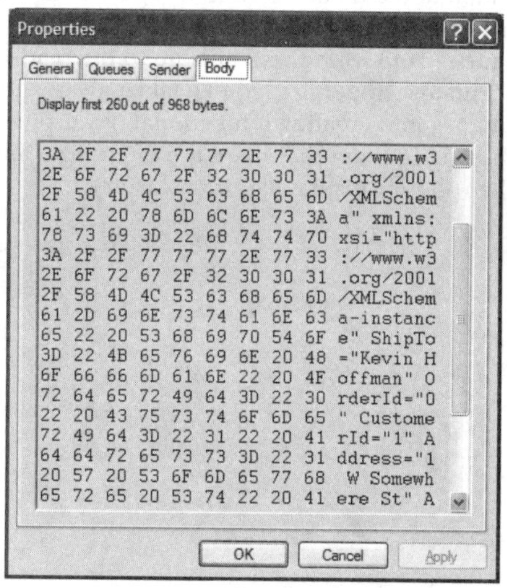

You can see the data in there that is our serialized order. In theory, there will be some process either on this machine or elsewhere connected to the MSMQ sub-system that will peel off these orders, store them locally, and keep track of updates. Each time something happens (such as an item coming in stock or an order shipping), the fulfillment system would then use the information (such as `OrderId`) contained in the order to post status change updates to the database. We didn't write this backend, but the code for it would be fairly simple and you can reuse our CMP data-tier and the MSMQ code from the `OrderClient` class to provide the backbone for such a fulfillment application.

Integrated Status

One of the other ways in which we can enhance this solution is to integrate the shipping and status services of other companies. We might want to provide links or fields in our database that contain UPS or FedEx tracking numbers that are supplied by the fulfillment backend. The user should be able to track the progress of packages that have been shipped so that problems can be resolved once the product has left the control of the website and the warhouse or third-party distributor.

Refactoring

Another thing that we noticed is that after building the entire order-handling pipeline, there was a large amount of code still residing in the presentation layer. After thinking about it, we found several places that we could combine into utility classes in our business tier, such as de-serializing the order class, or figuring out discount and coupon amounts and performing "sales math" rounding of percentages. All of that code could have been standardized and placed below the presentation tier for reusability and additional scalability. Perhaps when we need to go back to the order pipeline to add additional features we can work such re-factoring into our project schedule.

Summary

In this chapter we've had a look at the order pipeline and the process of turning a shopping cart into an order. After that, we had a look at the theory behind using asynchronous messaging systems such as MSMQ to communicate orders to a back-end fulfillment system. Our implementation ended at the writing of messages to the queue, and from there, it is up to the reader to write code that reads from the queue and performs status updates. Hopefully, you've taken away enough knowledge from this chapter to have a good idea of what goes into creating a functional order pipeline, fulfillment systems and displaying order history, keeping in mind that there are often legal and professional partnership requirements that dictate the rules for displaying order history.

CHAPTER 9

9

Community Building

If you ask a marketing or advertising person involved with commercial websites what the two most important things are to them, they'll tell you: getting new customers and retaining existing customers. Getting new customers is traditionally the job of the advertising and marketing people and programmers rarely have to worry about that kind of thing unless programming is required for an advertising campaign.

Making sure the customers keep coming back for more is something that programmers and site architects generally have a bit more control over. There are all kinds of things that you can do in order to make your customers want to come back, such as having good prices, or a good-looking, comfortable site with easy navigation; these are all things that generally fall under the umbrella of "user experience".

If the customer has a pleasant "user experience" then they will feel an attachment to your site that they might not feel with other sites. One thing you can do to create or enhance this experience is to provide a strong sense of community. This can be done any number of ways, and this chapter will talk about the problem of creating a sense of community, the GadgetsWarehouse.com design for building a community, and the source code for our implementation.

The Problem

The problem we're faced with is the need to create a strong sense of community for the customers of our web site. We need to make sure that there are enough features on the site that the customer wants to come back to make use of those features even if they're not necessarily looking to buy anything on that particular visit. However, we can't go too far, either. We need to make sure that we don't pile on so many features that the customer is overwhelmed and can't quite figure out what they should do with our site.

So, what exactly does a community for an e-commerce website look like?

Ratings

Ratings handling is actually a pretty broad subject. In short, what we're talking about is the customer's ability to supply some valued opinion about a product. Either they don't like a product, they do like a product, or they haven't expressed any interest in the product at all. A rating can result in something as simple as a number on a scale like 3 out of 5 stars, or it can be as complex as a preference engine that takes your interest in various products and uses that information to recommend products that you might like. Systems such as these are in place on some of the larger e-commerce sites like Amazon.com.

If we allow the customers to rate products, other customers can see those ratings and feel some kind of association with the other customers. It makes them feel as though they are part of a community joined by a common interest in products.

Reviews

Reviews are often coupled with ratings in terms of user interface, but they aren't the same thing. A rating is a simple numeric qualification for how much a customer likes a product. A review is a verbose description of that customer's opinion. It gives the customer a chance to explain to other customers *why* they rated a product the way they did. In general, if a system implements ratings, if will implement reviews, and vise versa.

By allowing the customers to voice their opinions you actually accomplish several things. First and foremost is that you are allowing your customers to give each other valuable information on products. Information supplied from a customer is generally trusted more than information supplied by a retailer. Another thing that it accomplishes is that it breaks down a barrier between you, the retailer, and them, the customer. By giving the customers the chance to interact with your site by posting their opinions of things, they feel that their opinion matters and that the people running your site might actually be watching and paying attention.

Discussions

Discussions go even further toward breaking down a barrier between the retailer and the customer. Discussions allow customers to freely converse with each other on your site. You are basically hosting their conversations. This goes further than just giving them the ability to review products and allows them to ask questions of other customers, respond to other customers' questions, and possibly even interact with staff members.

By allowing open discussions on your site, you are giving the users the opportunity to express themselves, and you're giving them the opportunity to communicate with other users on your site. This fosters a good sense of community on the site. In addition, by allowing customer discussion on your site, you are giving customers a reason to come back the next day. For example, if a customer posts a question on a particular discussion forum, they will be very likely to come back to your site to look and see if their question has been answered. Getting customers to come back to your site repeatedly even if they're not planning on buying anything does wonders for the livelihood of your site. If the customer comes back to check the forums and happens to see that something in their wish list has become available, they might just go ahead and buy that product and you might get additional revenue from your advertising partners that pay on a per-impression or per-click basis. Turning a community action into a sale is what everyone wants to see out of the community-building portion of your site.

The Design

The design for our community is two-fold. We're going to create a ratings and reviews system and a discussion system. Both of these systems will be centered on a product. Therefore, all discussions and reviews will revolve around products. First we'll take a look at the database design we need to support this system and then we'll take a look at some class diagrams of the code we think its going to take to get the job done.

We will not be allowing anonymous users to post reviews or discussions. We think this is excellent incentive for users to sign up and increase the size of the community. If a user without authentication wishes to contribute to the community, then they will have to become part of that community by registering a new account with the website.

Discussions

The discussions will all revolve around individual products. If you have been running any of the code provided in the previous chapters, then you have seen the navigation strip that provides customers with a web-based "tabbed dialog" style control. It allows them to switch between various views of data relating to one product. One of those views is the Discussions view. Customers will be able to add discussion messages to a particular product.

Reviews

Reviews are contained within another "tab" on the list of different product detail views, called "Ratings". Reviews and ratings have been combined into one feature. Therefore, when a customer reviews a product by supplying their opinion in a textbox, they will also be asked to supply a rating value to rank their satisfaction with the product.

The Database

The following is a diagram of the database tables we're going to be using for our community project:

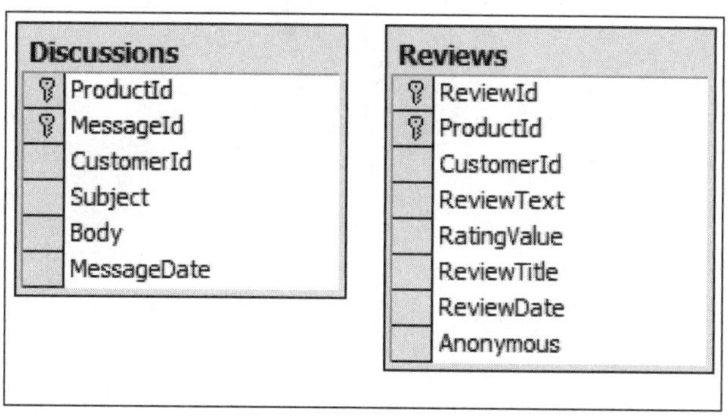

Discussions

The Discussions table holds all of the messages entered into discussion forums by the customers. In the traditional sense, discussions are separated into forums. Usually those forums are separated out into discussion threads. In our case, we don't actually have separate forums, and each thread of discussion is actually a single product. So, when someone adds to a discussion, they are adding to a discussion about a specific product. For an example of a more complete, and more generic, forum system, check out the previous book in this series, *Professional ASP.NET Website Programming – Problem – Design- Solution*, (Wrox Press ISBN 1-86100-693-4).

The information we're tracking about discussion messages is the customer who wrote the message, the subject, body, and the date the message was entered. Users without authentication are not allowed to contribute to any portion of the community, so they cannot write reviews or post messages in discussion forums. A production-ready system would also track the origin of the post, such as the IP address for security reasons.

Reviews

In our design, we're blending the concept of a review and a rating. Each time a customer writes a review on a product, they're also going to be supplying a rating value. This gives the customer the ability to express their like or dislike for a given product, as well as the opportunity to explain the reasoning behind their rating all on the same screen. It gives them the best of both worlds in the same page.

The information that we need to track on reviews is the ID of the customer supplying the review, the rating value, the text of the review, a title for the review, a date for the review, and the `anonymous` flag. The `anonymous` column is a bit flag that indicates whether or not the review is being posted anonymously. When a user posts a review anonymously, their real name will be hidden. Otherwise their name is attached to the review. Again, only authenticated users are allowed to participate in community features.

The Code

Now let's take a look at a class diagram of the classes that we're planning on creating.

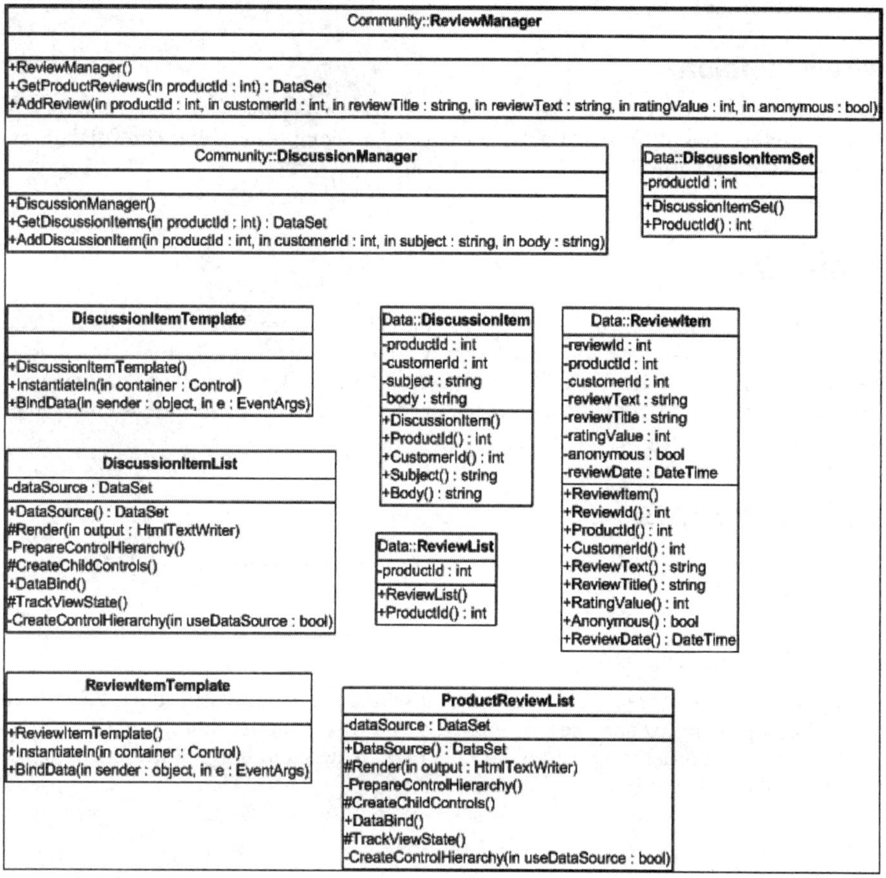

ReviewManager

The `ReviewManager` class provides all of the methods necessary for the presentation layer to handle reviews. It includes methods for retrieving a list of reviews and adding a new review to an existing product in the database. It does this using the persistence objects `ReviewItem` and `ReviewList`.

DiscussionManager

The `DiscussionManager` class provides all of the methods required to deal with discussions and discussion messages. It contains methods for selecting a list of discussion items that belong to a product as well as code to create new discussion items (messages). It does this through the `DiscussionItem` and `DiscussionItemSet` classes.

DiscussionItemTemplate

The `DiscussionItemTemplate` class is an `ITemplate` class that is responsible for rendering a single discussion message on the user interface. This class is used by the data-bound composite server control `DiscussionItemList`.

ReviewItemTemplate

The `ReviewItemTemplate` class is an `ITemplate` class that renders a review item on the user interface. This class is used by the `ProductReviewList` composite server control that renders all reviews associated with a product.

The Solution

As usual we'll start off our discussion of the solution with the stored procedures and the CMP metadata for our data tier. Then we'll talk about our main business component and finally the presentation tier. Our solution involves two pieces: reviews and discussions. Each of these items has its own "tab" on the product details listing so we'll be displaying the product pricing box and the product detail navigator on each of our pages.

Stored Procedures

The following is a list of the stored procedures we used for managing the data for our reviews and the product discussions.

Gw_Insert_DiscussionItem

This stored procedure will create a new message discussing a particular product. Each discussion item must consist of a product ID and the customer ID, as well as a subject and body. We want to keep the subjects fairly small in order to make the UI able to scale down to some of the smaller resolutions that might be present on laptops or set-top Web browsers.

```
CREATE PROCEDURE Gw_Insert_DiscussionItem
  @ProductId int,
  @CustomerId int,
  @Subject varchar(50),
  @Body text
AS
  INSERT INTO Discussions(ProductId, CustomerId, Subject, Body)
  VALUES(@ProductId, @CustomerId, @Subject, @Body)
GO
```

Gw_Select_ProductDiscussionItems

This stored procedure will retrieve all of the discussion items relating to a given product. It will retrieve all of the information needed by the user interface controls and order the display from oldest to newest. For each of the discussion items in the database for the given product, we want to retrieve the full name as well as user ID for the customer who posted the item. In addition, we need the subject, body, message date, and the customer's personal forum icon.

```
CREATE PROCEDURE Gw_Select_ProductDiscussionItems
  @ProductId int
AS

  SELECT ProductId, MessageId, Discussions.CustomerId, Subject, Body,
         MessageDate, Customers.UserId, Customers.FirstName,
         Customers.LastName, Customers.ForumImage
  FROM Discussions INNER JOIN Customers
  ON Discussions.CustomerId = Customers.CustomerId
  WHERE ProductId = @ProductId
  ORDER BY MessageDate
GO
```

Gw_Insert_ReviewItem

This stored procedure creates a new product review.

```
CREATE PROCEDURE Gw_Insert_ReviewItem
  @ProductId int,
  @CustomerId int,
  @ReviewText varchar(4000),
  @RatingValue int,
  @ReviewTitle varchar(100),
  @Anonymous bit
AS
  INSERT INTO Reviews(ProductId, CustomerId, ReviewText, RatingValue,
                      ReviewTitle, Anonymous)
  VALUES(@ProductId, @CustomerId, @ReviewText, @RatingValue,
         @ReviewTitle, @Anonymous)
GO
```

Gw_Select_ProductReviews

This procedure will select all of the reviews associated with a particular product and display them in order of newest to oldest, and with the rating value from best to worst for items reviewed on the same date.

```
CREATE PROCEDURE Gw_Select_ProductReviews
  @ProductId int
AS
  SELECT r.ReviewId, r.ProductId, r.CustomerId, r.ReviewText,
         r.RatingValue, r.ReviewTitle, r.ReviewDate, r.Anonymous,
         c.UserId, c.FirstName, c.LastName
  FROM Reviews r INNER JOIN Customers c ON r.CustomerId = c.CustomerId
  WHERE r.ProductId = @ProductId
  ORDER BY r.ReviewDate DESC, r.RatingValue DESC
GO
```

CMP Metadata

The following is the XML metadata configuration for all of the stored procedures used in our community-building classes. In order to keep this section from becoming its own chapter, I'll cut out a lot of this and just show one example stored procedure definition:

```
<ContainerMapping>
<ContainerMappingId>ProductReviews</ContainerMappingId>
<ContainedClass>ReviewList</ContainedClass>
<Select>
  <CommandName>Gw_Select_ProductReviews</CommandName>
  <Parameter>
    <ClassMember>ProductId</ClassMember>
    <ParameterName>@ProductId</ParameterName>
    <DbTypeHint>Int</DbTypeHint>
    <ParamDirection>Input</ParamDirection>
    <Size>4</Size>
  </Parameter>
</Select>
</ContainerMapping>
```

The Community Project

To manage our reviews and discussions, we're going to create a C# Class Library project called `Community`, and we'll add it to our main solution. We'll set the default namespace and output filename to `GW.Web.Community`. Also, we'll remove most of the information from `AssemblyInfo.cs` and link to the `SharedAssemblyInfo.cs` file that has the strong-name information and version attribute as we've done in all of our previous Class Library projects.

DiscussionManager

The `DiscussionManager` class is responsible for all things relating to the management of discussion messages. It contains code to create a new discussion item and code to retrieve a list of discussion items for a given product from the database.

```
using System;
using System.Reflection;
using System.Diagnostics;
using System.Data;

using GW.CMPServices;
using GW.MonitorServices;
using GW.MonitorServices.Logging;

using GW.Web.Community.Data;

namespace GW.Web.Community
{
  /// <summary>
  /// Summary description for DiscussionManager.
  /// </summary>
  public class DiscussionManager
```

```
    {
      public DiscussionManager()
      {
      }
```

The following method is pretty straightforward. We're creating an instance of the `SqlPersistenceContainer`, setting the parameter/property on the `DiscussionItemSet` class, and calling `Select`.

```
      public DataSet GetDiscussionItems( int productId )
      {
        DiscussionItemSet dis = new DiscussionItemSet();
        dis.ProductId = productId;

        SqlPersistenceContainer spc = new SqlPersistenceContainer(
           CMPConfigurationHandler.ContainerMaps["ProductDiscussionItems"] );
        spc.Select( dis );
        dis.FinalizeData();
        return dis.ResultSet;
      }
```

This next method takes the required data as arguments and creates a new discussion item.

```
      public void AddDiscussionItem( int productId, int customerId,
                                     string subject, string body )
      {
        DiscussionItem di = new DiscussionItem();
        di.ProductId = productId;
        di.CustomerId = customerId;
        di.Subject = subject;
        di.Body = body;

        SqlPersistenceContainer spc = new SqlPersistenceContainer(
                  CMPConfigurationHandler.ContainerMaps["DiscussionItem"] );
        spc.Insert( di );
      }
    }
  }
```

ReviewManager

The `ReviewManager` class is responsible for all management tasks relating to product reviews and ratings. It contains methods for creating product reviews and for selecting product reviews from the database.

```
  using System;
  using System.Data;

  using GW.CMPServices;
  using GW.MonitorServices;
  using GW.MonitorServices.Logging;
```

```
using GW.Web.Community.Data;

namespace GW.Web.Community
{
  /// <summary>
  /// Summary description for ReviewManager.
  /// </summary>
  public class ReviewManager
  {
    public ReviewManager()
    {
    }
```

This next method retrieves a list of reviews from the database for a particular product. As we saw in the stored procedure definition above, the results will contain all of the information necessary to populate the UI controls for displaying product reviews.

```
    public DataSet GetProductReviews( int productId )
    {
      ReviewList rl = new ReviewList();
      rl.ProductId = productId;

      SqlPersistenceContainer spc = new SqlPersistenceContainer(
                 CMPConfigurationHandler.ContainerMaps["ProductReviews"] );
      spc.Select( rl );
      rl.FinalizeData();
      return rl.ResultSet;
    }
```

This next method will create a new product review. It takes all of the information that has been obtained from the website and from the input form and calls `Insert` on the `SqlPersistenceContainer` to invoke the `Gw_Insert_ReviewItem` stored procedure.

```
    public void AddReview( int productId, int customerId,
                           string reviewTitle, string reviewText,
                           int ratingValue, bool anonymous )
    {
      ReviewItem ri = new ReviewItem();

      ri.ProductId = productId;
      ri.CustomerId = customerId;
      ri.ReviewText = reviewText;
      ri.ReviewTitle = reviewTitle;
      ri.RatingValue = ratingValue;
      ri.Anonymous = anonymous;

      SqlPersistenceContainer spc = new SqlPersistenceContainer(
                    CMPConfigurationHandler.ContainerMaps["ReviewItem"] );
      spc.Insert( ri );
    }
  }
}
```

DiscussionItem

The `DiscussionItem` class is a `PersistableObject` representing a single discussion message.

```
using System;
using System.Data;
using GW.MonitorServices.Logging;
using GW.MonitorServices;
using GW.CMPServices;

namespace GW.Web.Community.Data
{
  /// <summary>
  /// Summary description for DiscussionItem.
  /// </summary>
  public class DiscussionItem : PersistableObject
  {
    private int productId;
    private int customerId;
    private string subject;
    private string body;

    public DiscussionItem()
    {
    }

    public int ProductId
    {
      get { return productId; }
      set { productId = value; }
    }

    public int CustomerId
    {
      get{ return customerId; }
      set { customerId = value; }
    }

    public string Subject
    {
      get { return subject; }
      set { subject = value; }
    }

    public string Body
    {
      get { return body; }
      set { body = value; }
    }
  }
}
```

ReviewList

The `ReviewList` is a `PersistableObjectSet` class that represents a list of product reviews returned from the database.

```
using System;
using System.Reflection;
using System.Diagnostics;

using GW.CMPServices;
using GW.MonitorServices;
using GW.MonitorServices.Logging;

namespace GW.Web.Community.Data
{
  /// <summary>
  /// Summary description for ReviewList.
  /// </summary>
  public class ReviewList : PersistableObjectSet
  {
    private int productId;

    public ReviewList()
    { }

    public int ProductId
    {
      get { return productId; }
      set { productId = value; }
    }
  }
}
```

ReviewItem

The `ReviewItem` class is a `PersistableObject` that represents a single product review.

```
using System;
using System.Reflection;
using System.Diagnostics;

using GW.CMPServices;
using GW.MonitorServices;
using GW.MonitorServices.Logging;

namespace GW.Web.Community.Data
{
  /// <summary>
  /// Summary description for ReviewItem.
  /// </summary>
  public class ReviewItem : PersistableObject
  {
    private int reviewId;
    private int productId;
```

```
private int customerId;
    private string reviewText;
    private string reviewTitle;
    private int ratingValue;
    private bool anonymous;
    private DateTime reviewDate;

    public ReviewItem()
    {
    }

    public int ReviewId
    {
      get { return reviewId; }
      set { reviewId = value; }
    }

    public int ProductId
    {
      get { return productId; }
      set { productId = value; }
    }

    public int CustomerId
    {
      get { return customerId; }
      set { customerId = value; }
    }

    public string ReviewText
    {
      get { return reviewText; }
      set { reviewText = value; }
    }

    public string ReviewTitle
    {
      get { return reviewTitle; }
      set { reviewTitle = value; }
    }

    public int RatingValue
    {
      get {return ratingValue; }
      set {ratingValue = value; }
    }

    public bool Anonymous
    {
      get { return anonymous; }
      set { anonymous = value; }
      }
    }
```

```
    public DateTime ReviewDate
    {
      get { return reviewDate; }
      set { reviewDate = value; }
    }
  }
}
```

DiscussionItemSet

The `DiscussionItemSet` class is a `PersistableObjectSet` class representing a result set containing discussion items.

```
using System;
using System.Data;

using GW.CMPServices;
using GW.MonitorServices;
using GW.MonitorServices.Logging;

namespace GW.Web.Community.Data
{
  /// <summary>
  /// Summary description for DiscussionItemSet.
  /// </summary>
  public class DiscussionItemSet : PersistableObjectSet
  {
    private int productId;

    public DiscussionItemSet()
    {
    }

    public int ProductId
    {
      get { return productId; }
      set { productId = value; }
    }
  }
}
```

Presentation Layer

This next section covers all of the classes for the various controls that we need in order to display product discussions and reviews to the users. We need server controls that display product reviews and discussion items. In addition to that, we're going to need template classes that control the display and rendering of a single product review or discussion item within a bound list of items.

DiscussionItemTemplate

The `DiscussionItemTemplate` class is responsible for providing the rendering code required to display a single discussion message within the context of the composite server control that displays discussions.

```
using System;
using System.Web;
using System.Web.UI;
using System.Web.UI.WebControls;
using System.ComponentModel;
using System.Collections;
using System.Diagnostics;
using System.Data;
using System.Drawing;
using System.Text;

namespace GW.Web.Community.Controls
{
  /// <summary>
  /// Summary description for ReviewItemTemplate.
  /// </summary>
  public class DiscussionItemTemplate : ITemplate
  {
    public DiscussionItemTemplate() { }
```

In the `InstantiateIn` method, we're going to create a generic placeholder for our rendered HTML text. To do this in the most efficient way possible, we'll use a `Literal`. We could use a `Label` but there is more overhead involved in using a `Label`, especially when all we need is something to which we can attach an event handler for the `DataBinding` event.

```
    public void InstantiateIn( Control container )
    {
      Literal l = new Literal();
      l.DataBinding += new EventHandler(this.BindData);
      container.Controls.Add( l );
    }
```

The `BindData` method is called when an instance of this template is bound to a row of data. The end result that we're looking for is a string of HTML to output within the context of the `DataList` in which this item template is being displayed. We have two options here: we can create a `StringBuilder` and build our HTML manually, or we can use instances of ASP.NET controls and allow them to supply their own rendering. While the latter option may seem more appealing, it doesn't gain us any advantages. For each of the controls, we'd have to disable view state, and we'd be using an extraordinary amount of extra variables and memory. We opted for creating our HTML manually, since nothing we're rendering needs to respond to server-side events, and nothing we're rendering needs to persist its own viewstate.

Each time we render an individual discussion item, we're going to be displaying it in a bordered table.

```
    public void BindData( object sender, EventArgs e)
    {
      Literal l = (Literal)sender;
      DataListItem container = (DataListItem)l.NamingContainer;
      DataRowView currentRowView = (DataRowView) container.DataItem;

      StringBuilder sb = new StringBuilder();
```

```
        sb.Append("<table width=\"100%\" border=\"0\" cellspacing=\"1\" " +
                                                        "cellpadding=\"0\">");
        sb.Append("<tr>");
        sb.Append("<td width=\"100\" valign=\"top\" align=\"middle\">");
        sb.AppendFormat("  <b>{0}</b>  <br><img " +
                        "src=\"{1}\" border=\"0\" alt=\"Avatar\">",
                         currentRowView["UserId"].ToString(),
                         currentRowView["ForumImage"]);
        sb.Append("</td>");
        sb.Append("<td valign=\"top\" width=\"100%\">");
        sb.AppendFormat("Posted: <b>{0}</b>   Subject: " +
                        "<b><i>{1}</b></i>\n",
                        System.Convert.ToDateTime(
                          currentRowView["MessageDate"]).ToString(),
                        currentRowView["Subject"]);
        sb.Append("<hr size=\"1\" color=\"#000000\" width=\"100%\">");
        sb.AppendFormat("{0}</td>", currentRowView["Body"]);
        sb.Append("</tr></table>");

        l.Text = sb.ToString();
      }

    }

  }
```

The above code that creates HTML will render a discussion item that looks like this:

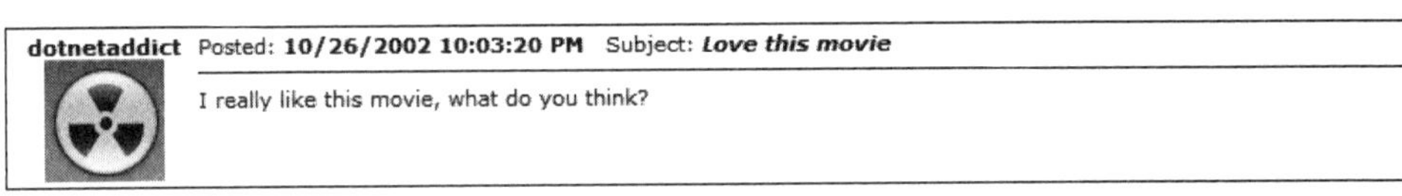

DiscussionItemList

The `DiscussionItemList` class is a composite server control that can be bound to a result set of discussion items. It will create the appropriate controls necessary to display a list of discussion items and use the appropriate template class for rendering an item. This is all accomplished by maintaining a `DataSource` property and an internal `DataList`. When the control is rendered the first time, it will bind the data source to its internal `DataList` and configure the `DataList` to render each item using an instance of the above template class. When the page is rendered via postback, the binding step is bypassed to allow the control to render itself from the viewstate.

Since you have already seen the template we're using for our server-side controls, we're going to skip right to the important method, `CreateControlHierarchy`.

```
    private void CreateControlHierarchy( bool useDataSource )
    {
      DataList dl = new DataList();
      dl.RepeatColumns = 1;
      dl.RepeatDirection = RepeatDirection.Vertical;
      dl.ID = "reviewList";
      dl.ItemTemplate = new DiscussionItemTemplate();
```

```
      dl.CellPadding = 2;
      dl.CellSpacing = 2;
      dl.ItemStyle.Width = new Unit(100, UnitType.Percentage);
      dl.ItemStyle.BorderStyle = BorderStyle.Solid;
      dl.ItemStyle.BorderColor = Color.Black;
      dl.ItemStyle.BorderWidth = new Unit(1, UnitType.Pixel);
      dl.AlternatingItemStyle.BackColor = Color.FromArgb(230, 223, 187);
      dl.Width = new Unit(100, UnitType.Percentage);

      Controls.Add( dl );

      if (useDataSource == true )
      {
        dl.DataSource = dataSource.Tables[0];
        dl.DataBind();
      }
    }
  }
}
```

ReviewItemTemplate

The `ReviewItemTemplate` class is an `ITemplate` class responsible for rending an individual review in the context of the `ProductReviewList` control. Like the previous template class, we're going to use manual HTML rendering to keep things quick and efficient. The `ReviewItemTemplate` will render itself in a bordered table. Within the table is the information for an invidual review, such as the rating, information on the reviewer (or the word Anonymous), and the text of the review. The rendered HTML looks like this:

```
using System;
using System.Web;
using System.Web.UI;
using System.Web.UI.WebControls;
using System.ComponentModel;
using System.Collections;
using System.Diagnostics;
using System.Data;
using System.Drawing;
using System.Text;

namespace GW.Web.Community.Controls
{
  /// <summary>
  /// Summary description for ReviewItemTemplate.
  /// </summary>
  public class ReviewItemTemplate : ITemplate
  {
    public ReviewItemTemplate() { }
```

```
    public void InstantiateIn( Control container)
    {
      Literal l = new Literal();
      l.DataBinding += new EventHandler(this.BindData);
      container.Controls.Add( l );
    }
```

The `BindData` method is called whenever an instance of this template is bound to a row of data. We'll take this row of data and convert it into a string of HTML representing the rendered output of a single item in the `DataList` that looks like the screenshot shown above.

```
    public void BindData( object sender, EventArgs e)
    {
      Literal l = (Literal)sender;
      DataListItem container = (DataListItem)l.NamingContainer;
      DataRowView currentRowView = (DataRowView) container.DataItem;

      StringBuilder sb = new StringBuilder();

      int ratingValue = System.Convert.ToInt32(
                                    currentRowView["RatingValue"] );
      bool anonymous = System.Convert.ToBoolean(
                                      currentRowView["Anonymous"] );
      DateTime dateReviewed = System.Convert.ToDateTime(
                                      currentRowView["ReviewDate"] );
      for (int i=0; i<ratingValue; i++)
      {
        sb.Append("<img src=\"images/litgear.gif\" " +
                               "align=\"absmiddle\" alt=\"Gear\">");
      }
      if (ratingValue < 5)
      {
        for (int j=0; j< (5-ratingValue); j++)
        {
          sb.Append("<img src=\"images/dimgear.gif\" " +
                               "align=\"absmiddle\" alt=\"Gear\">");
        }
      }


      sb.AppendFormat("  <b>{0}</b>, {1}",
        currentRowView["ReviewTitle"], dateReviewed.ToShortDateString() );

      sb.AppendFormat("\n<br>Reviewer: <b>{0}</b>",
                      anonymous ? "<i>Anonymous</i>" :
                      currentRowView["FirstName"].ToString() + " " +
                      currentRowView["LastName"].ToString() );

      sb.AppendFormat("\n<br><br>{0}<br><br>",
                      currentRowView["ReviewText"]);

      l.Text = sb.ToString();
    }
  }

  }
```

ProductReviewList

The ProductReviewList control is a composite server control that renders a list of product reviews. Because it is bound to an external data source, like all of our composite server controls, it can be used in any situation so that if we need to expand in the future we have a good chance of being able to reuse this control and others like it. As usual, we'll skip through the parts of the class that are part of our control template and skip to the method that does all the work:

```
        private void CreateControlHierarchy ( bool useDataSource )
        {
          DataList dl = new DataList();
          dl.RepeatColumns = 1;
          dl.RepeatDirection = RepeatDirection.Vertical;
          dl.ID = "reviewList";
          dl.ItemTemplate = new ReviewItemTemplate();
          dl.CellPadding = 2;
          dl.CellSpacing = 2;
          dl.ItemStyle.Width = new Unit(750, UnitType.Pixel);
          dl.ItemStyle.BorderStyle = BorderStyle.Solid;
          dl.ItemStyle.BorderColor = Color.Black;
          dl.ItemStyle.BorderWidth = new Unit(1, UnitType.Pixel);
          dl.AlternatingItemStyle.BackColor = Color.FromArgb(230, 223, 187);
          dl.Width = new Unit(750, UnitType.Pixel);

          Controls.Add( dl );

          if (useDataSource == true )
          {
            dl.DataSource = dataSource.Tables[0];
            dl.DataBind();
          }
        }
    }
}
```

ASP.NET Pages

Now that we've got our Community assembly written, let's take a look at the code for our web pages.

ProductForum.aspx

The ProductForum.aspx page controls the display of discussion items belonging to a specific product. It contains the product review list server control that displays a list of product reviews for the current product. We'll cut out the HTML for the navigation interfaces that apply to all of our pages so we can skip right to the important section of the page – we'll see the completed page in a moment anyway:

```
<%@ Page language="c#" Codebehind="ProductForum.aspx.cs"
    AutoEventWireup="false" Inherits="GW.Web.ProductForum" %>
<asp:Hyperlink ID="lnkNewMessage" Runat="server"
               text="Post new Message...">
</asp:Hyperlink><br><br>
<GWC:DiscussionItemList id="discussionItems"
                        runat="Server"></GWC:DiscussionItemList>
```

ProductForum.aspx.cs

The following is the code for the code-behind class for the `ProductForum` page:

```
using System;
using System.Collections;
using System.ComponentModel;
using System.Data;
using System.Drawing;
using System.Web;
using System.Web.SessionState;
using System.Web.UI;
using System.Web.UI.WebControls;
using System.Web.UI.HtmlControls;

namespace GW.Web
{
  /// <summary>
  /// Summary description for ProductForum.
  /// </summary>
  public class ProductForum : System.Web.UI.Page
  {
    protected System.Web.UI.WebControls.Label lblProductName;
    protected System.Web.UI.WebControls.Label lblShortDesc;
    protected GW.Web.ProductCatalog.Controls.ProductPricingBox prodPricing;
    protected System.Web.UI.WebControls.Panel pnlPricing;
    protected GW.Web.Community.Controls.DiscussionItemList discussionItems;
    protected System.Web.UI.WebControls.HyperLink lnkNewMessage;

    private int productId;
```

The `Page_Load` method will grab the sub-category ID, category ID, and product ID from the request. We know that they're in the request because the only links to this page have this information in the URL. Using this information, we can create a URL to the `AddMessage.aspx` page that allows users to post new messages (if they're authenticated).

```
    private void Page_Load(object sender, System.EventArgs e)
    {
      int categoryId;
      int subCategoryId;

      categoryId = System.Convert.ToInt32(Request["CategoryId"]);
      if (Request["SubcategoryId"] != null)
        subCategoryId = System.Convert.ToInt32(Request["SubcategoryId"]);
      else
        subCategoryId = -1;

      productId = System.Convert.ToInt32( Request["ProductId"] );
      // Put user code to initialize the page here
      if (!Page.IsPostBack)
      {
        LoadData();
```

```
        }
        lnkNewMessage.NavigateUrl = string.Format(
          "AddMessage.aspx?ProductId={0}&CategoryId={1}&SubcategoryId={2}",
          productId, categoryId, subCategoryId );
    }
```

LoadData is responsible for invoking the DiscussionManager class to retrieve a list of discussions to display on the page and performing the initial data binding.

```
      private void LoadData()
      {

        ProductCatalog.Data.Product curProduct =
               ProductCatalog.ProductCatalog.GetProductDetails( productId );
        lblProductName.Text = curProduct.Name;
        lblShortDesc.Text = curProduct.ShortDescription;

        prodPricing.DataSource = curProduct.SKUs;
        prodPricing.DataBind();

        Community.DiscussionManager dm = new Community.DiscussionManager();
        DataSet messages = dm.GetDiscussionItems( productId );

        discussionItems.DataSource = messages;
        discussionItems.DataBind();
      }

  }
```

All of this code combines to create an output of product forum messages that looks something like this:

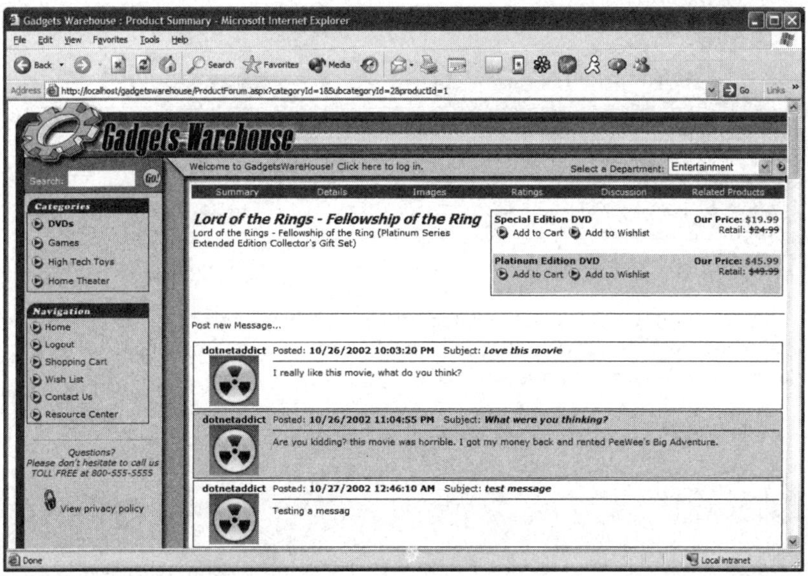

ProductRatings.aspx

The following code contains the HTML portion of the ProductRatings page. We'll just show the lines of code that include the server controls for displaying product ratings to keep things simple. All of the navigation and header/footer interface is the same as all other pages on the site.

```
<asp:HyperLink ID="lnkAddReview" Runat="server"
               Text="Write your own review...">&lt;/asp:HyperLink><br><br>
<GWC:ProductReviewList id="prodReviews" runat="server">
</GWC:ProductReviewList>
```

ProductRating.aspx.cs

The following is the source code listing for the code-behind class for the ProductRating page:

```
using System;
using System.Collections;
using System.ComponentModel;
using System.Data;
using System.Drawing;
using System.Web;
using System.Web.SessionState;
using System.Web.UI;
using System.Web.UI.WebControls;
using System.Web.UI.HtmlControls;

namespace GW.Web
{
  /// <summary>
  /// Summary description for ProductRatings.
  /// </summary>
  public class ProductRatings : System.Web.UI.Page
  {
    protected System.Web.UI.WebControls.Label lblProductName;
    protected System.Web.UI.WebControls.Label lblShortDesc;
    protected GW.Web.ProductCatalog.Controls.ProductPricingBox prodPricing;
    protected System.Web.UI.WebControls.Panel pnlPricing;
    protected GW.Web.Community.Controls.ProductReviewList prodReviews;
    protected System.Web.UI.WebControls.HyperLink lnkAddReview;
    private int productId;
```

The Page_Load method will retrieve the category and product information from the query string and use that to generate the URL required to add a product review. In addition, if the page has not been posted back, the LoadData method is invoked.

```
    private void Page_Load(object sender, System.EventArgs e)
    {
      int categoryId;
      int subCategoryId;

      categoryId = System.Convert.ToInt32(Request["CategoryId"]);
      if (Request["SubcategoryId"] != null)
```

```
        subCategoryId = System.Convert.ToInt32(Request["SubcategoryId"]);
      else
        subCategoryId = -1;

      productId = System.Convert.ToInt32( Request["ProductId"] );
      lnkAddReview.NavigateUrl = string.Format(
          "AddReview.aspx?ProductId={0}&CategoryId={1}&SubcategoryId={2}",
          productId, categoryId, subCategoryId );
      // Put user code to initialize the page here
      if (!Page.IsPostBack)
      {
        LoadData();
      }
    }

    private void LoadData()
    {
      ProductCatalog.Data.Product curProduct =
               ProductCatalog.ProductCatalog.GetProductDetails(productId );
      lblProductName.Text = curProduct.Name;
      lblShortDesc.Text = curProduct.ShortDescription;

      prodPricing.DataSource = curProduct.SKUs;
      prodPricing.DataBind();

      Community.ReviewManager rm = new Community.ReviewManager();
      DataSet productReviews = rm.GetProductReviews( productId );
      prodReviews.DataSource = productReviews;
prodReviews.DataBind();

    }

}
```

All of this code will produce output like this:

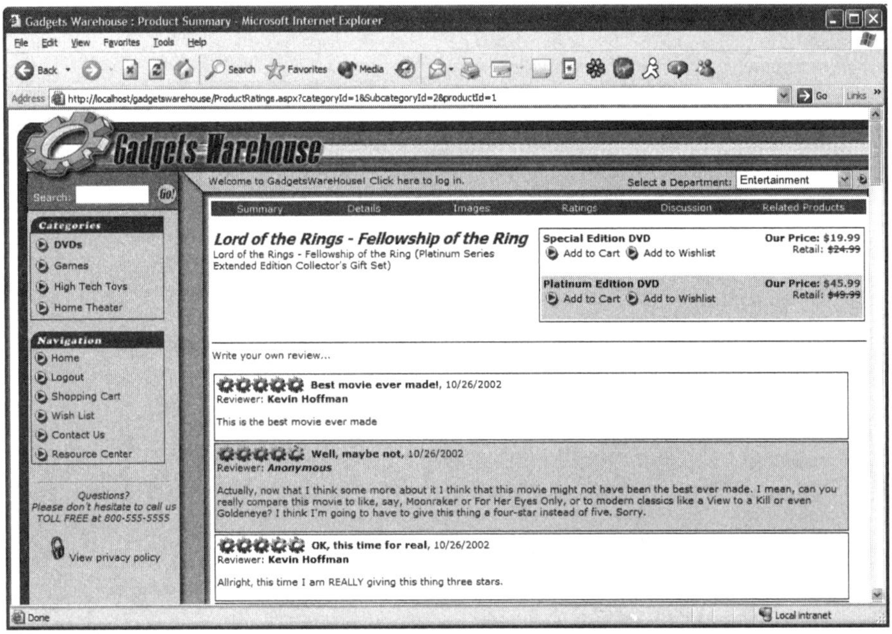

AddMessage.aspx

This is the code for the page that presents the user input form for adding a new discussion message. I've removed the redundant portions of the page:

```
<font color="Maroon" size="2" face="Tahoma">
<b><i>New Product Discussion Message:</i></b></font><br><br>
<table width="100%" border="0" cellspacing="2" cellpadding="1">
  <tr>
    <td width="100" align="right">Subject:</td>
    <td>
      <asp:TextBox ID="txtSubject" Runat="server"
                   size="50" MaxLength="50"></asp:TextBox>
    </td>
  </tr>
  <tr>
    <td align="right" valign="top">Message:</td>
    <td>
      <asp:TextBox ID="txtMessage" Runat="server"
                   width="400px" Height="100px"></asp:TextBox>
    </td>
  </tr>
  <tr>
    <td><br></td>
    <td>
      <asp:Button ID="btnSubmit" Runat="server"
                  Text="Submit"></asp:Button> 
      <asp:Button ID="btnCancel" Runat="server" Text="Cancel"></asp:Button>
```

AddMessage.aspx.cs

The following is the code-behind class for the `AddMessage` user input form page:

```
using System;
using System.Collections;
using System.ComponentModel;
using System.Data;
using System.Drawing;
using System.Web;
using System.Web.SessionState;
using System.Web.UI;
using System.Web.UI.WebControls;
using System.Web.UI.HtmlControls;

using GW.MonitorServices;
using GW.MonitorServices.Logging;
using GW.Web.ProductCatalog;

namespace GW.Web
{
  /// <summary>
  /// Summary description for AddMessage.
  /// </summary>
  public class AddMessage : System.Web.UI.Page
  {
    protected System.Web.UI.WebControls.Label lblProductName;
    protected System.Web.UI.WebControls.Label lblShortDesc;
    protected GW.Web.ProductCatalog.Controls.ProductPricingBox prodPricing;
    protected System.Web.UI.WebControls.TextBox txtSubject;
    protected System.Web.UI.WebControls.TextBox txtMessage;
    protected System.Web.UI.WebControls.Button btnSubmit;
    protected System.Web.UI.WebControls.Button btnCancel;

    int categoryId;
    int subCategoryId;
    int productId;
    int customerId;
```

The `Page_Load` method retrieves the category, subcategory, and product ID from the query string. These are needed to properly format the navigation interface as well as determine the product to which the new message will apply. The customer ID is obtained by converting the Forms Authentication user name to an integer. We don't need to perform an authentication check on the user here because our `web.config` file *requires* the user to be authenticated to view this page.

```
private void Page_Load(object sender, System.EventArgs e)
    {
      categoryId = System.Convert.ToInt32(Request["CategoryId"]);
      if (Request["SubcategoryId"] != null)
        subCategoryId = System.Convert.ToInt32(Request["SubcategoryId"]);
      else
        subCategoryId = -1;
      productId = System.Convert.ToInt32(Request["ProductId"]);
```

```
    customerId = System.Convert.ToInt32( User.Identity.Name );

    // Put user code to initialize the page here
    if (!Page.IsPostBack)
    {
      Load_Data();
    }
  }
```

The Load_Data method retrieves the current product from the database and populates the information in the product pricing box.

```
  private void Load_Data()
  {
    ProductCatalog.Data.Product curProduct =
            ProductCatalog.ProductCatalog.GetProductDetails( productId );
    lblProductName.Text = curProduct.Name;
    lblShortDesc.Text = curProduct.ShortDescription;

    prodPricing.DataSource = curProduct.SKUs;
    prodPricing.DataBind();

  }
```

This method responds to the Submit button. It will create a new discussion item and then perform the re-direct back to the original product view by invoking the Cancel button's event handler.

```
  private void btnSubmit_Click( object sender, EventArgs e )
  {
    Community.DiscussionManager dm = new Community.DiscussionManager();
    dm.AddDiscussionItem( productId, customerId, txtSubject.Text,
                          txtMessage.Text );
    btnCancel_Click( sender, e );
  }
```

The Cancel button's event handler will re-direct the user back to the product forum page from which they came.

```
  private void btnCancel_Click( object sender, EventArgs e )
  {
    Response.Redirect( string.Format(
      "ProductForum.aspx?ProductId={0}&CategoryId={1}&SubcategoryId={2}",
      productId, categoryId, subCategoryId ) );
  }

}
```

AddReview.aspx

The following is the code for the AddReview user input form. As usual, I'm only including the relevant portion of the HTML to render the page:

```
<table width="100%" border="0" cellspacing="2" cellpadding="2">
  <tr>
    <td width="250" align="right">
      How would you rate this product?:
    </td>
    <td>
      <asp:DropDownList ID="cboGears" Runat="server">
        <asp:ListItem Value="1">1</asp:ListItem>
        <asp:ListItem Value="2">2</asp:ListItem>
        <asp:ListItem Value="3">3</asp:ListItem>
        <asp:ListItem Value="4">4</asp:ListItem>
        <asp:ListItem Value="5">5</asp:ListItem>
      </asp:DropDownList> Gears. (1 = Worst, 5 = Best)
    </td>
  </tr>
  <tr>
    <td align="right">
      Post Review Anonymously
    </td>
    <td>
      <asp:CheckBox ID="chkAnonymous" Runat="server"></asp:CheckBox>
    </td>
  </tr>
  <tr>
    <td align="right">
      Enter a title for your review:
    </td>
    <td>
      <asp:TextBox id="txtTitle" Runat="server"
                   MaxLength="100" size="50"></asp:TextBox>
    </td>
  </tr>
  <tr>
    <td align="right" valign="top">
      Enter the text for your review:<br>
      <i>(4,000 characters max.)</i>
    </td>
    <td>
      <asp:TextBox id="txtReview" Height="100px" Runat="server"
                   MaxLength="4000" TextMode="MultiLine" Width="400px">
      </asp:TextBox>
    </td>
  </tr>
  <tr>
<td><br>
    </td>
    <td>
      <asp:Button ID="btnSubmit" Runat="server" Text="Submit Review">
      </asp:Button> <asp:Button ID="btnCancel" text="Cancel"
                                   Runat="server"></asp:Button>
```

AddReview.aspx.cs

The following is the code-behind class for the `AddReview` user input form page:

```
using System;
using System.Collections;
using System.ComponentModel;
using System.Data;
using System.Drawing;
using System.Web;
using System.Web.SessionState;
using System.Web.UI;
using System.Web.UI.WebControls;
using System.Web.UI.HtmlControls;

using GW.MonitorServices;
using GW.MonitorServices.Logging;
using GW.Web.ProductCatalog;
using GW.Web.Community;

namespace GW.Web
{
  /// <summary>
  /// Summary description for AddReview.
  /// </summary>
  public class AddReview : System.Web.UI.Page
  {
    protected System.Web.UI.WebControls.Label lblProductName;
    protected System.Web.UI.WebControls.Label lblShortDesc;
    protected GW.Web.ProductCatalog.Controls.ProductPricingBox prodPricing;
    protected System.Web.UI.WebControls.Button btnSubmit;
    protected System.Web.UI.WebControls.Button btnCancel;
    protected System.Web.UI.WebControls.DropDownList cboGears;
    protected System.Web.UI.WebControls.TextBox txtReview;
    protected System.Web.UI.WebControls.TextBox txtTitle;
    protected System.Web.UI.WebControls.CheckBox chkAnonymous;

    int categoryId;
    int subCategoryId;
    int productId;
```

The `Page_Load` method retrieves the usual query string parameters that are required for formatting the navigation user controls and the product ID on which the new review will be supplied. If the page is not a postback, the data will be loaded and bound. We don't need to check for user authentication here because our `web.config` file is set up to prevent anonymous access to this page.

```
    private void Page_Load(object sender, System.EventArgs e)
    {
      categoryId = System.Convert.ToInt32(Request["CategoryId"]);
      if (Request["SubcategoryId"] != null)
        subCategoryId = System.Convert.ToInt32(Request["SubcategoryId"]);
      else
```

```
        subCategoryId = -1;
      productId = System.Convert.ToInt32(Request["ProductId"]);

      // Put user code to initialize the page here
      if (!Page.IsPostBack)
      {
        Load_Data();
      }
    }

    private void Load_Data()
    {
      ProductCatalog.Data.Product curProduct =
ProductCatalog.ProductCatalog.GetProductDetails( productId );
      lblProductName.Text = curProduct.Name;
      lblShortDesc.Text = curProduct.ShortDescription;

      prodPricing.DataSource = curProduct.SKUs;
      prodPricing.DataBind();

    }
```

The **Cancel** button's event handler simply re-directs the user back to the page from which they came.

```
    private void btnCancel_Click(object sender, EventArgs e)
    {
     Response.Redirect( string.Format(
      "ProductRatings.aspx?ProductId={0}&CategoryId={1}&SubcategoryId={2}",
      productId, categoryId, subCategoryId ) );
    }
```

The **Submit** button's event handler will create a new review and then re-direct the user back to their original page by invoking the **Cancel** button's event handler.

```
    private void btnSubmit_Click(object sender, EventArgs e)
    {
      Community.ReviewManager rm = new Community.ReviewManager();
      rm.AddReview(
        productId,
        System.Convert.ToInt32( User.Identity.Name ),
        txtTitle.Text,
        txtReview.Text,
        System.Convert.ToInt32( cboGears.SelectedItem.Value ),
        chkAnonymous.Checked );
      btnCancel_Click( sender, e );
  }
    }
  }
```

Room for Improvement

There are a lot of interesting things that you can do to enhance the code in this chapter. For example, we implemented a very small discussion system where users can post and read messages, and that's about it. Full-featured forum management software allows users to customize their own signatures, avatars (personal icons), edit their own messages, perform searches, and do dozens of other things. There are forum software packages that have as much code as our entire site and then some.

The reviews also could use some improvement as a personal exercise for you when learning the code. You could modify them so that the user has the ability to see a list of all of the products they've reviewed. You could try to add a "my collections" type of interface where the user can rate products that they want differently from products that they already own. This could eventually end up providing background data for a recommendation engine to recommend products to customers. The possibilities are endless, and as long as you see that what we've provided is more of a starting block than an end point, you will be able to produce some truly robust, amazing results.

Another thing that might be a valuable exercise in expanding on the site is to create a user profile page. Typically, commerce websites will have a My Account page of some kind, where the customer can specify their preferences. In addition to being able to change their personal data, you might want to allow them to change their preferences for the community sections, such as customizing the icon that appears next to their posts and other display settings.

Our community system is fairly open. The discussion section is unmoderated, and reviews that users supply are directly placed on the website. This type of thing can lead to Internet vandalism where people submit offensive reviews and forum posts. To avoid that type of abuse of the site, you might want to add additional fields to the database and code to the administration site that allows for moderated discussion forums and reviews, requiring a member of the site staff to approve each of the reviews.

An addition that you could make to the `DiscussionManager` and `ReviewManager` classes is a profanity filter. By requiring the text being submitted for a new discussion item or review to be passed through such a filter, you could prevent quite a bit of abuse of the system before your staff would even have to review the item. Any new posts or reviews that failed the profanity filter would be rejected automatically and the user informed as to why.

Again, along the lines of protecting your site from abuse: you might want to consider preventing the customer from reviewing the same product twice. That kind of protection is fairly simple to code and would prevent a customer from overloading your system with reviews that would require hours and hours of extra time for the moderators on your staff to sift through.

Summary

This chapter was an effort to show you some of the issues tackled when creating a community-building solution. We took a look at some of the problems and aspects of community management, and then we took a look at the design for our reviews, ratings, and discussion forum solution. Finally, we took an extensive look at the source code for our reviews and discussions solutions. Hopefully, you now have a good idea of why it is important for site developers and designers to consider community development as well as how various aspects of community development can be designed and developed to provide a rich user experience for your customers.

CHAPTER 10

10

Affiliates and Partners

By now you probably have a good picture of what kinds of services and features your website is going to provide and why. The main reason for doing all of this is of course, to make money. You figure out your profit by subtracting your expenses from your earnings. It's obviously more complex than that, but that's the general idea. The main way of making money is selling products. You can sell more products by expanding the *reach* of your website, which grabs more customers.

This chapter is all about working with affiliates and creating partnerships. These things will expand the influence and reach of your website. Evidence of your website will be visible outside your site, allowing you to increase the number of potential visitors to your site. In this chapter we'll talk about the problems involved in creating affiliates and partnerships and the issues involved in dealing with them. Then we'll talk about the design we came up with to solve that problem, and finally we'll go through the code involved in handling our affiliate programs.

The Problem

The problem that we are faced with here is that we cannot underestimate the value of spreading out the reach of our website. We need our presence to be visible on more sites than just our own. While this can be done with pure advertising and banner ads, a more effective answer is by creating partnerships. There are literally millions of websites available for customers to choose from. If you are selling something as generic as "Gadgets" (as our fictitious website is), you might be lost in an infinite wasteland of keyword searches. For example, type the word "gadget" into a search engine and see how many hundreds of thousands of hits you see. Through the use of partnerships, your site can be reachable from more than one location, which increases the chances that people might stumble onto your own small piece of Internet real-estate.

What kinds of partnerships are there? While there really is an indefinite number of ways to arrange partnerships with other sites and companies, the following is a list of some of the more common ways of supporting partnerships.

Even Trade

An **even trade partnership** is where two sites agree to mutually support each other. This is generally the cheapest kind of partnership. Content sites will often enter into these kinds of partnerships by creating "web rings", where a host of related sites will all agree to post links to each other. Another type of even trade partnership is where a partner site will agree to funnel all traffic of a certain type to your site in exchange for you doing the same to them.

For example, assume that your website sells all kind of electronic gizmos but you don't sell batteries. Another site that sells nothing but batteries might be looking to form a partnership. You could arrange to direct your customers to the battery site after they finish checking out, while the battery site could direct their customers to your site after checking out with a batch of batteries. Both sites win in the arrangement, and as such, this kind of arrangement is either made for free or very cheaply. The only real maintenance task in an arrangement like this is that you might want to track the sales that originated from the other company's site. This is just a simple example, and doesn't necessarily mean that such "gadget and battery" partnerships actually exist. Typically, sites partner with other sites that do not sell similar products to avoid cross-competition.

Cross-Sells and Commissions

Another extremely common form of partnership is one where sales are referred to your site from another location. This is often referred to as a cross-sell or a *commission* sale. The reason for calling it a commission sale is that this arrangement is usually sealed by an agreement that will provide a kickback or commission to the referring site based on sales.

For example, let's say that we know of a content site called gadgetfan.com. It is a site for the gadget enthusiast, and it has a vast amount of content for gadget lovers. If we made our product catalog available in some way to that site, and we gave its users the ability to hit our site to buy the various products they might be displaying on their content site, we would definitely owe them something. Indeed, we would probably arrange to pay gadgetfan.com a certain percentage of all of the sales that are generated by customers coming to the site from gadgetfan.com.

This kind of traffic usually comes from content sites or SIG (Special Interest Group) sites. It is also possible to have partnerships with your own customers. Many sites provide the ability for customers to refer other customers to the site and earn small amounts of credit based on sales generated from those referrals. Amazon.com's partnership program accomplishes this and it has been very successful for it. It makes its customers happy, thus increasing the feeling of community and return visits. It also makes a bit of money for Amazon.com and gives its customers some useful discounts.

The Design

The design of our affiliate system is going to be fairly simple. Essentially, we're going to have two features: referrals and a Web Service. The referral system will allow affiliates to link into our site. Once they've linked to our website, we'll keep track of which affiliate and affiliate campaign the current user came from. This information will then be attached to the order so that we can track total sales for each affiliate and affiliate campaign. This gives us enough information to pay out the commissions we've contracted for. The Web Service is provided as a value-add for affiliates, giving them the ability to query our product catalog to enhance the content of their own site with live product information from our database.

Before we get started on the design, let's define some terms so we know what we're working with:

Affiliate

An affiliate is any single person or company that is affiliated with our site. This means that it could be a website, a group of websites owned by a parent company, a single person, one of our customers, virtually anyone. Each affiliate will have contact information that we'll need to maintain so that we can properly deal with contracts, commission payments, and (hopefully not all that often) collecting on overdue fees, payments, or defaulted contractual obligations.

Campaign

A campaign is just that. It is a single partnership or advertising campaign undertaken with a particular affiliate. The reason we need to maintain the campaigns is 90% legal and financial and 10% architectural. There are going to be many times throughout the life of our e-commerce site that we're going to have partnerships. Each of those partnerships will (hopefully) last a long time. For obvious reasons, we're going to want to be able to keep track of the difference in traffic between an affiliate referring sales for a particular movie, and an affiliate referring sales for some kind of holiday promotion, for example.

By using a campaign, we can set up a promotion with our affiliate that we can track individually. This promotion will have a specific "home" page on our site, either a category listing or a product detail page, or maybe even a custom page that we built specifically for a customer. Just because our site is flexible and scalable, we shouldn't be naïve enough to think that we're going to get away without custom-making pages for partnerships and advertising campaigns. The use of campaigns will allow us to see which of our affiliates are producing the most results, and which affiliates we might actually be losing money or business on.

It will be the unique identifier belonging to a particular campaign that will be placed in the order for us to keep track. From the campaign identifier we can link back up to a particular affiliate. Campaigns can be triggered by hitting a special campaign home page.

The Database

The database design should be pretty simple to accomplish. We need to add various tables to keep track of affiliates and affiliate campaigns. In addition, we need to modify the `Orders` table so that we can link an affiliate campaign with a specific order. If no affiliate campaign is active when the order takes place, a value of `-1` will be used for the `CampaignId` on the order.

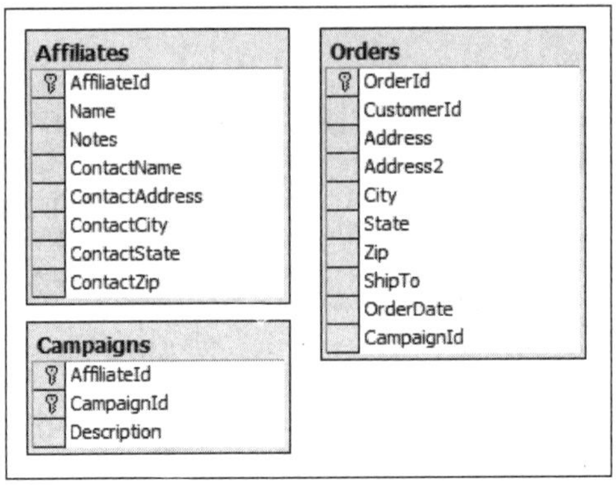

The Code

There are two separate pieces of code that we need to design: The affiliate management code and the Web Service. We're going to be providing a Web Service that will provide affiliates with the ability to access our product catalog and product search programmatically. The following is the class diagram for our `Affiliates` project:

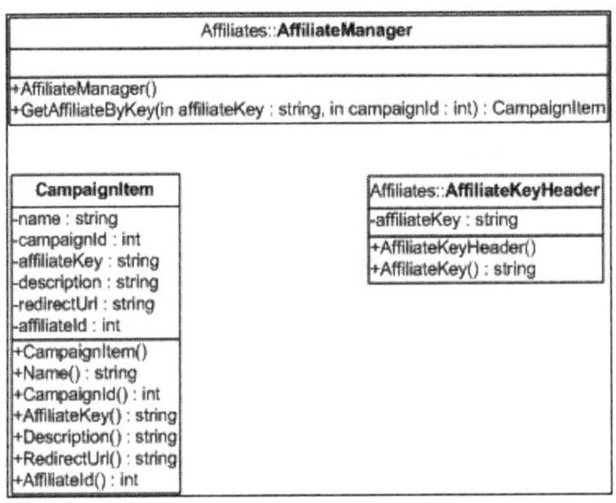

The Solution

Now that we've taken a look at the design for our affiliate solution, let's take a look at the source code we created for affiliate handling. Keep in mind that most of the hard work behind affiliate management is typically done by people other than the programmers. These people deal with working up the contracts, contacting potential affiliates, and generating the affiliate reports that let financial people make decisions on those affiliations. All that typically remains for us developers to do is to make sure that the affiliation code is there and it works. We simply need to do enough bookkeeping to keep the salespeople and legal types happy, and make sure they have access to the bookkeeping that we've been doing.

Before we get into the solution code, let's take a look at how it all gets put together. This next screenshot is a shot from a completely fictitious affiliate:

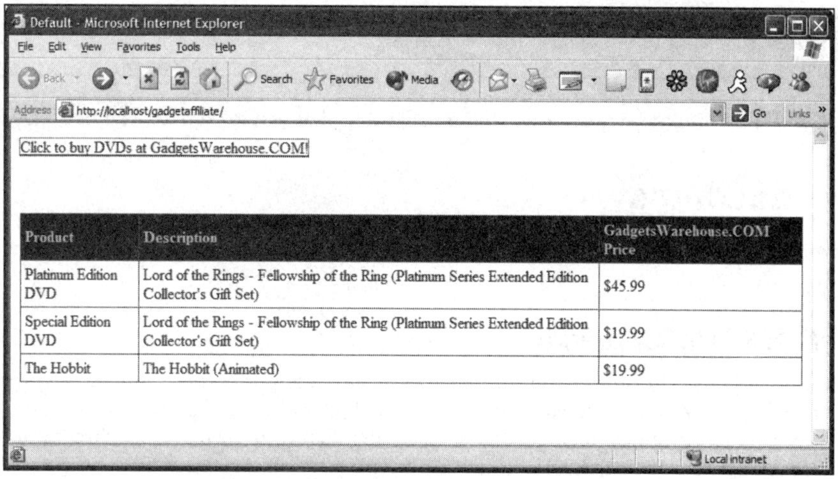

As you can see here, this affiliate not only has a link to our DVD section, but also can display the details of the product catalog within our DVD category, which it received through the Web Service we will be building.

When the customer clicks the link to buy DVDs from us, they are taken to `CampaignRedirector.aspx`, which stores the campaign of the affiliate link in a cookie so that it can be used in creating affiliate orders, and then redirects the user to the page indicated by the campaign. In our case, the user is then presented with the DVD category browse:

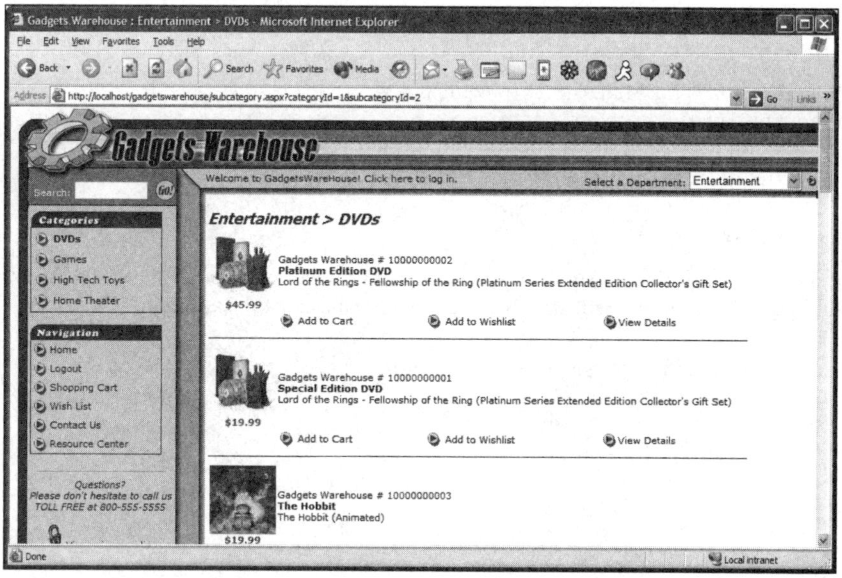

If we scroll down to the trace information, we can see that after having hit the `CampaignRedirector.aspx` page, we now have a new cookie:

Cookies Collection		
Name	**Value**	**Size**
ASP.NET_SessionId	gke0ubbtb1pd2a45a0qbip45	42
CampaignId	1	12

The campaign ID in this cookie is stored with our order if we happen to complete an order from this session.

Stored Procedures

The following is the list of stored procedures that we needed in order to get our affiliate re-direction home page to work:

Gw_Select_AffiliateCampaign

The `Gw_Select_AffiliateCampaign` procedure retrieves an individual campaign from the database based on the affiliate's key and the campaign ID. If the key and campaign ID are accurate, then the campaign information is returned so that the website can determine where to redirect the customer, and create the campaign cookie.

```
CREATE PROCEDURE Gw_Select_AffiliateCampaign
  @AffiliateKey varchar(50),
  @CampaignId int,
  @Name varchar(50) out,
  @Description varchar(50) out,
  @RedirectUrl varchar(500) out,
  @AffiliateId int out
AS

  SELECT @AffiliateId = a.AffiliateId, @Name = a.Name,
         @Description = c.Description, @RedirectUrl = c.RedirectUrl,
         a.AffiliateKey
  FROM Affiliates a INNER JOIN Campaigns c
  ON a.AffiliateId = c.AffiliateId
  WHERE a.AffiliateKey = @AffiliateKey AND c.CampaignId = @CampaignId
GO
```

Gw_Insert_Order

We've modified the insert order stored procedure to take a campaign identifier as an additional parameter. Unaffiliated orders will simply supply a `-1` value for the campaign ID.

```
CREATE PROCEDURE Gw_Insert_Order
  @CustomerId int,
  @Address varchar(100),
  @Address2 varchar(100),
  @City varchar(50),
  @State varchar(2),
  @Zip varchar(14),
  @ShipTo varchar(50),
  @CampaignId int,
  @OrderId int out
AS
  INSERT INTO Orders(CustomerId, Address, Address2, City, State,
```

```
                    Zip, ShipTo, CampaignId)
             VALUES(@CustomerId, @Address, @Address2, @City, @State,
                    @Zip, @ShipTo, @CampaignId)

   SET @OrderId = @@IDENTITY
GO
```

Affiliates CMP Metadata

The following is the CMP metadata for the `web.config` file for our affiliate campaign stored procedure.

```
<ContainerMapping>
  <ContainerMappingId>AffiliateCampaign</ContainerMappingId>
  <ContainedClass>CampaignItem</ContainedClass>
  <Select>
    <CommandName>Gw_Select_AffiliateCampaign</CommandName>
    <Parameter>
      <ClassMember>AffiliateKey</ClassMember>
      <ParameterName>@AffiliateKey</ParameterName>
      <DbTypeHint>Varchar</DbTypeHint>
      <ParamDirection>Input</ParamDirection>
      <Size>50</Size>
    </Parameter>
    <Parameter>
      <ClassMember>CampaignId</ClassMember>
      <ParameterName>@CampaignId</ParameterName>
      <DbTypeHint>Int</DbTypeHint>
      <ParamDirection>Input</ParamDirection>
      <Size>4</Size>
    </Parameter>
    <Parameter>
      <ClassMember>Name</ClassMember>
      <ParameterName>@Name</ParameterName>
      <DbTypeHint>Varchar</DbTypeHint>
      <ParamDirection>Output</ParamDirection>
      <Size>50</Size>
    </Parameter>
    <Parameter>
      <ClassMember>Description</ClassMember>
      <ParameterName>@Description</ParameterName>
      <DbTypeHint>Varchar</DbTypeHint>
      <ParamDirection>Output</ParamDirection>
      <Size>50</Size>
    </Parameter>
    <Parameter>
      <ClassMember>RedirectUrl</ClassMember>
      <ParameterName>@RedirectUrl</ParameterName>
      <DbTypeHint>Varchar</DbTypeHint>
      <ParamDirection>Output</ParamDirection>
      <Size>500</Size>
    </Parameter>
```

```
    <Parameter>
      <ClassMember>AffiliateId</ClassMember>
      <ParameterName>@AffiliateId</ParameterName>
      <DbTypeHint>Int</DbTypeHint>
      <ParamDirection>Output</ParamDirection>
      <Size>4</Size>
    </Parameter>
  </Select>
</ContainerMapping>
```

We also need to modify the CMP metadata for our insert order stored procedure. This is one of the main advantages of the CMP architecture – we don't have to do that much work to make changes to the existing system:

```
<ContainerMapping>
  <ContainerMappingId>Order</ContainerMappingId>
  <ContainedClass>Order</ContainedClass>
  <Insert>
    <CommandName>Gw_Insert_Order</CommandName>
    <Parameter>
      <ClassMember>CustomerId</ClassMember>
      <ParameterName>@CustomerId</ParameterName>
      <DbTypeHint>Int</DbTypeHint>
      <ParamDirection>Input</ParamDirection>
      <Size>4</Size>
    </Parameter>
    <Parameter>
      <ClassMember>Address</ClassMember>
      <ParameterName>@Address</ParameterName>
      <DbTypeHint>Varchar</DbTypeHint>
      <ParamDirection>Input</ParamDirection>
      <Size>100</Size>
    </Parameter>
    <Parameter>
      <ClassMember>Address2</ClassMember>
      <ParameterName>@Address2</ParameterName>
      <DbTypeHint>Varchar</DbTypeHint>
      <ParamDirection>Input</ParamDirection>
      <Size>100</Size>
    </Parameter>
    <Parameter>
      <ClassMember>City</ClassMember>
      <ParameterName>@City</ParameterName>
      <DbTypeHint>Varchar</DbTypeHint>
      <ParamDirection>Input</ParamDirection>
      <Size>50</Size>
    </Parameter>
    <Parameter>
      <ClassMember>State</ClassMember>
      <ParameterName>@State</ParameterName>
      <DbTypeHint>Varchar</DbTypeHint>
      <ParamDirection>Input</ParamDirection>
      <Size>2</Size>
```

```
      </Parameter>
      <Parameter>
        <ClassMember>Zip</ClassMember>
        <ParameterName>@Zip</ParameterName>
        <DbTypeHint>Varchar</DbTypeHint>
        <ParamDirection>Input</ParamDirection>
        <Size>14</Size>
      </Parameter>
      <Parameter>
        <ClassMember>ShipTo</ClassMember>
        <ParameterName>@ShipTo</ParameterName>
        <DbTypeHint>Varchar</DbTypeHint>
        <ParamDirection>Input</ParamDirection>
        <Size>50</Size>
      </Parameter>
      <Parameter>
        <ClassMember>CampaignId</ClassMember>
        <ParameterName>@CampaignId</ParameterName>
        <DbTypeHint>Int</DbTypeHint>
        <ParamDirection>Input</ParamDirection>
        <Size>4</Size>
      </Parameter>
      <Parameter>
        <ClassMember>OrderId</ClassMember>
        <ParameterName>@OrderId</ParameterName>
        <DbTypeHint>Int</DbTypeHint>
        <ParamDirection>Output</ParamDirection>
        <Size>4</Size>
      </Parameter>
    </Insert>
  </ContainerMapping>
```

The Affiliates Project

Next we created a C# Class Library called `Affiliates`. It has a default namespace of `GW.Web.Affiliates` and an output filename of `GW.Web.Affiliates`. As usual, we modified the `AssemblyInfo.cs` file to remove the version information and the key file data and *linked* to the `SharedAssemblyInfo.cs` file.

AffiliateManager

The `AffiliateManager` class is the main workhorse for the affiliate system. It is responsible for providing all of the interface methods required by the presentation tier.

```
using System;
using System.Data;
using System.Reflection;

using GW.CMPServices;
using GW.MonitorServices;
using GW.MonitorServices.Logging;
```

```
using GW.Web.Affiliates.Data;

namespace GW.Web.Affiliates
{
  public class AffiliateManager
  {
    public AffiliateManager()
    {
      // TODO: Add constructor logic here
    }
```

When an affiliate comes to our main redirection page, they will supply their affiliate key, not a numeric identifier. This is to prevent malicious people from "accidentally" supplying someone else's affiliate. If they can use numeric IDs, they can just pick random numbers and get in. Because our affiliate keys are GUIDs, it would take an intruder a considerable amount of time to randomly stumble on an affiliate key. This also explains the choice of `Varchar` for storing the type of affiliate key in the `Gw_Select_AffiliateCampaign` stored procedure, instead of a simple integer for this value. This next method retrieves an affiliate based on the affiliate key and campaign ID supplied to the campaign redirector.

```
    public CampaignItem GetAffiliateByKey( string affiliateKey,
                                           int campaignId )
    {
      SqlPersistenceContainer spc = new SqlPersistenceContainer(
            CMPConfigurationHandler.ContainerMaps["AffiliateCampaign"] );
      CampaignItem ci = new CampaignItem();
      ci.AffiliateKey = affiliateKey;
      ci.CampaignId = campaignId;
      spc.Select( ci );
      return ci;
    }
  }
}
```

CampaignItem

`CampaignItem` is a `PersistableObject` that represents the results of the campaign item selection stored procedure. It is used for single campaign retrieval operations.

```
using System;
using System.Data;
using System.Reflection;
using System.Diagnostics;

using GW.CMPServices;
using GW.MonitorServices;
using GW.MonitorServices.Logging;

namespace GW.Web.Affiliates.Data
{
  /// <summary>
  /// Summary description for CampaignItem.
  /// </summary>
```

```
  public class CampaignItem : PersistableObject
  {
    private string name;
    private int campaignId;
    private string affiliateKey;
    private string description;
    private string redirectUrl;
    private int affiliateId;

    public CampaignItem()
    {
      // TODO: Add constructor logic here
    }

    public string Name
    {
      get { return name; }
      set { name = value; }
    }

    public int CampaignId
    {
      get { return campaignId; }
      set { campaignId = value; }
    }

    public string AffiliateKey
    {
      get { return affiliateKey; }
      set{ affiliateKey = value; }
    }

    public string Description
    {
      get{ return description; }
      set{ description = value; }
    }

    public string RedirectUrl
    {
      get { return redirectUrl; }
      set { redirectUrl = value; }
    }

    public int AffiliateId
    {
      get { return affiliateId; }
      set { affiliateId = value; }
    }
  }
}
```

AffiliateKeyHeader

The `AffiliateKeyHeader` is a `SoapHeader` class that we need for the Web Service to retrieve the `affiliate` identifier from the SOAP header when Web Service methods are invoked. We use the information in the SOAP header to identify the affiliate that is requesting the operation. This allows us to identify the source of the request for an affiliate operation.

```
using System;
using System.Web;
using System.Web.Services;
using System.Web.Services.Protocols;

namespace GW.Web.Affiliates
{
  /// <summary>
  /// Summary description for AffiliateKeyHeader.
  /// </summary>
  public class AffiliateKeyHeader : SoapHeader
  {
    private string affiliateKey;

    public AffiliateKeyHeader()
    {
      // TODO: Add constructor logic here
    }

    public string AffiliateKey
    {
      get { return affiliateKey; }
      set { affiliateKey = value; }
    }
  }
}
```

CampaignRedirector.aspx

This is the almost-empty HTML portion of the campaign redirector. The campaign redirector is essentially a "portal" for campaign requests. An affiliate website might have a campaign set up where it provides a link to a particular category on our website. In order to track the fact that the link was from an affiliate campaign, rather than linking to our category home page (`Category.aspx`), they will provide a link to `CampaignRedirector.aspx` with the campaign ID and affiliate key. Based on the campaign ID and affiliate key, the redirector will redirect the customer to the appropriate page.

```
<%@ Page language="c#" Codebehind="CampaignRedirector.aspx.cs"
    AutoEventWireup="false" Inherits="GW.Web.CampaignRedirector" %>
<!DOCTYPE HTML PUBLIC "-//W3C//DTD HTML 4.0 Transitional//EN" >
<HTML>
  <HEAD>
    <title>CampaignRedirector</title>
    <meta name="GENERATOR" Content="Microsoft Visual Studio 7.0">
    <meta name="CODE_LANGUAGE" Content="C#">
    <meta name="vs_defaultClientScript" content="JavaScript">
```

```
    <meta name="vs_targetSchema"
          content="http://schemas.microsoft.com/intellisense/ie5">
  </HEAD>
  <body>
    <form id="CampaignRedirector" method="post" runat="server">
    </form>
  </body>
</HTML>
```

CampaignRedirector.aspx.cs

This is the code-behind class that is responsible for obtaining the campaign information from the database and redirecting the customer to the appropriate "home" page for the campaign. In addition, the campaign identifier will be written to a cookie.

```
using System;
using System.Collections;
using System.ComponentModel;
using System.Data;
using System.Drawing;
using System.Web;
using System.Web.SessionState;
using System.Web.UI;
using System.Web.UI.WebControls;
using System.Web.UI.HtmlControls;

using System.Diagnostics;
using System.Reflection;

using GW.Web.Affiliates;
using GW.Web.Affiliates.Data;
using GW.MonitorServices.Logging;
using GW.MonitorServices;

namespace GW.Web
{
  /// <summary>
  /// Summary description for CampaignRedirector.
  /// </summary>
  public class CampaignRedirector : System.Web.UI.Page
  {
    private void Page_Load(object sender, System.EventArgs e)
    {
      string affiliateKey;
      int campaignId;

      affiliateKey = Request["affiliateKey"];
      campaignId = System.Convert.ToInt32( Request["campaignId"] );
```

As we saw in the code for the affiliate manager, the `GetAffiliateByKey` method is used to retrieve an affiliate as long as the key and campaign ID are valid. If they are valid, then the campaign ID is written to a cookie (used for completing an order based on an affiliation) and the customer is then redirected to the appropriate page.

```
        AffiliateManager am = new AffiliateManager();
        CampaignItem ci = am.GetAffiliateByKey( affiliateKey, campaignId );
        GWTrace.Trace( TraceLevel.Verbose, "ci.AffiliateId : {0}",
                       ci.AffiliateId );

        Response.Cookies.Add( new HttpCookie("CampaignId",
                              campaignId.ToString() ) );

        Response.Redirect( ci.RedirectUrl );

      }

      #region Web Form Designer generated code
      override protected void OnInit(EventArgs e)
      {
        //
        // CODEGEN: This call is required by the ASP.NET Web Form Designer.
        //
        InitializeComponent();
        base.OnInit(e);
      }

      /// <summary>
      /// Required method for Designer support - do not modify
      /// the contents of this method with the code editor.
      /// </summary>
      private void InitializeComponent()
      {
        this.Load += new System.EventHandler(this.Page_Load);

      }
      #endregion
    }
  }
```

AffiliateService.asmx.cs

The following is the code that runs behind our simple affiliate Web Service. It allows affiliates to query our category list and run quick searches against our database. The main function of the affiliate code in this chapter is the redirector that we saw above, which will provide us with the functionality needed to track which orders originated from an affiliate campaign. As a value-add feature to enhance the experience of partnerships, we've made our product catalog browsing ability available programmatically to enable affiliate sites to display more detailed information about our products.

```
using System;
using System.Collections;
using System.ComponentModel;
using System.Data;
using System.Diagnostics;
using System.Web;
using System.Web.Services;
using System.Web.Services.Protocols;
```

```
using GW.MonitorServices;
using GW.MonitorServices.Logging;
using GW.CMPServices;

using GW.Web.Affiliates;
using GW.Web.ProductCatalog;
using GW.Web.Products;
using GW.Web.Wishlist;

namespace GW.Web
{
  /// <summary>
  /// Summary description for AffiliateService.
  /// </summary>
  [WebService(Namespace="http://www.gadgetswarehouse.com")]
  public class AffiliateService : System.Web.Services.WebService
  {
    public AffiliateKeyHeader affiliateKeyHeader;

    public AffiliateService()
    {
      //CODEGEN: This call is required by the ASP.NET Web Services Designer
      InitializeComponent();
    }

    #region Component Designer generated code

    //Required by the Web Services Designer
    private IContainer components = null;

    /// <summary>
    /// Required method for Designer support - do not modify
    /// the contents of this method with the code editor.
    /// </summary>
    private void InitializeComponent()
    {
    }

    /// <summary>
    /// Clean up any resources being used.
    /// </summary>
    protected override void Dispose( bool disposing )
    {
      if(disposing && components != null)
      {
        components.Dispose();
      }
      base.Dispose(disposing);
    }

    #endregion
```

By using the `SoapHeader` attribute here, we can retrieve the `AffiliateKey` from the `SOAP` header. If we wanted to expand the functionality of our service to log individual requests for information from our database, we could use the information in the SOAP header to attach that log of requests to the affiliates requesting the information.

```
      [WebMethod(false)]
      [SoapHeader("affiliateKeyHeader")]
      public DataSet GetProductCategories(  )
      {
        DataSet newData = new DataSet();

        newData.Merge( ProductCatalog.ProductCatalog.GetCategories() );
        return newData;
      }

      [WebMethod(false)]
      [SoapHeader("affiliateKeyHeader")]
      public DataSet GetProductBrowseList( int categoryId )
      {
        return ProductCatalog.ProductCatalog.GetProductBrowseList(
                                                              categoryId );
      }

      [WebMethod(false)]
      [SoapHeader("affiliateKeyHeader")]
      public DataSet QuickProductSearch( string searchKey )
      {
        return ProductCatalog.ProductCatalog.QuickSearch( searchKey );
      }
    }
  }
```

FinalCheckout.aspx.cs

As we mentioned before, in order for us to fulfill our contractual obligations with regards to affiliate campaigns, we need to make sure that we log all sales that originate from an affiliate site so that we can provide the affiliates with a report as well as any commissions that might be due them. We're going to do this by adding the `CampaignId` to the `Order` object as well as to the `Order` table and `Gw_Insert_Order` stored procedure. Below, we check the contents of the `CampaignId` cookie. If it exists, then we will record the campaign ID with the order, otherwise we will record the value `-1`.

```
  private void btnComplete_Click(object sender, System.EventArgs e)
  {
    pnlFinalCheckout.Visible = false;

    XmlSerializer xs = new XmlSerializer(
                                typeof( GW.Web.OrdersClient.Data.Order ));
    StringReader sr = new StringReader(ViewState["CurrentOrder"].ToString());
    currentOrder = (GW.Web.OrdersClient.Data.Order)xs.Deserialize( sr );

    if (Request.Cookies["CampaignId"] != null)
      currentOrder.CampaignId = System.Convert.ToInt32(
```

```
                                          Request.Cookies["CampaignId"].Value );
      else
        currentOrder.CampaignId = -1;

      OrderClient oc = new OrderClient(
        System.Configuration.ConfigurationSettings.AppSettings["OrderQueue"] );
      oc.SubmitOrder( currentOrder );

      lblFinalSummary.Visible = true;
    }
```

Sample Affiliate Client

The following code is a snippet from the code-behind class of the page we saw at the beginning of *The Solution* section. It is for a website that has a web reference to our affiliate service. This site is also listed in our affiliates table in the database, as it has its own affiliate key and has a campaign ID – both of these are required to make full use of our Web Service and `CampaignRedirector.aspx` page. The following is the listing of relevant code for the code-behind for the `default.aspx` page on the sample affiliate's website:

```
public class _Default : System.Web.UI.Page
{
protected System.Web.UI.WebControls.HyperLink lnkAffiliate;
protected System.Web.UI.WebControls.DataGrid dgProducts;

private void Page_Load(object sender, System.EventArgs e)
{
  // Put user code to initialize the page here
  if (!Page.IsPostBack)
  {
    LoadData();
  }
}
```

Here we are making use of the SOAP header that is required. We need to have this SOAP header populated so that the Web Service can keep track of the activity of the various affiliates. This way, our site can identify the most and least active affiliates, and which affiliates might be potentially abusing the system by using it far too often and impacting on our site's performance.

```
public void LoadData()
{
  gadgetswarehouse.AffiliateService svc = new
                                 gadgetswarehouse.AffiliateService();
  gadgetswarehouse.AffiliateKeyHeader keyHeader = new
                                 gadgetswarehouse.AffiliateKeyHeader();
  keyHeader.AffiliateKey =
  System.Configuration.ConfigurationSettings.AppSettings["GWAffiliateKey"];
  svc.AffiliateKeyHeaderValue = keyHeader;
```

Through previous uses of the Web Service and obtaining the list of categories, we know that the DVD category is ID #2. In a realistic scenario we would want to wrap this inside some error handling code since we are at the mercy of another company's database and that database's reliability.

```
    DataSet ds = svc.GetProductBrowseList( 2 );
    dgProducts.DataSource = ds;
    dgProducts.DataBind();

    lnkAffiliate.NavigateUrl = "http://localhost/gadgetswarehouse/" +
        "CampaignRedirector.aspx?AffiliateKey=" +
        keyHeader.AffiliateKey +    "&CampaignId=" +
        System.Configuration.ConfigurationSettings.AppSettings[
                                                "GWCampaignId"];
}
```

Room for Improvement

The implementation that we've created is fairly minimal. What we've done is provide a way to track the sales that are being generated as a result of partnership campaigns with other companies, websites, or even customers and other individuals. This gives us the ability to make our product catalog available to the affiliates, gives our affiliates the ability to search our product catalog, and the ability to link their marketing campaigns to a URL on our site so that we can track resulting sales.

We don't want to get ourselves into the business of creating reporting tools, but if we felt ambitious we could create some kind of report that is e-mailed to the various affiliates and our own financial departments at timed intervals to make things easier for everyone in the long run. Another thing we could do is provide a web page or some code that ranks the affiliates based on how much sales they produced in the past month, six months, or a year. This might be an excellent exercise, though the skills required are definitely more toward the SQL and DBA department than the .NET and C# area.

Another thing that we might do to improve the affiliate management system is provide something in the Web Service that allows affiliates to create their own campaigns. They could supply the URL they wanted the redirect to go to and they could supply a name for the campaign. The possibilities for expanding the affiliate system are plentiful, only limited by the time and resources you have or your company has.

Summary

This chapter was all about affiliates and partnerships. We discussed the importance of creating partnerships and alliances, and building affiliates to spread your website's presence across the web to give it more survivability, lasting power, and a larger visible amount of "real estate" usage. Then, we talked about our design for an affiliate management solution. After that, we took a look at the source code we used to implement our own design for an affiliate handling system. We saw how to implement some of the common tasks required for dealing with affiliates in an e-commerce scenario.

This chapter is also the last chapter that produces code that a customer will see. The next chapter, *Administration*, will show how to build a site administration system that can be used by programmers and managers alike.

CHAPTER 11

11

Administration

At this point, if you've downloaded and installed the sample code, you're probably looking at a fairly complete site right now. It allows customers to browse the product catalog, examine product details, put items in the cart and wish list, and has many other features. Up until this point, all of the data that has been driving the website has been manually entered either using SQL Enterprise Manager or using the Query Analyzer tool. You can also pre-load the website's database with the SQL Server 2000 database backup provided in the download package.

This chapter is all about administration. We'll take a look at the problem of creating an administration tool and the issues that are involved. Then we'll take a look at the design alternatives facing us when creating an administration tool and the design that we decided to implement. Finally, we'll walk you through the source code to our administration application.

The Problem

The problem here that we're trying to solve is the ability to administer and maintain the data that drives our application. Not everyone should have access to the database, and even those who do may not be able to reliably enter data directly into the database without causing enormous data integrity failures. This means that programmers or database administrators are typically the only people who are ever allowed to enter data directly into the database.

This is also not the best solution. Programmers are better off spending their time programming and not doing data entry. People who perform data entry tasks come far cheaper than programmers, so we want to be able to use data entry people or even temporary employees if need be to perform data entry. To do this, these people need some kind of application they can use in order to get data into the system in a secure, reliable way that enforces all of the rules and restrictions of our database. In addition to enforcing all of the appropriate rules, we need our application to be easy enough to use so that someone who has no experience with our particular line of work or our database (say, temporary employees or data entry clerks) can quickly learn the application and start entering data. We should be able to hand someone a page from a catalog or a link from a manufacturer's website and they should be able to use the information in front of them to enter data into our website.

We also need to make sure that whatever design we come up with will be sufficient in terms of security. We need to make sure that we deal with limiting access to the administration site, and how much we want to differentiate the abilities of individual administrative users.

The Design

It might seem like a fairly simple matter just to whip up an administration application for the various types of data we're maintaining in the application. Unfortunately, that is not the case. There are several different things that we need to decide on that make a drastic impact on the development of the application in general.

The first and foremost is security: how will we secure the application so that it won't "fall into the wrong hands"? The last thing you need is for a customer to get a hold of your administration application and change prices. Once you've secured the application so that only authorized personnel can use it, do you add more security within the application? For example, do you want your application to accept a username and a password so that each user of the application has a varying set of permissions?

The design for our administrative application is going to limit access through Windows authentication. By using Windows authentication, we can guarantee that the only people who even have a chance of getting into the website are those that are authenticated on our intranet in some way. This rules out an enormous portion of potential attackers. Secondly, we're going to require that any user attempting to use our website be part of a specific NT group. This gives us the ability to specifically choose which people on our corporate network will be allowed to use the system.

Once you've dealt with security as a design issue, you need to deal with location. It is possible to have the administration application reside somewhere else other than the main application server. This may in fact be the type of behavior you want from the application. Once you have decided on the location, you then need to decide on a platform: Are you going to use Remoting to communicate with your business objects? Are you going to use Web Services? Are you going to use ASP.NET or Windows Forms? All of these are questions you need to answer when you are building the design for your administration application.

Finally, one thing that we often forget about when we're in the artificial world of sample applications: time and money. How much time, money, resources, and effort can you spend working on this application? This will factor greatly into your design. It is not unheard of for administrative applications to take more time and resources to develop than the original application took. You'll need to figure out how to balance the tradeoff between administrative features and time spent working on those features by doing a cost-benefit analysis.

One thing that we need to consider in our design is the database. The business logic that we coded throughout the book was very much geared toward mostly read-only operations. For example, we didn't code anything that allows us to create new products, or categories, or create and modify coupons and discounts. While coding, we just assumed that this would be handled by some administration system. As a result, we don't have stored procedures or business methods for dealing with this type of data operation, and we'll need to make sure that we create those for our solution.

The following is an analysis of four of the main ways in which you can accomplish an administrative application designed to administer an ASP.NET website by reusing the website's business components. One thing you'll want to do here is talk to the network and IT administrators. In general, the method you're going to use for connecting to your administration site is going to be strongly influenced by the network configuration of firewalls, DMZs, routers, proxies, and more technical issues to which programmers generally don't have much exposure.

After we discuss the different kinds of designs available to us, we'll move on to the design we decided to go with.

Remoting

Our main goal in producing an administration application is to reuse the application's business tier. We want to do this so that we know that everything we do in the administration application will mimic as much as possible actions taken by a user. We also want to be able to see the same things users see when they perform queries against our database. The best way to do this is to make sure that we reuse not only the same stored procedures but the same business-tier code.

It is extremely tempting to utilizing Remoting to accomplish this. We could simply set up the business tier classes to be hosted by some Remoting host (either a console application, IIS, or a Windows service, etc.). By doing this, our application (either Windows Forms or ASP.NET) could remotely communicate with the application business tier to perform all of its tasks. The Remoting host would provide a point of entry for Remoting calls through a configuration file that contained references to the object instances being hosted.

The advantage here is that our administrative application can be anywhere so long as it has network access to the Remoting host. The disadvantage is that, depending on what we need to do, we might need to put some assemblies in the Global Assembly Cache to make them available to the Remoting system. Another thing we would need to take into account is security – we'd need to guarantee that our application and *only* our application could communicate with the business tier, and prevent intruders or potential hackers from imitating the behavior of the administrative UI and accessing the business tier directly. If would-be hackers were to figure out that we'd exposed some functionality via Remoting, they could write some classes to tamper with our database.

Local Windows Forms

The best way to get the most interactive and powerful user interface for any application is to use Windows Forms. By using Windows Forms, we can take advantage of quick, fast-responding UI features like tab pages, controls that re-populate when you change the values of other controls, and much more. This interface advantage also applies to a Remoting solution.

What makes the "Local" Windows Forms application different is that it references the application's business tier directly. This means that it must be installed on and run from the same machine on which the web application has been installed, or the entire business tier of the web application would need to be distributed to the client machine, and a "stub" created to load all of the CMP metadata from something other than the `web.config` file. This has both advantages and disadvantages.

One of the main advantages is security. You can tie the security of your application to the security of the machine on which the web application is running. In other words, you are free to worry about application features and can secure your application simply by making the physical location of your web server a secure location. Another advantage is speed. With the business tier residing directly on the same machine as the Windows-based user interface, the response time of the application should be quite good, and a large amount of quick-responding interactivity could be programmed that wouldn't be possible in other types of client applications.

This same fact also has a downside: access. By making the application run physically on the website, you either need to have physical access to the machine or you need to be able to use a tool like terminal services to get into the machine. Having physical access to a web server is sometimes tricky, as the actual machines are often located in remote data centers, nowhere near the office where the programmers and network administrators work. You also won't have physical access to a machine if you're using a third-party hosting company that provides customers with space and resources for a monthly fee. Also, allowing terminal services connections to a machine running your web server can be fraught with danger and is only something you should do if you are sure it is 100% secure.

Web Services

If you have decided to keep the administration application remote, and decided against the use of Remoting for whatever reason another logical alternative is the use of Web Services. You can either create a web application or a Windows Forms application to communicate with the Web Service. Again, your concern will have to be security. You'll need to make sure that people cannot make use of the Web Service when they are not authorized, which includes using techniques to prevent people from writing code that pretends to be your application to gain access to your product catalog and other vital data.

Security is even more of a concern with Web Services than with Remoting. If you are implementing a remote administration application that uses Web Services as a backend, you need to make sure that backend is secure. Securing a Web Service application may not be as difficult a task as it has been in the recent past. With the release of the WSE (Web Services Enhancements for .NET), programmers will have access to code that implements the new WS-Security standard, which allows for things like digitally signing SOAP envelopes, support for multiple security tokens with hashed passwords, and much more. Another advantage of this solution is that you can have access to the administration application from virtually anywhere, from a PocketPC through the Compact Framework.

ASP.NET Administration

Finally, the other most common option for creating an administration tool is to create another web application. In order to have access to the main application's business tier, this application would have to reside on the same machine as the commerce website. The simplicity here is both the advantage and disadvantage. While it might be quick and easy to create an administration application, especially if we have many reusable ASP.NET controls, it also won't benefit from the advantages of a rich interface that you can find in Windows, or from the flexibility of supplying administrative methods via Web Services.

This application has the advantage of being able to reuse many of the visual controls that we created for the main application, as well as the ability to reuse the business tier. By being a web application, it also has the benefit of allowing people to access it even from small devices like PDAs or Cell Phones through WAP, for example.

You can secure this application in many ways, including requiring Windows Authentication, which would effectively allow you to limit access to the application only to people authenticated on your network. Beyond that, you can test for membership in Windows NT groups, so you can create a group of administrators and only allow application access to those users.

ASP.NET administration is the option we decided to use. We can easily create references to the existing business assemblies because they're already part of our main web application solution. We don't have to worry about placing our assemblies in the Global Assembly Cache, or the concerns that have to be dealt with for Web Services as well as Remoting. In addition, we can secure our application using Windows Authentication, which should prevent quite a bit of tampering attempts from the "outside world", since the application shouldn't even be visible to anyone outside the intranet.

The Solution

The solution to the design we came up with is straightforward, but there is a lot of code to complete. In the interest of keeping this chapter down to a reasonable size, we're not going to cover all of the possible things that we can do with the administration system.

What we will cover is how to administer products and categories, as well as how to secure the administrative application. This should give you enough of an idea of how to build the administrative framework to suit your own needs.

Stored Procedures

The following is a list of the stored procedures that we developed in order to facilitate our administrative application. Our sample administrative application provides the ability to administer products and categories. Additional code for administering other areas of the site can be added as an exercise. Because so much of the main web application that customers see is read-only, we had to develop special procedures for inserting and updating data that normal customers should not be allowed to use.

Gw_Insert_Category

The `Gw_Insert_Category` stored procedure is used for creating a new category. If the parent category supplied is `-1`, it will use a `NULL` value to indicate a top-level category.

```
CREATE PROCEDURE Gw_Insert_Category
  @Description varchar(50),
  @Notes text,
  @ParentCategoryId int
AS
  IF @ParentCategoryId = -1
    INSERT INTO Categories(Description, Notes, ParentCategoryId)
                VALUES(@Description, @Notes, NULL)
  ELSE
```

```
    INSERT INTO Categories(Description, Notes, ParentCategoryId)
                VALUES(@Description, @Notes, @ParentCategoryId)
GO
```

Gw_Update_Category

The following procedure will update an existing category. We can change the category's description, notes, and even the parent category. By changing the parent category of a category, we can effectively move an entire product tree from one location to another without much hassle.

```
CREATE PROCEDURE Gw_Update_Category
  @CategoryId int,
  @Description varchar(50),
  @Notes text,
  @ParentCategoryId int
AS
  IF @ParentCategoryId = -1
    UPDATE Categories SET Description = @Description,
                          Notes = @Notes,
                          ParentCategoryId = NULL
    WHERE CategoryId = @CategoryId
  ELSE
    UPDATE Categories SET Description = @Description,
                          Notes = @Notes,
                          ParentCategoryId = @ParentCategoryId
    WHERE CategoryId = @CategoryId
GO
```

Gw_Update_Product

The following stored procedure will commit changes such as the category, name, or description of an existing product to the database.

```
CREATE PROCEDURE Gw_Update_Product
  @ProductId int,
  @CategoryId int,
  @Name varchar(50),
  @ShortDescription varchar(100),
  @LongDescription varchar(4000)
AS
  UPDATE Products SET Name = @Name,
                      ShortDescription = @ShortDescription,
                      LongDescription = @LongDescription,
                      CategoryId = @CategoryId
  WHERE ProductId = @ProductId
GO
```

CMP Metadata

The following is a list of the changes we've had to make to the `web.config` to support the above stored procedures. Remember that we're using the `web.config` file because ASP.NET is already configured to restart the application if the file changes. We want the application to restart anytime anyone changes the information in the database. This next section was added to the `ProductSkus` container mapping section:

```
<Delete>
  <CommandName>Gw_Delete_SKU</CommandName>
  <Parameter>
    <ClassMember>SKU</ClassMember>
    <ParameterName>@SKU</ParameterName>
    <DbTypeHint>Varchar</DbTypeHint>
    <ParamDirection>Input</ParamDirection>
    <Size>11</Size>
  </Parameter>
</Delete>
<Update>
  <CommandName>Gw_Update_SKU</CommandName>
  <Parameter>
    <ClassMember>SKU</ClassMember>
    <ParameterName>@SKU</ParameterName>
    <DbTypeHint>Varchar</DbTypeHint>
    <ParamDirection>Input</ParamDirection>
    <Size>11</Size>
  </Parameter>
  <Parameter>
    <ClassMember>Description</ClassMember>
    <ParameterName>@Description</ParameterName>
    <DbTypeHint>Varchar</DbTypeHint>
    <ParamDirection>Input</ParamDirection>
    <Size>50</Size>
  </Parameter>
  <Parameter>
    <ClassMember>RetailPrice</ClassMember>
    <ParameterName>@RetailPrice</ParameterName>
    <DbTypeHint>Money</DbTypeHint>
    <ParamDirection>Input</ParamDirection>
    <Size>8</Size>
  </Parameter>
  <Parameter>
    <ClassMember>ActualPrice</ClassMember>
    <ParameterName>@ActualPrice</ParameterName>
    <DbTypeHint>Money</DbTypeHint>
    <ParamDirection>Input</ParamDirection>
    <Size>8</Size>
  </Parameter>
</Update>
```

The following section was added to the `SingleProduct` container mapping:

```
<Update>
<CommandName>Gw_Update_Product</CommandName>
  <Parameter>
    <ClassMember>ProductId</ClassMember>
    <ParameterName>@ProductId</ParameterName>
    <DbTypeHint>Int</DbTypeHint>
    <ParamDirection>Input</ParamDirection>
    <Size>4</Size>
  </Parameter>
  <Parameter>
```

```
      <ClassMember>CategoryId</ClassMember>
      <ParameterName>@CategoryId</ParameterName>
      <DbTypeHint>Int</DbTypeHint>
      <ParamDirection>Input</ParamDirection>
      <Size>4</Size>
    </Parameter>
    <Parameter>
      <ClassMember>Name</ClassMember>
      <ParameterName>@Name</ParameterName>
      <DbTypeHint>Varchar</DbTypeHint>
      <ParamDirection>Input</ParamDirection>
      <Size>50</Size>
    </Parameter>
    <Parameter>
      <ClassMember>ShortDescription</ClassMember>
      <ParameterName>@ShortDescription</ParameterName>
      <DbTypeHint>Varchar</DbTypeHint>
      <ParamDirection>Input</ParamDirection>
      <Size>100</Size>
    </Parameter>
    <Parameter>
      <ClassMember>LongDescription</ClassMember>
      <ParameterName>@LongDescription</ParameterName>
      <DbTypeHint>Varchar</DbTypeHint>
      <ParamDirection>Input</ParamDirection>
      <Size>4000</Size>
    </Parameter>
  </Update>
```

Finally, the following section of code was added to the `CategorySet` container mapping in `web.config` to allow us to update a category:

```
  <Update>
    <CommandName>Gw_Update_Category</CommandName>
    <Parameter>
      <ClassMember>CategoryId</ClassMember>
      <ParameterName>@CategoryId</ParameterName>
      <DbTypeHint>Int</DbTypeHint>
      <ParamDirection>Input</ParamDirection>
      <Size>4</Size>
    </Parameter>
    <Parameter>
      <ClassMember>Description</ClassMember>
      <ParameterName>@Description</ParameterName>
      <DbTypeHint>Varchar</DbTypeHint>
      <ParamDirection>Input</ParamDirection>
      <Size>50</Size>
    </Parameter>
    <Parameter>
      <ClassMember>Notes</ClassMember>
      <ParameterName>@Notes</ParameterName>
      <DbTypeHint>Text</DbTypeHint>
      <ParamDirection>Input</ParamDirection>
      <Size>8000</Size>
```

```
    </Parameter>
    <Parameter>
      <ClassMember>ParentCategoryId</ClassMember>
      <ParameterName>@ParentCategoryId</ParameterName>
      <DbTypeHint>Int</DbTypeHint>
      <ParamDirection>Input</ParamDirection>
      <Size>4</Size>
    </Parameter>
  </Update>
```

Categories.aspx

Let's take a look at the `Categories.aspx` page. The following screenshot shows the page in the default state. You can see that we can either edit an existing category or we can create a new one.

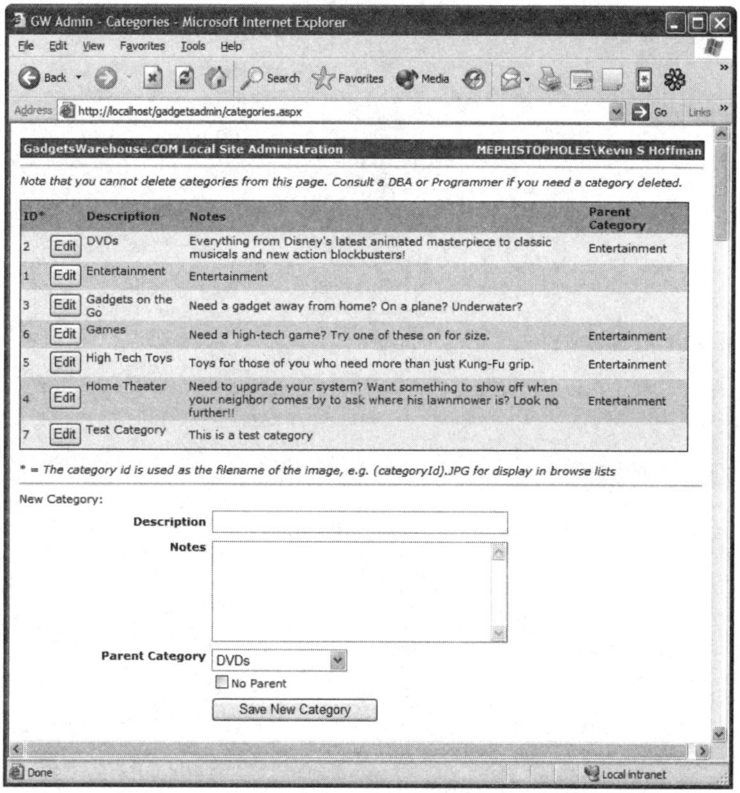

This page contains the HTML designer portion of the category management page:

```
<%@ Page language="c#" Codebehind="Categories.aspx.cs" AutoEventWireup="false"
Inherits="GadgetsAdmin.Categories" %>
<%@ Register tagprefix="GWUser" Tagname="AdminHeader"
Src="Controls/AdminHeader.ascx" %>
```

```
<!DOCTYPE HTML PUBLIC "-//W3C//DTD HTML 4.0 Transitional//EN" >
<HTML>
  <HEAD>
    <title>GW Admin - Categories</title>
    <meta content="Microsoft Visual Studio 7.0" name="GENERATOR">
    <meta content="C#" name="CODE_LANGUAGE">
    <meta content="JavaScript" name="vs_defaultClientScript">
    <meta content="http://schemas.microsoft.com/intellisense/ie5"
          name="vs_targetSchema">
    <LINK href="Styles/main.css" type="text/css" rel="stylesheet">
  </HEAD>
  <body>
    <form id="Categories" method="post" runat="server">
      <GWUSER:ADMINHEADER id="adminHeader"
                          runat="server"></GWUSER:ADMINHEADER>
      <i>Note that you cannot delete categories from this page. Consult
         a DBA or Programmer if you need a category deleted.</i><br>
      <br>
```

This next section of code defines the DataGrid we use for displaying the category list:

```
      <asp:DataGrid id="dgCategories" runat="server"
                    AutoGenerateColumns="False" BorderColor="Black"
                    BorderWidth="1px" BackColor="LightGoldenrodYellow"
                    CellPadding="2" GridLines="None" ForeColor="Black">
        <SelectedItemStyle ForeColor="GhostWhite"
                           BackColor="DarkSlateBlue"></SelectedItemStyle>
        <AlternatingItemStyle BackColor="PaleGoldenrod">
        </AlternatingItemStyle>
        <HeaderStyle Font-Bold="True" BackColor="Tan"></HeaderStyle>
        <FooterStyle BackColor="Tan"></FooterStyle>
        <PagerStyle HorizontalAlign="Center" ForeColor="DarkSlateBlue"
                    BackColor="PaleGoldenrod"></PagerStyle>
        <Columns>
```

This next section defines the ID column. We set it up so that it will be read-only in both the view and the edit state. We use a Label control in the edit state to make the ID of the row accessible via a call to FindControl:

```
          <asp:TemplateColumn HeaderText="ID*" HeaderStyle-Font-Bold=true>
            <ItemTemplate>
              <%# DataBinder.Eval( Container.DataItem, "CategoryId") %>
            </ItemTemplate>
            <EditItemTemplate>
              <asp:Label ID="lblCategoryId" Runat="server"
                         Text='<%# DataBinder.Eval( Container.DataItem,
                                                    "CategoryId") %>'>
              </asp:Label>
            </EditItemTemplate>
          </asp:TemplateColumn>
```

This next section of code shows the setup of another template column. We're displaying the description of the category as raw text in the default grid control state. However, in edit mode, we display the category description in an editable `Textbox` control.

```
<asp:EditCommandColumn ButtonType="PushButton" C
                       CancelText="Cancel" EditText="Edit"
                       UpdateText="Update">
</asp:EditCommandColumn>
<asp:TemplateColumn HeaderText="Description"
                    HeaderStyle-Font-Bold="True"
                    ItemStyle-Width="100px"
                    HeaderStyle-Width="100px"
                    ItemStyle-VerticalAlign="top">
  <ItemTemplate>
    <%# DataBinder.Eval( Container.DataItem, "Description") %>
  </ItemTemplate>
  <EditItemTemplate>
    <asp:TextBox ID="txtDescription" Runat="server"
                 Text='<%# DataBinder.Eval( Container.DataItem,
                                            "Description") %>'>
    </asp:TextBox>
  </EditItemTemplate>
</asp:TemplateColumn>
<asp:TemplateColumn HeaderText="Notes"
                    HeaderStyle-Font-Bold="True"
                    ItemStyle-Width="400px"
                    HeaderStyle-Width="400px">
  <ItemTemplate>
    <%# DataBinder.Eval( Container.DataItem, "Notes") %>
  </ItemTemplate>
  <EditItemTemplate>
    <asp:TextBox ID="txtNotes" Runat="server"
                 TextMode="MultiLine" Width="400px"
                 Height="100px"
                 Text='<%# DataBinder.Eval( Container.DataItem,
                                                "Notes") %>'>
    </asp:TextBox>
  </EditItemTemplate>
</asp:TemplateColumn>
<asp:TemplateColumn HeaderText="Parent Category"
                    HeaderStyle-Font-Bold="True"
                    ItemStyle-Width="100px"
                    HeaderStyle-Width="100px">
  <ItemTemplate>
    <%# GetCategoryName( DataBinder.Eval( Container.DataItem,
                         "ParentCategoryId")) %>
  </ItemTemplate>
  <EditItemTemplate>
    <asp:DropDownList ID="cboCategories"
                      Runat="server"
                      DataValueField="CategoryId"
                      DataTextField="Description">
 DataSource='<%# GetParentCategories( System.Convert.ToInt32(
                          DataBinder.Eval(Container.DataItem,
```

```
                                                    "CategoryId"))) %>'
            </asp:DropDownList>
            <asp:CheckBox ID="chkNoParent" Runat="server" Text="No Parent"
                  Checked='<%# ParentIsNull( System.Convert.ToInt32(
                  DataBinder.Eval(Container.DataItem, "CategoryId"))) %>'>
            </asp:CheckBox>
          </EditItemTemplate>
        </asp:TemplateColumn>
      </Columns>
    </asp:DataGrid><br>
    * = <i>The category id is used as the filename of the image,
    e.g. (categoryId).JPG for display in browse lists</i>
    <hr>
    New Category:<br>
    <table width="500" border="0" cellspacing="2" cellpadding="2">
      <tr>
        <td width="200" align="right">
          <b>Description</b>
        </td>
        <td width="300">
          <asp:TextBox ID="txtNewDescription" Width="300px"
                       Runat="server"></asp:TextBox>
        </td>
      </tr>
      <tr>
        <td align="right" valign="top" width="200">
          <b>Notes</b>
        </td>
        <td valign="top">
          <asp:TextBox ID="txtNewNotes" Width="300px"
                       Height="100px" Runat="server"
                       TextMode="MultiLine"></asp:TextBox>
        </td>
      </tr>
      <tr>
        <td align="right" width="200" valign="top">
          <b>Parent Category</b>
        </td>
        <td valign="top">
          <asp:DropDownList ID="cboNewCategories"
                            Runat="server"></asp:DropDownList><br>
          <asp:CheckBox ID="chkNoNewParent" Runat="server"
                        Text="No Parent"></asp:CheckBox>
        </td>
      </tr>
      <tr>
        <td><br>
        </td>
        <td>
          <asp:Button ID="btnSaveNew" Runat="server"
                      Text="Save New Category"></asp:Button>
        </td>
      </tr>
    </table>
```

```
    </form>
  </body>
</HTML>
```

Categories.aspx.cs

Here is the source code listing for the code-behind class that drives the category manager. It illustrates how we're handling the various events generated by our editable `DataGrid`, as well as providing an event handler to respond to the user clicking the button to create a new category. Note that all our code for administration of our website goes into the `GadgetsAdmin` namespace.

```
using System;
using System.Collections;
using System.ComponentModel;
using System.Data;
using System.Drawing;
using System.Web;
using System.Web.SessionState;
using System.Web.UI;
using System.Web.UI.WebControls;
using System.Web.UI.HtmlControls;
using System.Diagnostics;

using GW.Web.ProductCatalog;
using GW.MonitorServices;
using GW.MonitorServices.Logging;

namespace GadgetsAdmin
{
  /// <summary>
  /// Summary description for Categories.
  /// </summary>
  public class Categories : System.Web.UI.Page
  {
    protected System.Web.UI.WebControls.TextBox txtNewDescription;
    protected System.Web.UI.WebControls.TextBox txtNewNotes;
    protected System.Web.UI.WebControls.DropDownList cboNewCategories;
    protected System.Web.UI.WebControls.CheckBox chkNoNewParent;
    protected System.Web.UI.WebControls.Button btnSaveNew;
    protected System.Web.UI.WebControls.DataGrid dgCategories;

    private void Page_Load(object sender, System.EventArgs e)
    {
      // Put user code to initialize the page here
      if (!Page.IsPostBack)
      {
        LoadData();
      }
    }

    void LoadData()
    {
```

By calling GetChildCategories here with a -1, we are asking for all of the categories in the system, without regard to the parent categories. This is because we want to be able to edit all of the categories without having to deal with a tree view. However, if we were working with a Windows interface, a tree view would have been significantly easier to manage.

```
    DataTable categories = ProductCatalog.GetChildCategories(-1);
    cboNewCategories.DataSource = categories;
    cboNewCategories.DataTextField = "Description";
    cboNewCategories.DataValueField = "CategoryId";
    cboNewCategories.DataBind();
    Cache["Categories"] = categories;
    dgCategories.DataSource = categories;
    dgCategories.DataBind();
  }

  #region Web Form Designer generated code
  override protected void OnInit(EventArgs e)
  {
    //
    // CODEGEN: This call is required by the ASP.NET Web Form Designer.
    //
    InitializeComponent();
    base.OnInit(e);
  }

  /// <summary>
  /// Required method for Designer support - do not modify
  /// the contents of this method with the code editor.
  /// </summary>
  private void InitializeComponent()
  {
    this.dgCategories.CancelCommand += new
              System.Web.UI.WebControls.DataGridCommandEventHandler(
                                      this.dgCategories_CancelCommand);
    this.dgCategories.EditCommand += new
                 System.Web.UI.WebControls.DataGridCommandEventHandler(
                                        this.dgCategories_EditCommand);
    this.dgCategories.UpdateCommand += new
                 System.Web.UI.WebControls.DataGridCommandEventHandler(
                                      this.dgCategories_UpdateCommand);
    this.btnSaveNew.Click += new
                         System.EventHandler(this.btnSaveNew_Click);
    this.Load += new System.EventHandler(this.Page_Load);

  }
  #endregion
```

By now you should be fairly familiar with how to use an editable DataGrid, so you should also be familiar with seeing the various methods that respond to the button event handlers as well as various methods in the code-behind class that are called from within a data binding context to perform additional operations. Essentially, the DataGrid is first rendered in read-only mode. By clicking the Edit button, the grid will be placed in edit mode; in this mode all template columns with an EditItemTemplate defined will render themselves, bringing up our editable text box, and so on. Once in edit mode, the grid will also display the Save and Cancel buttons, all of which we can assign event handlers to. The following is a list of the various events we're responding to on the DataGrid:

```
private void dgCategories_EditCommand(object source,
                  System.Web.UI.WebControls.DataGridCommandEventArgs e)
{
  dgCategories.EditItemIndex = e.Item.ItemIndex;
  LoadData();
}

public DataView GetParentCategories( int categoryId )
{
  DataTable categories = ProductCatalog.GetCategories();
  // may use cache
  DataView dv = new DataView( categories );
  dv.RowFilter = "CategoryId <> " + categoryId.ToString();
  return dv;
}
```

The `GetCategoryName` method is used by the ASPX page to obtain the name of a particular parent category ID. In order to avoid a complex and slow self-join on the `Categories` table to produce the name of the current category and the name of its parent, we use the following method to perform a look up on the parent category's name at bind-time:

```
public string GetCategoryName( object parentCategoryId )
{
  if (parentCategoryId == DBNull.Value)
    return "";
  int parentCatId = (int)parentCategoryId;
  DataTable categories = ProductCatalog.GetCategories();
  // may use cache
  DataRow parentRow = categories.Select("CategoryId = " +
                                   parentCatId.ToString())[0];
  return parentRow["Description"].ToString();
}
```

The `ParentIsNull` method is used by the data binder to determine if the current category has a null parent, which means that it is a top-level category.

```
public bool ParentIsNull( int categoryId )
{
  DataTable categories = ProductCatalog.GetCategories(); // may use cache
  DataRow currentRow = categories.Select("CategoryId = " +
                                       categoryId.ToString())[0];
  if (currentRow["ParentCategoryId"] == DBNull.Value)
    return true;
  else
    return false;
}
```

Canceling an edit operation is actually pretty easy. We set the `EditItemIndex` on the `DataGrid` to `-1`, and then perform the data-binding operation. It is a good thing to remember that a `DataGrid` cannot change states (go from read to edit or the other way around) without being re-bound.

```
private void dgCategories_CancelCommand(object source,
                System.Web.UI.WebControls.DataGridCommandEventArgs e)
{
  dgCategories.EditItemIndex = -1;
  LoadData();
}
```

The `UpdateCommand` method will update the currently edited category. It will take the value of the No Parent checkbox, the value of the Description textbox and the current ID of the selected category, and use these to perform the database update operation. Once the update is complete, we set `EditItemIndex` to `-1` (bringing the grid back to read-only mode) and then we re-bind the data in the grid.

```
private void dgCategories_UpdateCommand(object source,
                System.Web.UI.WebControls.DataGridCommandEventArgs e)
{
  DataGridItem dgi = e.Item;
  Label lblCategoryId = (Label)dgi.FindControl("lblCategoryId");
  GWTrace.Trace( TraceLevel.Verbose, "CategoryId: {0}",
                lblCategoryId.Text);
  int categoryId = Int32.Parse( lblCategoryId.Text );
  CheckBox chkNoParent = (CheckBox)dgi.FindControl("chkNoParent");
  DropDownList cboParent =
                  (DropDownList)dgi.FindControl("cboCategories");
  TextBox txtDescription = (TextBox)dgi.FindControl("txtDescription");
  TextBox txtNotes = (TextBox)dgi.FindControl("txtNotes");
  GWTrace.Trace( TraceLevel.Verbose, "Selected Parent Category: {0}",
                 cboParent.SelectedItem.Value);

  int parentCategoryId = chkNoParent.Checked ? -1 :
                            Int32.Parse(cboParent.SelectedItem.Value);
      ProductCatalog.UpdateCategory( categoryId, txtDescription.Text,
                                     txtNotes.Text, parentCategoryId);
  dgCategories.EditItemIndex = -1;
  LoadData();
}

private void btnSaveNew_Click(object sender, System.EventArgs e)
{
  int parentCategoryId = chkNoNewParent.Checked ? -1 :
                    Int32.Parse(cboNewCategories.SelectedItem.Value);
  ProductCatalog.CreateCategory( txtNewDescription.Text,
                                 txtNewNotes.Text, parentCategoryId );

  LoadData();
}
}
}
```

EditProduct.aspx

Before we take a look at the HTML designer and code-behind class for the `EditProduct` page, let's take a look at a screenshot of the page in action:

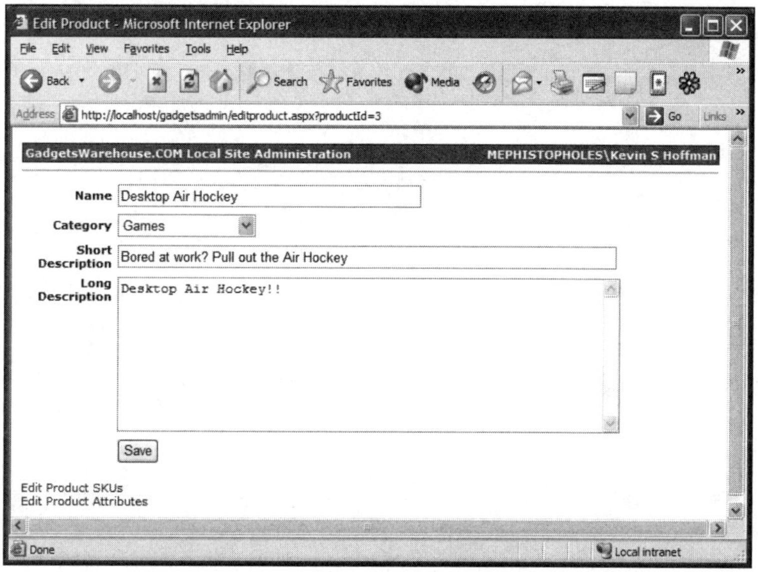

The following is the HTML designer portion of the page that controls single-product editing and provides additional links for working with product attributes and product SKUs:

```
<%@ Register tagprefix="GWUser" Tagname="AdminHeader"
    Src="Controls/AdminHeader.ascx" %>
<%@ Page language="c#" Codebehind="EditProduct.aspx.cs"
    AutoEventWireup="false" Inherits="GadgetsAdmin.EditProduct" %>
<!DOCTYPE HTML PUBLIC "-//W3C//DTD HTML 4.0 Transitional//EN" >
<HTML>
  <HEAD>
    <title>Edit Product</title>
    <meta name="GENERATOR" Content="Microsoft Visual Studio 7.0">
    <meta name="CODE_LANGUAGE" Content="C#">
    <meta name="vs_defaultClientScript" content="JavaScript">
    <meta name="vs_targetSchema"
        content="http://schemas.microsoft.com/intellisense/ie5">
    <link rel="stylesheet" href="Styles/main.css" type="text/css">
  </HEAD>
  <body>
    <form id="EditProduct" method="post" runat="server">
      <GWUser:AdminHeader id="adminHeader" runat="server" />
      <table width="600" border="0" cellspacing="2" cellpadding="2">
        <tr>
          <td width="100" align="right">
            <b>Name</b>
          </td>
          <td width="500">
            <asp:TextBox ID="txtName" Runat="server"
                         Width="301px"></asp:TextBox>
          </td>
        </tr>
```

```
      <tr>
        <td align="right">
          <b>Category</b>
        </td>
        <td>
          <asp:DropDownList ID="cboCategories"
                            Runat="server"></asp:DropDownList>
        </td>
      </tr>
      <tr>
        <td align="right">
          <b>Short Description</b>
        </td>
        <td>
          <asp:TextBox ID="txtShortDescription" Runat="server"
                       Width="496px"></asp:TextBox>
        </td>
      </tr>
      <tr>
        <td align="right" valign="top">
          <b>Long Description</b>
        </td>
        <td width="500" valign="top">
          <asp:TextBox ID="txtLongDescription" Width="500px"
                       Height="150px" TextMode="MultiLine"
                       Runat="server"></asp:TextBox>
        </td>
      </tr>
      <tr>
        <td><br>
        </td>
        <td>
          <asp:Button ID="btnSave" Runat="server"
                      Text="Save"></asp:Button>
        </td>
      </tr>
    </table>
    <br>
    <asp:LinkButton ID="lnkSKUs" Runat="server"
                    Text="Edit Product SKUs"></asp:LinkButton><br>
    <asp:LinkButton ID="lnkAttributes" Runat="server"
                    Text="Edit Product Attributes"></asp:LinkButton>
  </form>
 </body>
</HTML>
```

EditProduct.aspx.cs

The following is the code-behind class for the product-editing page. It provides the event handler that performs the actual product update as well as the code that loads the product to be edited:

```
using System;
using System.Collections;
```

```
using System.ComponentModel;
using System.Data;
using System.Drawing;
using System.Web;
using System.Web.SessionState;
using System.Web.UI;
using System.Web.UI.WebControls;
using System.Web.UI.HtmlControls;

using GW.Web.ProductCatalog;
using GW.Web.ProductCatalog.Data;
using GW.MonitorServices;
using GW.MonitorServices.Logging;

namespace GadgetsAdmin
{
  /// <summary>
  /// Summary description for EditProduct.
  /// </summary>
  public class EditProduct : System.Web.UI.Page
  {
    protected System.Web.UI.WebControls.TextBox txtName;
    protected System.Web.UI.WebControls.TextBox txtShortDescription;
    protected System.Web.UI.WebControls.Button btnSave;
    protected System.Web.UI.WebControls.LinkButton lnkSKUs;
    protected System.Web.UI.WebControls.LinkButton lnkAttributes;
    protected System.Web.UI.WebControls.TextBox txtLongDescription;
    protected System.Web.UI.WebControls.DropDownList cboCategories;

    private int productId;

    private void Page_Load(object sender, System.EventArgs e)
    {
      productId = Int32.Parse(Request["ProductId"]);
      // Put user code to initialize the page here
      if (!Page.IsPostBack)
      {
        LoadData();
      }
    }

    public void LoadData()
    {
      Product prod = ProductCatalog.GetProductDetails( productId );
      txtName.Text = prod.Name;
      txtShortDescription.Text = prod.ShortDescription;
      txtLongDescription.Text = prod.LongDescription;

      DataTable cats = ProductCatalog.GetCategories();
      cboCategories.DataSource = cats;
      cboCategories.DataValueField = "CategoryId";
      cboCategories.DataTextField = "Description";
      cboCategories.DataBind();
      cboCategories.Items.FindByValue(
```

```
                      prod.CategoryId.ToString() ).Selected = true;
    }

    #region Web Form Designer generated code
    override protected void OnInit(EventArgs e)
    {
      //
      // CODEGEN: This call is required by the ASP.NET Web Form Designer.
      //
      InitializeComponent();
      base.OnInit(e);
    }

    /// <summary>
    /// Required method for Designer support - do not modify
    /// the contents of this method with the code editor.
    /// </summary>
    private void InitializeComponent()
    {
      this.btnSave.Click += new System.EventHandler(this.btnSave_Click);
      this.lnkSKUs.Click += new System.EventHandler(this.lnkSKUs_Click);
      this.lnkAttributes.Click += new
                        System.EventHandler(this.lnkAttributes_Click);
      this.Load += new System.EventHandler(this.Page_Load);

    }
    #endregion

    private void btnSave_Click(object sender, System.EventArgs e)
    {
      int categoryId;

      if (cboCategories.SelectedItem == null)
        categoryId = Int32.Parse( cboCategories.Items[0].Value );
      else
        categoryId = Int32.Parse( cboCategories.SelectedItem.Value );

      ProductCatalog.UpdateProduct( productId, categoryId, txtName.Text,
                                    txtShortDescription.Text,
                                    txtLongDescription.Text );

    }

    private void lnkSKUs_Click(object sender, System.EventArgs e)
    {
      Response.Redirect("ProductSkus.aspx?ProductId=" +
                                              productId.ToString());
    }

    private void lnkAttributes_Click(object sender, System.EventArgs e)
    {
      Response.Redirect("ProductAttributes.aspx?ProductId="+
                                               productId.ToString());
    }
  }
}
```

ProductSKUs.aspx

The `ProductSKUs.aspx` page contains an editable `DataGrid` much like the categories editor we have already examined. Let's take a look at it in action:

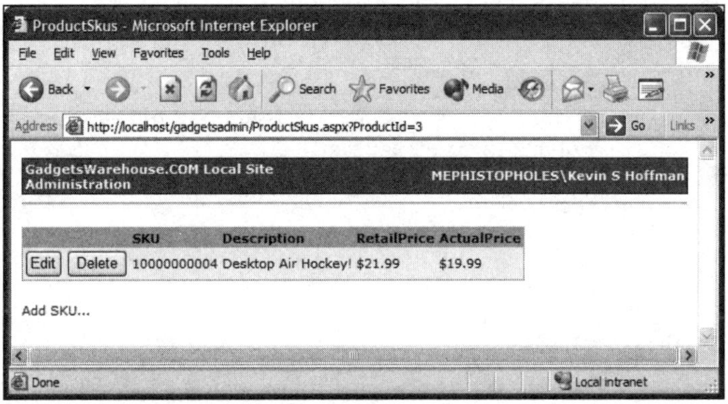

The following is the HTML designer portion of the product SKU editor, and it is similar to the HTML designer code from the Categories editor:

```
<%@ Page language="c#" Codebehind="ProductSkus.aspx.cs" AutoEventWireup="false"
    Inherits="GadgetsAdmin.ProductSkus" %>
<%@ Register tagprefix="GWUser" Tagname="AdminHeader"
    Src="Controls/AdminHeader.ascx" %>
<!DOCTYPE HTML PUBLIC "-//W3C//DTD HTML 4.0 Transitional//EN" >
<HTML>
  <HEAD>
    <title>ProductSkus</title>
    <meta name="GENERATOR" Content="Microsoft Visual Studio 7.0">
    <meta name="CODE_LANGUAGE" Content="C#">
    <meta name="vs_defaultClientScript" content="JavaScript">
    <meta name="vs_targetSchema"
          content="http://schemas.microsoft.com/intellisense/ie5">
    <link rel="stylesheet" href="Styles/main.css">
  </HEAD>
  <body>
    <form id="ProductSkus" method="post" runat="server">
      <GWUser:AdminHeader id="adminHeader"
                    runat="server"></GWUser:AdminHeader>
      <br>
        <asp:DataGrid id="dgSKUs" runat="server" BorderColor="Tan"
                    BorderWidth="1px" BackColor="LightGoldenrodYellow"
                    CellPadding="2" GridLines="None" ForeColor="Black"
                    AutoGenerateColumns="False">
          <SelectedItemStyle ForeColor="GhostWhite"
                       BackColor="DarkSlateBlue"></SelectedItemStyle>
          <AlternatingItemStyle BackColor="PaleGoldenrod">
          </AlternatingItemStyle>
          <HeaderStyle Font-Bold="True" BackColor="Tan"></HeaderStyle>
          <FooterStyle BackColor="Tan"></FooterStyle>
          <PagerStyle HorizontalAlign="Center" ForeColor="DarkSlateBlue"
```

```
            BackColor="PaleGoldenrod"></PagerStyle>
    <Columns>
      <asp:BoundColumn DataField="ProductId" Visible="False">
      </asp:BoundColumn>
      <asp:EditCommandColumn CancelText="Cancel"
                             ButtonType="PushButton" EditText="Edit"
                             UpdateText="Update">
      </asp:EditCommandColumn>
      <asp:ButtonColumn Text="Delete"
                        ButtonType="PushButton"></asp:ButtonColumn>
      <asp:TemplateColumn HeaderText="SKU"
                          HeaderStyle-Font-Bold="True">
        <ItemTemplate>
          <asp:Label ID="lblSKU" Runat="server"
           Text='<%# DataBinder.Eval(Container.DataItem, "SKU") %>'>
          </asp:Label>
        </ItemTemplate>
      </asp:TemplateColumn>
      <asp:TemplateColumn HeaderText="Description"
                          HeaderStyle-Font-Bold="true">
        <ItemTemplate>
          <asp:Label ID="lblDescription" Runat="server"
                     Text='<%# DataBinder.Eval(Container.DataItem,
                                                "Description") %>'>
          </asp:Label>
        </ItemTemplate>
        <EditItemTemplate>
          <asp:TextBox ID="txtDescription" Runat="server"
                       Text='<%# DataBinder.Eval(Container.DataItem,
                                                "Description") %>'>
          </asp:TextBox>
        </EditItemTemplate>
      </asp:TemplateColumn>
      <asp:TemplateColumn HeaderText="RetailPrice"
                          HeaderStyle-Font-Bold="true">
        <ItemTemplate>
          <asp:Label ID="lblRetailPrice" Runat="server"
                     Text='<%# DataBinder.Eval(Container.DataItem,
                                    "RetailPrice", "{0:c}") %>'>
          </asp:Label>
        </ItemTemplate>
        <EditItemTemplate>
          <asp:TextBox ID="txtRetailPrice" Width="50px" Runat="server"
                       Text='<%# DataBinder.Eval(Container.DataItem,
                                                "RetailPrice") %>'>
          </asp:TextBox>
        </EditItemTemplate>
      </asp:TemplateColumn>
      <asp:TemplateColumn HeaderText="ActualPrice"
                          HeaderStyle-Font-Bold="true">
        <ItemTemplate>
          <asp:Label ID="lblActualPrice" Runat="server"
                     Text='<%# DataBinder.Eval(Container.DataItem,
                                   "ActualPrice", "{0:c}") %>'>
```

```
                </asp:Label>
              </ItemTemplate>
              <EditItemTemplate>
                <asp:TextBox ID="txtActualPrice" Width="50px" Runat="server"
                             Text='<%# DataBinder.Eval(Container.DataItem,
                                                    "ActualPrice") %>'>
                </asp:TextBox>
              </EditItemTemplate>
            </asp:TemplateColumn>
          </Columns>
        </asp:DataGrid></P>
      <P>
        <asp:LinkButton id="lnkAddSKU" runat="server">Add SKU...
        </asp:LinkButton></P>
    </form>
  </body>
</HTML>
```

ProductSKUs.aspx.cs

The following is the code-behind class that drives the product SKU editor. It provides all of the DataGrid event handling:

```
using System;
using System.Collections;
using System.ComponentModel;
using System.Data;
using System.Drawing;
using System.Web;
using System.Web.SessionState;
using System.Web.UI;
using System.Web.UI.WebControls;
using System.Web.UI.HtmlControls;

using GW.MonitorServices;
using GW.MonitorServices.Logging;
using GW.Web.ProductCatalog;
using GW.Web.ProductCatalog.Data;

namespace GadgetsAdmin
{
  /// <summary>
  /// Summary description for ProductSkus.
  /// </summary>
  public class ProductSkus : System.Web.UI.Page
  {
    protected System.Web.UI.WebControls.DataGrid dgSKUs;
    protected System.Web.UI.WebControls.LinkButton lnkAddSKU;
    private int productId;

    private void Page_Load(object sender, System.EventArgs e)
    {
      productId = Int32.Parse(Request["ProductId"]);
```

```
    // Put user code to initialize the page here
    if (!Page.IsPostBack)
    {
      LoadData();
    }
  }

  public void LoadData()
  {
    Product prod = ProductCatalog.GetProductDetails( productId );
    dgSKUs.DataSource = prod.SKUs;
    dgSKUs.DataBind();
  }

  #region Web Form Designer generated code
  override protected void OnInit(EventArgs e)
  {
    //
    // CODEGEN: This call is required by the ASP.NET Web Form Designer.
    //
    InitializeComponent();
    base.OnInit(e);
  }

  /// <summary>
  /// Required method for Designer support - do not modify
  /// the contents of this method with the code editor.
  /// </summary>
  private void InitializeComponent()
  {
    this.dgSKUs.CancelCommand += new
               System.Web.UI.WebControls.DataGridCommandEventHandler(
                                               this.dgSKUs_CancelCommand);
    this.dgSKUs.EditCommand += new
                System.Web.UI.WebControls.DataGridCommandEventHandler(
                                                 this.dgSKUs_EditCommand);
    this.dgSKUs.UpdateCommand += new
                System.Web.UI.WebControls.DataGridCommandEventHandler(
                                              this.dgSKUs_UpdateCommand);
    this.dgSKUs.DeleteCommand += new
                  System.Web.UI.WebControls.DataGridCommandEventHandler(
                                               this.dgSKUs_DeleteCommand);
    this.Load += new System.EventHandler(this.Page_Load);

  }
  #endregion

  private void dgSKUs_DeleteCommand(object source,
                  System.Web.UI.WebControls.DataGridCommandEventArgs e)
  {
    DataGridItem dgi = e.Item;
    string sku = ((Label)dgi.FindControl("lblSKU")).Text;
    ProductCatalog.DeleteSKU( sku );
  }
```

```
    private void dgSKUs_EditCommand(object source,
                System.Web.UI.WebControls.DataGridCommandEventArgs e)
    {
      dgSKUs.EditItemIndex = e.Item.ItemIndex;
      LoadData();
    }

    private void dgSKUs_CancelCommand(object source,
                System.Web.UI.WebControls.DataGridCommandEventArgs e)
    {
      dgSKUs.EditItemIndex = -1;
      LoadData();
    }

    private void dgSKUs_UpdateCommand(object source,
                 System.Web.UI.WebControls.DataGridCommandEventArgs e)
    {
      DataGridItem dgi = e.Item;
      string sku = ((Label)dgi.FindControl("lblSKU")).Text;
      string description =
                 ((TextBox)dgi.FindControl("txtDescription")).Text;
      string retail = ((TextBox)dgi.FindControl("txtRetailPrice")).Text;
      string actual = ((TextBox)dgi.FindControl("txtActualPrice")).Text;

      ProductCatalog.UpdateSKU( sku, description,
                         System.Convert.ToDecimal( retail ),
                         System.Convert.ToDecimal( actual ) );
      dgSKUs.EditItemIndex = -1;
      LoadData();
    }
  }
}
```

Security

Now that we've looked at some of the code involved in the actual administration of the site, let's move on to how to secure the code against unauthorized personnel. As we mentioned in the design section, we're using Windows authentication. This form of authentication requires the user to be a valid Windows user. In addition, we're going to be enforcing a particular Windows group membership.

Web.config

The following modification is made to the `web.config` file so that users are required to authenticate via Windows authentication. Again, keep in mind that we're working on an entirely different web application here, and we are not working on the `GadgetsWarehouse` web project. The impersonation is required so that attempts to query the current login user return the actual user and not the ASPNET system account:

```
<authentication mode="Windows">
</authentication>
<identity impersonate="true"/>
```

AdminHeader.ascx.cs

The AdminHeader user control displays the current logged in user's name in the header as well as performs a check. It checks to see if the currently logged in user is a member of the local group "GW Admin". If the user is not part of that NT group, the page will display Access Denied and execution will terminate.

```
namespace GadgetsAdmin.Controls
{
  using System;
  using System.Data;
  using System.Drawing;
  using System.Security;
  using System.Security.Principal;
  using System.Web;
  using System.Web.UI.WebControls;
  using System.Web.UI.HtmlControls;

  /// <summary>
  ///    Summary description for AdminHeader.
  /// </summary>
  public abstract class AdminHeader : System.Web.UI.UserControl
  {
    protected System.Web.UI.WebControls.Label lblLogin;

    private void Page_Load(object sender, System.EventArgs e)
    {
      // Put user code to initialize the page here
```

On these next two lines of code, we're creating a WindowsPrincipal, which represents a specific user. We'll create a WindowsIdentity, which represents that user's Windows identity. We'll use these to determine who the user is and whether or not they belong to the "GW Admin" group that we are using to indicate authorized users. This group is a local machine group, but it could just as easily be another domain group.

```
      WindowsPrincipal wp = (WindowsPrincipal)Context.User;
      WindowsIdentity wi = (WindowsIdentity)Context.User.Identity;

      lblLogin.Text = wi.Name;
      if ( !wp.IsInRole( System.Environment.MachineName + "\\GW Admin") )
      {
        Response.Write("Access <b>denied.</b>");
        Response.End();
      }
    }

    #region Web Form Designer generated code
    override protected void OnInit(EventArgs e)
    {
      //
      // CODEGEN: This call is required by the ASP.NET Web Form Designer.
      //
      InitializeComponent();
```

```
        base.OnInit(e);
      }

      ///     Required method for Designer support - do not modify
      ///     the contents of this method with the code editor.
      /// </summary>
      private void InitializeComponent()
      {
        this.Load += new System.EventHandler(this.Page_Load);

      }
      #endregion
    }
  }
```

Summary

At the beginning of this chapter, we explored some of the problems and concerns associated with building administration applications, such as location, security, reliability, and availability – concerns that are prevalent among many applications today, not just administration tools. Then, we explored some of the design alternatives that we could choose between when building our application. Finally, we chose one of the designs and implemented an ASP.NET-based administration tool that provides a secure and reliable way to maintain our site's data.

CHAPTER 12

12

Conclusion

Now that we've finished coding our sample e-commerce site, we're going to take this chapter to review some of the things that we went over throughout the book. If you followed the book over a long period of time, some of the material from the earlier chapters might not be as fresh in your mind as the later chapters.

As usual, we're going to go through defining the problem, illustrating a design, and completing a solution. However, in this chapter we'll review each of those sections from throughout the entire book. It should give you a good review of the issues we faced when building the site and refresh the "big picture" and give us a chance to step back and look at the website as a whole.

The Problem

The problem we were faced with was the daunting task of creating a complete and functioning e-commerce website. The problem, with regard to the entire site, was to create a list of features that we thought would please the customers, generate revenue, and still be realistic enough to achieve in the short amount of time that we had for development.

Additionally, we needed to break down the list of tasks involved in creating this website into manageable units like Core Services, the Product Catalog, and so on. From there, we created our design and from the design we created our solution. The following is a quick review of some of the problems we faced in building the various aspects of our website:

Core Services

We were faced with many problems when creating this portion of our website. Any application is only as good as the foundation on which it is built. Because of that fact, we knew we needed quality. We also needed a solution that would be reliable, easy to maintain, and scalable. We also wanted to create a suite of core services that could be used easily by other programmers, and would be easy to understand for programmers of varied backgrounds.

Product Catalog

There are quite a few problems involved with the product catalog. The problem we needed to solve was that we needed a catalog to store all of our products. We recognized the fact that the catalog would need to be very fast and efficient, since most of the tasks a user performs on the e-commerce site would touch the product catalog somehow. We also know that the nature of commerce is such that things are always changing. We needed to build a product catalog that would be flexible enough to support a current line of products, as well as support the addition of new products, and new types of products as they become available. The key to defining our problem was to recognize that customers might tolerate deficiencies in other portions of our application, but they won't buy anything from us if our product catalog is difficult to use, slow, unresponsive, or broken.

Coupled with the problems inherent in building a product catalog are the issues surrounding product searches. The issues we discussed revolved around the fact that we need to be able to allow customers to find products they're looking for quickly and easily, but we can't do so at the expense of system performance. The main problem was determining the balance between features that are useful to the search, and those that could negatively impact performance, and therefore make our search unacceptable to customers.

Shopping Cart

One point we tried to make is that the website is only as good as its weakest module. Therefore, we got a bit repetitive claiming that each chapter was the most important up to that point. In the shopping cart chapter, we covered some of the problems involved in creating a shopping cart. We needed to make the shopping cart easy to use. The main goal was making the number of clicks from any page into the shopping cart minimal, and making the shopping cart useable by both anonymous and registered users. We discussed the fact that if the customer finds a problem with our shopping cart, it is very likely that they will not buy anything from us.

Wish List

The wish list solved the problem of hesitant buyers, or those who might be saving up for things. By providing a wish list facility, those buyers can store a list of what they're interested in, and return to it when they have the desire or the money to complete the purchase. We needed to make sure that the wish list was reliable, and could hold any type of product, and would be, as usual, as user friendly as we could make it.

Discounts and Coupons

In this chapter we discussed the problems involved in discounting and coupons. We discussed problems like how to store discounts and coupons, as well as how to deliver coupons to customers. Promotions, sales, discounts, and coupons all encourage customers to buy, because they feel they're getting a better deal on a product than if they had just simply bought it without regard to the sale. We need to be able to provide enough promotional content that customers are encouraged to come back to the site, but not so much that we don't make a profit on anything we sell. Despite certain rare exceptions to this rule, e-commerce sites simply cannot function without making a profit.

Order Fulfillment

Order fulfillment presents us with a problem with a very large scope. There is a myriad of things that need to be considered: are we building our own fulfillment system or are we integrating with something that is already being used (like a pre-existing in-house order management system or something commercial like JD Edwards)? Do we have our own warehouse or are we using third-party shipping? How will the customers know about the status of their orders? We also recognize that there are legal and financial issues involved with order fulfillment and we need to make sure that nothing about our process of handling orders is going to upset customers or violate any regulations. Customers need to be informed about the status of their order as soon as possible.

Community Building

An active, thriving community on a website will do more for that site's well-being than any amount of advertising or marketing could, and costs less. When we considered the problem of building a community, we needed to find ways to incorporate community-building tools such as ratings, reviews, and discussion forums in such a way that the focus of the community was still on commerce and buying our products.

Affiliates and Partners

We recognized that a website generally cannot survive on its own, and needs to create partnerships. The problem with partnerships is how do you create them without giving the affiliate more than you receive? We also recognized the need to track affiliate activity. In order to pay affiliates what they're due (and to receive what we're due) we need to keep track of partnership activities.

Administration

Administering the data and configuration of the site should be a painless task. The problem of administration is that changing data on the website can often be so painstaking and lengthy a process that it ends up costing the site too much to change its content. We know that varied content is one of the things that keeps a site alive. Therefore, we need to be able to administer the site in such a way that programmers and DBAs do not have to spend their time changing data by hand, and people more familiar with the content such as marketers and buyers can write the content for the site.

The Design

The design of our website had to take into account a lot of factors. Every single time we approached a problem, we needed to figure out how much of the problem we were going to solve with the design at hand. It is always a big tradeoff when deciding on the design for your application. You can't please everyone, and you can't include every single feature, so we need to be able to prioritize the features in terms of the most benefit versus cost of implementing each feature. Features that we know we just can't tackle without putting more important features behind schedule we have to cut.

Programmers are typically a very talented and ambitious crowd. One skill that programmers need to learn, no matter what kind of application they're developing is the ability to restrain themselves from shouting "I can do that!" when someone suggests a feature. If you do that in a meeting with project managers, "I can do that" will very quickly become "Do that in three weeks or you'll be sorry".

Designing an application that requires fast time-to-market, reliability, scalability, and availability is not an easy task, by any means. I can't stress enough that a good solid design will help to soften the blow of even the worst coding mistakes. However, a poor design will *never* be able to hide behind the work of a talented programmer.

Let's take a look at a site map that illustrates most of the features of our entire website from a conceptual, high-level point of view. After that we'll recap the designs we came up with for the different features of GadgetsWarehouse.com:

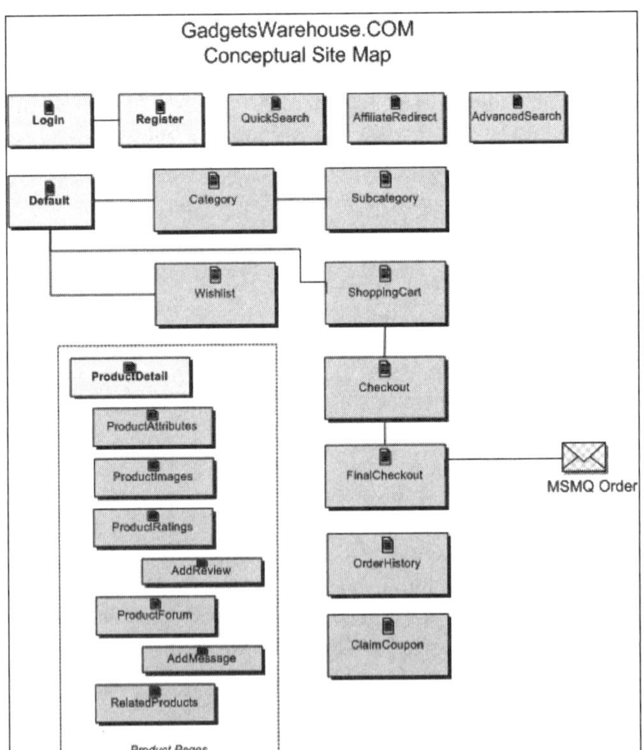

Core Services

I've probably said that every single chapter was the most important chapter, but the chapter detailing the core services is more important than the others. Whenever you sit down at a design meeting to figure out what the design is really going to look like for your website, you absolutely need to include an underlying infrastructure that provides basic services for all of the code in your application. There are many reasons for this, most of which we already went over. The idea is to provide a central point through which your entire application will go through to accomplish common tasks such as database access, activity monitoring, tracing, security, and authentication.

Once your core services have been thoroughly tested and optimized, you can use that as a reliable foundation on which you can build the rest of your application. If you need to make changes to any of the core services, they should be easy to make and should have very little impact on the rest of your application.

Product Catalog

Any retailer will tell you that making money is all about moving the product. If the customer can't find what they're looking for, if what they're looking for doesn't look good, or you don't have the product in stock, they're going to leave your store. The same thing is true for on-line sales, only the competition is far stronger. In a day when customers can hit a single website and within 10 seconds comparison shop a single product at thirty different retailers, you need to make sure that your site's product catalog does its job perfectly.

So, what is the job of the product catalog? The job of an e-commerce product catalog is to allow customers to search for a specific product and browse categories in a quick, easy and straightforward way, and to allow the customer to examine all aspects of a product. Some product catalogs allow customers to compare multiple products within the same site for features and price.

Shopping Cart

Once we managed to design our product catalog and the features that are available within it, we had to design the shopping cart. A shopping cart is the last thing the customer sees before they part with their hard-earned money and turn a cart into an order. Therefore, the design for a shopping cart needs to stress user-friendliness and ease of use over almost everything except reliability. Our design for a shopping cart was one that allowed anonymous customers to put items into a cart that would be moved to their new account after they registered. This allowed the quickest possible path from a new customer finding a product they wanted to the actual purchase. This model is a fairly common one and most people who do a lot of online shopping consider it a standard.

Wish Lists

Where shopping carts are available to allow the customer to purchase something right away, we need to recognize the fact that customers might want to think about a purchase for a while before committing to it. We should be all too happy to help them do this, so long as they come back to our site to make the final purchase. If the customer knows they have a wish list on our site that has all of the things they've been thinking about getting themselves or for other people as gifts, they are far more likely to buy those items from our site as opposed to going somewhere else. It is all about convenience. Customers will do the most convenient thing for them, so the trick is to make the functionality of our website simply be the most convenient thing for the customer. This includes the ability to track products they're thinking about buying and updating their wish list display to reflect that they purchased an item on the list.

Discounting and Coupons

Nothing sells like a sale. No matter how much we all claim to be immune to the power of a sale, we're all suckers for the big, fancy, shining signs. If we walk into a store with no intention to buy anything, some hidden impulse compels us to even just consider buying an item if it is on sale. How many times have you been in a store with someone and heard the famous argument for buying an item, "But ... it's on sale..."?

Retailers count on this impulse, and in fact need it to make ends meet. Can you remember the last time you walked into a store and *didn't* see something on sale? E-commerce is the same way: customers expect to find sales, and retailers expect to have them. Whether you discount new items that you want to sell a lot of, or old items that you need cleared out of your warehouse, you will always have something on sale in your store, or you're doing something wrong.

Our design took this into consideration and gave us a flexible system for dealing with discounts and coupons, two different ways of giving the customers a reduction in price and making them feel as though they got a good deal. All of this goes toward getting the customer to come back for their next purchase. We also provided the ability for a customer to claim a coupon only once. This prevents abuse of the coupons and reduces the negative impact of "coupon sites", that post e-commerce coupon codes for everyone to use, even if they weren't the target audience of the promotion.

Order Fulfillment

When we were thinking about the design for our order fulfillment, we had a few things that we needed to account for: legal issues, order history, and de-coupled fulfillment. As for legal issues, we needed to be able to produce a 100% accurate detailed record of every single change to the order status that took place. We weren't sure what legal requirements there might have been for keeping records, so we decided to keep as much as possible. The concept of storing every change to an order status as a separate record we felt was unique and provided some real benefits to the customer.

In order to deal with de-coupled order fulfillment we decided to use messaging, specifically MSMQ. This allowed us to connect our order fulfillment system, which could have been anything from another Win2k server to an AS/400 mainframe running some large fulfillment software. By using the MSMQ system, we could transmit orders to that system without worrying about the implementation of the system.

Community Building

Our design for community building had one main goal: encourage the customer to come back to the site as often as possible, even if they're not going to buy anything. The way in which we wanted to accomplish this goal was to provide a way for the customer to interact with and leave their mark on the website. This would be accomplished by creating a ratings and review system for products as well as public discussion forums based on the products in the catalog. This would encourage the customers to come back and check reviews of products they might be considering as well as check to see if there are any new messages posted on a product in which they are interested.

Affiliates and Partners

One thing that we needed to stress when building the design for affiliate handling was how important it is to create lasting partnerships as an e-commerce site. It is all about real estate. If your store is a traditional shop that people walk into and has a roof, then nothing short of a natural disaster is going to take that store away, and people will be able to find it fairly easily. The Internet is a different story entirely. A website is simply a tiny island in a really, really, really big ocean. Your devoted customers will always remember how to get to your island, and they are extremely valuable, but your biggest concern is the customers who can easily forget where your island is and go to another one for their shopping. By establishing partnerships between other islands, you effectively increase your real estate and increase the chance that people can find their way to your island.

It may not be the best metaphor, but the design for affiliates and partnerships is much simpler than the concept that they simply must be supported by the website. Our affiliate design is fairly simple: an affiliate directs a customer to a specific URL on our site, we record who the affiliate is and if that session turns into a completed order, we'll be able to compensate the affiliate accordingly.

Administration

The design of our administration system was something that took quite a bit of discussion. We needed to find some way to administer all of the various features we've coded throughout the entire book, and we needed to do it in a way that was fast, efficient, secure, and such that administering the site wouldn't take the system down, and failures on the administrative site wouldn't cause failures on the production site. The design was probably the biggest challenge for this section.

The Solution

As we built this website, our goals were to promote best practices. We wanted to illustrate principals of good code reuse, good object-oriented programming and design principles, as well as scalable, efficient data access and multi-tier enterprise application programming.

We've already seen the source code for virtually the entire website. There are a few piece of code that we left out that are just there to tidy up the loose ends that you'll be able to see when you download the full solution from http://www.wrox.com. For now, we'll take this next section of the chapter and discuss some of the complex, new, or just plain cool code that we used in order to accomplish the various pieces of our website.

Core Services

The code for our core services uses a few tricks and techniques that you might not have had much exposure to already. The first point of interest is that we're using a concept called *Container-Managed Persistence.* You might remember from this early chapter that CMP is a concept in which the data (persistable) objects have absolutely no knowledge of the data source. They themselves do not invoke stored procedures nor do they contain any data that ties them to one particular data source. There are many benefits to this setup; some of the more obvious ones are that you can easily change and re-configure your data source without having to recompile business objects. By de-coupling the business object and the data source, you can more easily directly map design to classes, creating a much more object-oriented business tier.

We also used a bit of reflection in order to get the CMP code to work properly. In addition, we used an embedded resource file to store a list of pre-defined error message strings that we can easily upgrade to be multi-lingual in the future.

Product Catalog

The code for the product catalog introduced a heavy load of ASP.NET controls, including user controls, composite server controls, and templated `DataGrid` columns. We used `DataGrid` and `DataList` controls, and all kinds of other really interesting ASP.NET techniques. The code contained in this module contains a lot of useful information for ASP.NET novices and experts alike.

Shopping Cart

The shopping cart is a key part of any e-commerce application. We used plenty of `DataGrid` code including templated columns, and we used a large amount of interesting and useful techniques for creating column summaries and running totals, and performing behind-the-scenes code logic within databinder evaluation methods. The code for the shopping cart not only displayed cart items, but it also displayed relevant discounts and running discount totals, it displayed a coupon, and would display the final price in the shopping cart. Again, there are quite a few techniques and design patterns in the solution to the shopping cart that apply not only to shopping carts, but to many other problems programmers have to solve with ASP.NET.

Wish Lists

The code for wish lists introduced us to working with editable columns and rows in a `DataGrid`, a very useful and handy technology. The code behind the wish list system dealt with adding items from product pages to a customer's wish list, viewing the list, and editing a single item in the list. We saw a lot of useful code in this chapter that will help in any wish list implementation as well as other ASP.NET tasks.

Discounting and Coupons

The discounting and coupon system involved some fairly complex code. We really got to explore the inner workings of data binding and using custom methods on the code-behind page to create running totals, and discount and coupon sums. We also saw how to gradually build an order while rendering the contents of the shopping cart so we didn't have to perform the same discounting and sum calculations twice.

Order Fulfillment

To build on what we created for the discounting and coupons, we added more code to the shopping cart. We also saw some complex code to deal with passing complex data between several pages in a chain. This kind of code comes in handy for checkout pipelines, wizards, and complex multi-page data entry forms.

Beyond the shopping cart, we had a look at some code that adds an order to an MSMQ Queue. This gave us an opportunity to look at a fully XML-serialiazable class, code for operating an MSMQ Queue, as well as code for order history. The order history code is worthy of mentioning on its own, as it showed a very interesting way of accomplishing a master-detail view on the same page. We used a `DataGrid` that was embedded in a `<div>` tag that had some style attributes on it that would cause it to appear in a scrollable `IFRAME`, allowing all of the customer's past orders to appear in a fixed height on the screen so they could find a single order and click on it to display the details and items for that order.

Community Building

The chapter on community building introduced us to the code that drives a fully-functioning ratings, reviews, and discussion system. The code we used can be expanded to produce recommendation engine systems, which recommend various products to customers based on their ratings, as well as robust forum software. These days, lots of customers are looking to find communities around something, and we illustrated some code that will allow your site to hopefully provide just the community your customers are looking for.

Affiliates and Partners

By this point, a lot of the code in the site might start to look fairly familiar and routine. The affiliate section didn't introduce any drastic new code techniques or design patterns, but it did illustrate the need to take care of the appropriate bookkeeping that needs to be done in order to fulfill contractual obligations and arrangements with business partners.

Administration

The administration section didn't show us all that much in terms of new ASP.NET code. However, it did reinforce the fact that we can re-use much of the techniques and patterns we developed when building this site for internal users as well as the general public. We saw how to secure an administration site above and beyond what the standard website can do in terms of authentication.

Room for Improvement

The purpose of this book wasn't to provide you a complete, ready-to-go website. Not only would that not teach you anything, but we would certainly be charging more for the book than we are now. The goal of books like this is not just to show you the end-result code, but to show you the *process* of getting to the end-result code.

We feel that if you know the process of creating a website like this, and you understand the essential underlying techniques, then you will be able to go off on your own and improve on what we've done here. You might refer to this code as a reference, but what you do when you close this book will be your own. This ability to customize and extend our solution is far more useful to you than simply purchasing a complete solution.

As such, the solution we came up with has plenty of room for improvement. We left it that way deliberately. The first thing that can be improved is the error handling system. Improvements can be made in usability and the interface, new features can be added, and existing features can be enhanced. Half of the fun in developing a site like this is to exercise your own ability to go beyond what we've already done and create something new that might benefit you, your company, or the general public.

In addition, we deliberately did not discuss taking payments from customers. There are many APIs and redirections that can take place at the end of the checkout process to validate the customer's credit card information and record the purchase. The framework we've laid down and techniques we've illustrated should be enough for you to integrate whatever payment method you're using into the site.

Summary

Each chapter was a complete breakdown of what we needed to accomplish in order to build a complete module. First, we discussed the problem we were attempting to solve. Then, we discussed the possible design alternatives and discussed the design we came up with for GadgetsWarehouse.com. Finally, we walked you through the code that we implemented to bring life to each design in each of the chapters. After the chapters were completed, we added a few touchups to the site to make it flow a bit more smoothly; and the complete code can be downloaded from www.wrox.com.

INDEX

Index

A Guide to the Index

The index is arranged hierarchically, in alphabetical order, with symbols preceding the letter A. Most second-level entries and many third-level entries also occur as first-level entries. This is to ensure that users will find the information they require however they choose to search for it.

Symbols

A

B

C

D

E

F

G

M

N

O

P

Q

R

S

T

U

V

W

Notes

Programmer to Programmer™

Registration Code: 8031YA74BPBPA601

Wrox writes books for you. Any suggestions, or ideas about how you want information given in your ideal book will be studied by our team. Your comments are always valued at Wrox.

Free phone in USA 800-USE-WROX
Fax (312) 893 8001

UK Tel.: (0121) 687 4100 Fax: (0121) 687 4101

ASP.NET E-Commerce Programming – Registration Card

Name ______________________

Address ______________________

____

____

____

City ____________ State/Region ____________

Country ____________ Postcode/Zip ____________

E-Mail ______________________

Occupation ______________________

How did you hear about this book?

- ❐ Book review (name) ____________
- ❐ Advertisement (name) ____________
- ❐ Recommendation ____________
- ❐ Catalog ____________
- ❐ Other ____________

Where did you buy this book?

- ❐ Bookstore (name) ____________ City ____________
- ❐ Computer store (name) ____________
- ❐ Mail order ____________
- ❐ Other ____________

What influenced you in the purchase of this book?

❐ Cover Design ❐ Contents ❐ Other (please specify):

____

How did you rate the overall content of this book?

❐ Excellent ❐ Good ❐ Average ❐ Poor

What did you find most useful about this book? ____________

____

____

What did you find least useful about this book? ____________

____

____

Please add any additional comments. ____________

____

____

What other subjects will you buy a computer book on soon?

____

What is the best computer book you have used this year?

Note: This information will only be used to keep you updated about new Wrox Press titles and will not be used for any other purpose or passed to any other third party.

wrox

Programmer to Programmer™

Note: If you post the bounce back card below in the UK, please send it to:

Wrox Press Limited, Arden House, 1102 Warwick Road,
Acocks Green, Birmingham B27 6HB. UK.

Computer Book Publishers

NO POSTAGE
NECESSARY
IF MAILED
IN THE
UNITED STATES

BUSINESS REPLY MAIL

FIRST CLASS MAIL PERMIT#64 CHICAGO, IL

POSTAGE WILL BE PAID BY ADDRESSEE

WROX PRESS INC.,
29 S. LA SALLE ST.,
SUITE 520
CHICAGO IL 60603-USA